Out of the Blue

The moral right of Corinne Brazier and Steve Rice to be identified as the authors of this work has been asserted in accordance with the Copyright, Designs and Patents Act of 1988.

Picture copyright is stated where known and every effort has been made to trace and contact all copyright holders. The authors will be pleased to make good any omission or rectify any mistakes brought to their attention at the earliest opportunity.

Contents

Foreword

Once again I have the great privilege of providing the foreword to another excellent book by Corinne and Steve ably supported by volunteers from the West Midlands Police Museum.

It is hard to imagine today the police going out on strike, but that is what happened in 1919 here in Birmingham and in other cities across the country.

This book tells the story of the strike, centred on Birmingham, but just as importantly why this event has not been repeated. After the First World War a policeman's lot (and it was generally then) was not always a happy one. Many factors caused those who went out on strike to do so and this book tells the human story of those officers, their motivations and the consequences for their lives from the strike. The changes that arose from the strike that have made such an event impossible in our minds today: significant improvements in pay and conditions and the foundation of the Police Federation.

It is important at a challenging time for policing we reflect carefully on our history and remember that those who serve should never be taken for granted.

I offer my sincere thanks for all who have helped to create this important work.

David Thompson QPM LLB

Chief Constable of West Midlands Police

Introduction

In 1919 a significant event happened. The culmination of poor working conditions, authoritarian management, below average pay and a general feeling of discontent that had been brewing for some time, led the Birmingham City Police to do something they had never done before (and have never done since): they went on strike.

The 1918 police strike, which had led to the Home Office agreeing to all the demands of the Police and Prison Officers Union, was still fresh in the Birmingham officers' memories. Many of them would have thought that even better was to come and supported the national call to go out on strike.

What ended up not working out in their favour, was that the recommendations of the Desborough Committee and the Police Act 1919 had been rushed through Parliament, leading all officers to receive £10 in back pay (not an insignificant sum in 1919) within their pay packets on 1 August, and many other improvements in pay and working conditions.

With the government seeming to have listened to the demands and taken action to significantly improve the lives of police officers around the country, a great deal of officers did not want to risk this promising future and besides, many had wives and children to consider.

When the call to strike came to Birmingham, out of an alleged eight hundred membership, and a force of just over 1,400, only 120 officers went on strike. All were dismissed, and no appeals for leniency or reinstatement were granted.

There is very little information in the public domain about the police strikes, and even less information about the Birmingham element of the 1919 strike. On the 100th anniversary of both the strike and the creation of the Police Federation – we wanted to change that, and to explain what led some very brave and highly commended officers to risk everything for a cause which most would think had already been addressed before they even left their posts.

We are indebted to several of the West Midlands Police Museum volunteers who have spent hours researching the lives of these men and helped to make this book a reality – huge thanks go to Dave Shergold, Sandra Gill and Linda Fraser who did the lion's share of the research on the men. We are

also grateful to Jon Langley, Berni May, Debbie Menzel and Helen Kirkman for their support and to Malcolm Fraser and Dave Shergold for proof reading.

For further reading on the police strikes, we recommend *'The Night the Police Went on Strike'* by Gerald W Reynolds and Anthony Judge, 1968 and *'Police Strike'* by A V Sellwood, 1978 and for further information about the Birmingham City Police Force - *'150 Years of Policing Birmingham'* by John Reilly, 1989 and *'Invisible Men: The secret lives of Police Constables in Liverpool, Manchester and Birmingham'* by Joanne Klein, 2010.

Steve Rice & Corinne Brazier

West Midlands Police

The Beginning

Full-time, professional policing commenced in Britain in 1829 when Home Secretary Sir Robert Peel created the Metropolitan Police. The basic ethos of his thinking was that policing would be effective when done through the consent of the public, not the authority of the state. The nine 'Peelian Principles' outlined to every officer as part of their 'General Instructions' from 1829 onwards, upon which the philosophy of Peel's police was based, stated:

1) The police must prevent crime and disorder (as opposed to focussing on more severe punishments to deter offenders)
2) The ability of the police to perform their duties is dependent upon public approval and respect of police actions and behaviour
3) Police must secure the willing co-operation of the public in voluntary observance of the law to be able to secure and maintain the respect of the public
4) The degree of co-operation of the public that can be secured diminishes proportionately to the necessity of the use of physical force
5) Police seek and preserve public favour not by pandering to public opinion but by constantly demonstrating absolute impartial service to the law
6) Police use physical force to the extent necessary to secure observance of the law or to restore order only when the exercise of persuasion, advice and warning is found to be insufficient
7) Police, at all times, should maintain a relationship with the public that gives reality to the historic tradition that the police are the public and the public are the police; the police being only members of the public who are paid to give full-time attention to duties which are incumbent on every citizen in the interests of community welfare and existence
8) Police should always direct their action strictly towards their functions and never appear to usurp the powers of the judiciary
9) The test of police efficiency is the absence of crime and disorder not the visible evidence of police action in dealing with it

These principles remain relevant today and are woven throughout the values of West Midlands Police. In essence, they describe how the police have to be honest, impartial, fair and just. How the police **are** the public and how they must strive to prevent crime and disorder with the support and co-operation of the public.

What these principles do not cover is how the public will treat the police. Who will protect the police from violence? Who will ensure they are given a reasonable wage to enable them to feed themselves and their families? Who will ensure they are given fair working conditions? The police often see the public at their worst: violent, drunk, abusing their loved ones or complete strangers and out of control. They also have to be there to support members of the public through the most dreadful situations – when they are victims of abuse, sexual assault, road traffic accidents and drug overdoses. Thousands have died whilst on duty and hundreds have been killed in the line of duty. Who will give the police the support they need? Today, in 2019, the Police Federation looks after rank and file officers and the Superintendents Association takes care of superintendents and chief superintendents.

In this book we tell the story of how the Police Federation came about – the demands from the police for fair pay and working conditions and the national context that encouraged and indulged the police strike of 1919.

Birmingham City Police – the early days

At the very beginning, in November 1839, Birmingham was not yet a city and it was the Birmingham Borough Police that first took control of the streets following Chartist rioting, which took place after the Chartist petition arguing for better rights for the working class had failed.

The Birmingham force was officially created on the 20 November 1839 Francis Burgess, a local barrister, was appointed as the first Police Commissioner for Birmingham and his force had a strength of 260 men. Officers were paid 17s a week and worked a seven day week. Unmarried constables were required to live in single quarters within police premises, be back within the station at a certain time of the evening and not be involved in any kind of scandal that could bring the force into disrepute. In short most elements of their life were controlled by supervision. Lord Normanby's 1840 regulations regarding pay (which only applied to county forces but were observed by most boroughs) with a maximum weekly pay of 21s remained in force until 1866 when it went up to 23s. In 1874 the Birmingham Borough Police were 'agitating for an increase in pay'[i]. 1886 changes increased weekly wages to 29s, but a man had to serve for eight years to attain this.[ii]

In 1887 policemen were allowed to vote in Parliamentary elections and six years later, they were given the right the vote in municipal elections.[iii]

By the time Birmingham was granted city status in 1889 the establishment and strength of the force was 550. At the end of the 19th Century the establishment had risen to 700 but the actual strength was 685. The introduction of a monthly leave day in 1883 required 15 extra men and the increase in legislation and police duties meant the men were spread even thinner[iv].

After several attempts at introducing legislation governing police pensions, the 1890 Police Act included a requirement for Watch Committees to give pensions to officers who had completed 25 years' service (15 years' service were required for medical pensions). Prior to this they had been given at the Watch Committee's discretion. Special pensions were provided for officers unable to work through injury on duty and for the widows and children of officers killed in the line of duty.

The 1890 Police Act also introduced various educational requirements – which led to a distinction between pre and post 1890 officers, with younger officers often looking down on their less educated (but more experienced) colleagues.

The Birmingham police operated a class system within ranks – whereby constables and sergeants could move up a class based on length of service, merit and an examination. Likewise, officers could find themselves moved down a class for misconduct. Constables would generally start in the fifth class and could migrate all the way up to first class, progressing around one class each year if they were performing well, with each rise carrying a small pay increase and each move back down the classes carrying the equivalent drop in pay. The force also operated a system of merit stripes awarded for bravery, diligence and good police work for constables and sergeants – officers could earn extra pay for each stripe. Constables could be awarded up to three stripes and sergeants two.

For good police work, diligence and bravery – officers could be complimented in police orders (which were distributed to every station around the force), commended by the Chief Constable and/or the Watch Committee and awarded a monetary award - normally a guinea. Punishments generally consisted of reductions in pay and/or class, leave being stopped and warnings.

Officers were allocated a warrant number upon joining which remained the same throughout their service (changing only if they left and re-joined) but collar numbers changed as officers changed divisions or upon promotion to sergeant (officers above sergeant did not have collar numbers). Warrant numbers were chronological going right back to officer number one in 1839.

The boundaries of Birmingham expanded as the city grew during the end of the 19th Century and the start of the next – in 1891 Saltley, Ward End and Harborne were added – increasing the acreage by nearly 50%. Quinton followed in 1909 and the city almost trebled in size with the 1911 additions of Kings Norton, Northfield, Handsworth, Aston Manor, Erdington and Yardley[v].

In 1893 the Birmingham Police Aided Association was created with the main aim of providing boots and warm garments for destitute children. These were purchased with donations from organisations and from events organised by the police to generate funds. This helped to foster better relations with some of the poorest classes of society[vi].

In 1910 the Police (Weekly Rest Day) Act was passed after many years of being raised in Parliament. This finally entitled officers to have one day off per week. It was highlighted at Parliament that all other classes within society have one weekly rest day and a further half day holiday every week, but that the police were not even permitted one full day in seven. It was further pointed out by Viscount Ridley that the police were not allowed leave on bank holidays and that 'on the very days when the general community enjoys itself most, the police have to work the hardest'.[vii] Evidence was given by a police officer's wife which describes just how hard life could be for a policeman:

> "After having got a chill, having been out day after day in rain, fog, etc., clothes scarcely dry before they have to go out on duty again. After recovering from an illness, hardly knowing how to keep up till they go off duty (especially with those heavy overcoats). After days of nights of broken rest owing to the illness of wife or children, as soon as they come off duty, they have to turn to and help in the house, or look after a sick child while the wife goes out to do her shopping... a man is practically deprived of going anywhere with his wife and children. When the leave comes round, he is constantly obliged to spend it in mending boots, or doing things in the home which he has had no time to do on ordinary days... By the time the man has had his breakfast, it is time for the children to be put to bed, and there is no chance of turning out the room properly. It is often a great strain on the wife trying to keep the children quiet all day long during the night-duty month, and one day a week would be of the greatest benefit in relieving the strain, in enabling the wife to clean the rooms, and making it possible for the children to see something of their father at least once a week."[viii]

The select committee that considered the need for the weekly rest day in 1908 also looked at the issue regarding the right to confer – e.g. an official union. There was clearly a desire from the police for a place they could air their grievances and a need to have someone fighting for their rights, listening to their issues and ensuring improvements to their pay and working conditions. Former officers of Liverpool and the Metropolitan Police talked of the difficulties that existed at that time for officers to be able to hold meetings and discuss grievances and the worry that an individual officer could be singled out as a trouble maker for complaining about anything.[ix]

Whilst all this debate was going on about the police being given a basic entitlement of one day off in seven, legislation was fast increasing (18 Acts of Parliament affecting policing were introduced between 1900 and 1908[x]), motor vehicles were starting to become popular and cause problems requiring police intervention on roads and the suffragette movement was gaining momentum – the policeman's job was getting more complex and more demanding.

But through all this there were some things that were improving. Drinking on duty had been a significant issue across police forces throughout the 1800s. Not isolated to policing, many Victorians turned to alcohol to escape the troubles of poverty and hardship that families were often living in. Usually with large families, irregular wages and living in appalling and squalid housing – family life in Victorian Birmingham was particularly tough for most. It is unusual to find a record of a policeman in Birmingham working during the 1800s who does not have at least one blemish on his record for drinking alcohol whilst on duty. This trend was changing into the 20th Century across police forces – a Liverpool sergeant who retired in 1908 after 26 years' service stated *'When I joined the force, it was the exception to find one man who did not drink on duty. Today it is the exception to find one who does.[xi]'*

As well as being hard work and relatively low paid, policing Birmingham in the 1800s and early 1900s was also dangerous: there are records of two Birmingham night watchmen who were killed whilst on duty prior to the inception of the police force – Robert Twyford who was shot in 1806 and died in 1814 and Thomas Stych who was viciously assaulted on duty and died four weeks later in 1836.

A further nine officers were killed on duty between 1839 and 1919 and another six died whilst on duty.[xii] Of those who were killed:

- Three were due to train accidents whilst on special protection duty during World War One
- One was crushed in a stampede trying to evacuate a concert hall
- One was stabbed
- One fell off a fire escape after testing it following repairs
- Three were killed after making an arrest and trying to bring prisoners in, when they were assaulted and/or objects were thrown at them

Unlike other working class occupations, a police constable would find that all areas of his life were regulated, on and off duty: single men would live in single quarters at station houses, they had to be up and parading for duty at a certain time, complete educational classes as required, maintain a high level of cleanliness of their uniform and possessions, ensure they were home before curfew, ask for permission to leave the force area and not drink in the wrong public house or get involved in arguments[xiii]. Potential wives were thoroughly checked out by local officers prior to the Chief Constable giving permission for an officer to marry. But the regulation did not stop here: the officer had to ensure his wife and children did not get into disagreements with or upset neighbours or shop keepers. Any kind of gossip, scandal or incident that could bring the force into disrepute was taken very seriously.

The strength of the Birmingham Police had been typically under establishment since the late 1800s and this only got worse as it became apparent that even at full strength, there were not sufficient constables to deal with the expanding boundaries of Birmingham and the rising complexity of police work due to ever increasing legislation. In 1900 Her Majesty's Inspectorate of Constabulary highlighted during their inspection that the force was 200 officers short on the beat[xiv]. Chief Constable Charles Haughton Rafter KBE KPM convinced the Watch Committee to recruit additional constables and increase the establishment, but by 1913 the force was 300 officers short and he was asking constables to take recruiting papers home on leave with them, in the hope that they knew suitable individuals who could apply.[xv]

And still the complexity and variety of police work grew – in addition to patrolling beats, investigating complaints and crimes, catching burglars and thieves, officers had to keep public walkways safe, impound horses found straying, unfit for work or with drunk drivers. They protected schoolchildren crossing roads, took in lost children, *'wandering lunatics'* and stray animals. They rescued people locked in buildings, trapped by fire or poisoned by gas. They examined dead bodies found on their beat and performed first aid (which had become mandatory in most forces by about 1900). As telephones became more common, the police found themselves summoned to deal with more and more minor incidents such as noise trouble and *'naughty children'*, and still the role proliferated more[xvi].

By 1901 most other forces had granted a pay rise to their officers after years of complaints about insufficient police pay. The Birmingham force finally gave superintendents and inspectors a pay increase in October following successful petitions. Constables and sergeants however – received no pay rise. The A Division requested permission from Rafter to meet and put forward a delegation regarding pay, duty and leave. The same day a notice appeared in police orders where Rafter asserted his authority over the matter – stating that he did not appreciate *'anonymous circulars, furtive round-robins, unauthorised or secret meetings, and anonymous letters to the press were derogatory to the character and discipline of the Birmingham City Police and highly insubordinate'.*[xvii] He eventually gave permission for A Division to meet, but the petition was shelved during the Lloyd George riots in December and was then lost, with the men only getting their pay rise in July 1903. Even then the rise was inconsistent and did not grant any increase to some men – leading to the Watch Committee being called the meanest in the country by the Police Review!

There was further discontent with the Watch Committee over pay for policing a railway strike in 1913 – with the committee allowing one day's pay indiscriminately to all the men, ignoring the fact that that some had worked four days extra and some had not performed any extra duty. With the Watch Committee failing to listen to the concerns of their men – support for a police union began to mount.[xviii] Rumours of a police union in Birmingham in 1911 had apparently reached Rafter but nothing could be confirmed[xix]. After the pay protests following the railway strike a small union appeared in Birmingham – its aims were to ensure fair promotion, give legal representation in misconduct cases, fully reinstate the weekly rest day and achieve better pay and allowances. Whilst the men insisted this union was a legitimate organisation not breaching any force rules, Rafter disagreed – stating that any private meetings of policemen were contrary to regulations unless of a legitimate purpose cleared by him.[xx]

Sir Charles Haughton Rafter KBE KPM

Joining the Royal Irish Constabulary in 1883, Rafter was a district inspector within six months. He had held this post for 16 years when he applied to become the Chief Constable of Birmingham City Police. Out of eight short-listed candidates, Rafter was the only one who turned up to the interview in full dress uniform – which must have made quite an impression and tells a little about Rafter's military style and his obsession with discipline and appearance.

In 1900 Rafter set up a voluntary night school in Birmingham, supported by the Education Committee, later known as the Police Institute. This was one of the significant improvements he made in Birmingham which undeniably improved the education of the men, likely making them better officers, but arguably also exercised an element of control over them – with an expectation that men attended the classes.

PC LLOYD GEORGE 87D.

LLOYD GEORGE ESQ. MP
ESCAPED DISGUISED AS A LOYAL SUBJECT.

Rafter was recommended to the Birmingham Watch Committee as *'skilled in the preservation or restoration of peace in troubled districts where party feeling runs high'*[xxi]. This was tested early on when a riot broke out following an anti-Boer war speech at the town hall by radical MP David Lloyd George[xxii]. Anticipating trouble, Rafter ordered 400 officers on duty in and around the town hall which was just as well as a mob armed with stones, bricks and anything else they could get their hands on, smashed windows and street lamps and eventually were dispersed when the Birmingham officers commenced a baton charge. A young man sadly died during the aftermath of the riot and David Lloyd George was smuggled away dressed in the uniform of Police Constable Edward Taylor. This post card produced at the time is an artist's impression of what Lloyd George looked like in police uniform escaping from the rioters.

Rafter had to lead the force through many difficult times during his long tenure – including the significant reduction in numbers during the Great War, responsibility for Defence of the Realm regulations in Birmingham, trade unionism and strikes in a variety of industries, gangs and illegal racecourse bookmakers. He also brought about a number of key improvements in policing such as the introduction of women police in Birmingham, the first police run hostel for women and the introduction of juvenile courts. He was an early advocate for crime prevention measures and in addition, is credited with stamping out the infamous Peaky Blinder gangs of Birmingham.

Many officers bitterly resented Rafter's strict military-like rule and letters appeared in the Police Review throughout the early 1900s to this effect. Police orders in Birmingham reflect how specific and through he was regarding appearance, cleanliness and adhering to rules and regulations.

In 1901, Rafter took to police orders to highlight his dissatisfaction with his men's appearance – stating:

> *'The Chief Constables observes that the men on duty in uniform on the streets have lost the smart, tidy look which as a whole they presented on the recent government inspection. Their hair is uncut and much too long and very untidy. Their trousers are wrinkled and baggy at the knees, indicating that the uniform trousers are being worn when off duty which is forbidden.*
>
> *This must be corrected at once and the men must take a proper pride in their uniform and in turning out smart, tidy and clean.'*[xxiii]

It went on to state that the complaint was not limited to constables, with sergeants and inspectors also being guilty of an untidy appearance. Rafter stated that sergeants, inspectors and even superintendents should pay much more attention when inspecting the men before they went on duty, or they could also expect to be disciplined.

In November 1914 once again Rafter highlighted his displeasure with uncleanliness – after visiting Digbeth Police Station with renowned architect Aston Webb and noting that every window was dirty (and many contained words written by the hands of officers!) and that *'this grossly careless action must be rectified at once'!*[xxiv].

Digbeth Police Station © Tony Hisgett

Policing the Strikes

Throughout the early 1900s many different trades were coming out on strike demanding improved pay and working conditions – these included London bus conductresses, Lancashire mill workers, railwaymen and miners. Not to mention dock workers and the general transport strike in Liverpool that erupted into fierce violence in 1911, known locally as Bloody Sunday.

All the strikes had resulted in improvements for the workers – which would not have gone unnoticed by the police.[xxv]

In August 1911 the 2nd Battalion the Royal Munster Fusiliers were sent to Birmingham during the national railway strike. It was the first time railway staff nationally had walked out and the Prime Minister pledged that soldiers would be deployed to keep the trains running. Home Secretary Winston Churchill suspended the regulation that required local authorities to expressly request military support before it was sent. It only lasted two days but occurred shortly prior to the Llanelli Railway riots in which six people died after violence broke out between the strikers, the police and army[xxvi].

The strike arose from longstanding disputes between workers and railway companies. A meeting of the four main railway companies was arranged in Liverpool and the unions issued ultimatums to the companies. As well as Birmingham, troops were dispatched to London and 31 other towns across the country.

Mounted police lead the soldiers through the streets of Birmingham, August 1911

Left: Police and strikers outside Snow Hill Station 1911 – reproduced with the permission of the Library of Birmingham[xxvii]

Below: Police and strikers outside Midlands Railway Goods Station 1911 – reproduced with the permission of the Library of Birmingham[xxviii]

The 1911 general transport strike overlapped with the 1911 national railway strike referred to above. It was mainly focussed around Liverpool – but other cities were also affected. Snow Hill Station was almost brought to a standstill but for the workers who were part of the National Union of Railwaymen who were not on strike. Soldiers were brought into Liverpool and the resounding violence left two civilians dead. 100 Birmingham officers had also been sent to aid the Liverpool Police during this strike including PC Joseph Philips who received the King's Police Medal for his bravery when he risked his own safety to save the life of his superintendent who had been attacked by a mob.

K O.10.

A C Garton,

STRIKE DUTY AT GRAYS 1912

The Birmingham Police were sent to help police many other strikes across the country – such as the dock strikes in Hull in 1911 and Grays, Essex in 1912

Pictures: *Previous page: Birmingham Police at the Hull Docks Strike in 1911. There may be officers from other forces amongst the Birmingham men*

Above: Photo courtesy of Laurence Breakwell – showing Birmingham police officers alongside members of the Army and Navy

Right: Sergeant Charles Brown policing the strike at Grays in 1912

The docks in London and in the North were plagued with strikes throughout the early 1900s as arguments over wages, protected labour and workers' rights escalated. Tensions were high and there was significant violence across the country as workers downed their tools and the police were sent in.

STRIKE DUTY AT GRAYS 1912

Birmingham officers – potentially policing a strike during the 1910s, with thanks to the Russell family – descendants of Jack Allen, Thomas Mooney, Harry Paragreen, Billy Woodyatt and William Robinson

The Great War and the Impact on Policing

At the beginning of the war the weekly leave day was cancelled – all leave was stopped from August to October 1914, then changed to two days a month and then to a weekly rest day again from November 1914 to November 1915, before it reverted back to two days a month[xxix]. In Birmingham – pay was delayed for all these extra days worked – another cause of anger for the men working so hard to keep the streets of Birmingham safe during the war.

Many officers were military reservists and were therefore called to the colours immediately upon the outbreak of war. Others volunteered for His Majesty's Armed Forces with a large number being attested and joining the reserve list in December 1915, many of those being called up in 1918. The Birmingham Daily Gazette reported on 10 December 1915:

> 'The first batch of the Birmingham policemen under the group system were attested at Digbeth Police Station yesterday. The whole of the men of military age of the "A" and "R" divisions were asked to parade yesterday, and were acquainted with the Home Office order, after which those who wished were allowed to join. Practically every man present was attested and sworn in.'

A total of 571 officers left the Birmingham Police to join the Armed Forces during World War One and 56 made the ultimate sacrifice – never returning home or dying soon after their return as a direct result of wounds and sickness received in the battlefields. Several more officers (many former soldiers) were loaned to the Army as drill instructors in the Birmingham barracks. The force's strength dropped from 1164 in 1914 to 658 in 1918 – just above half of the authorised establishment of 1233[xxx]. The force utilised the First Police Reserve (fulltime paid officers – signed up for service for the duration of the war) and the Second Police Reserve (also known as the Special Constabulary – individuals willing to undertake police duty each week for no pay) to boost the numbers and ensure policing in Birmingham could continue.

The police assumed many new duties under emergency measures as soon as war broke out. They were required to 'arrest enemy aliens, guard vulnerable points, enforce lighting restrictions and deal with the consequences of air raids'.[xxxi] Armed police were sent to patrol special duty points such as train tunnels. As mentioned earlier three officers (a special constable and two members of the First Police Reserve) were killed during World War One in accidents whilst policing the train lines around Moor Street and New Street Stations. One of these was discovered by striking officer John Hodgkiss.

Pay did not keep up with wartime inflation and this caused many difficulties for the officers who remained to police the streets of Birmingham. A war bonus was introduced but this did not cover the rising cost of living and officer pay was looking smaller and smaller in comparison to the rising wages of munitions workers and other wartime occupations. By August 1918 the war bonus had risen to 19s a week.

Those officers that returned from the forces with little or no physical injuries often carried the mental scars of time spent in the trenches. Post-traumatic stress disorder (PTSD) was not fully understood during or immediately after the War, with the anxiety and mental trauma the men suffered when they attempted to return to normality being referred to as shell-shock. For officers such as Constable Harry Evans, invalided out of the military due to shell shock, they were simply posted back to a division. Harry recovered and served with Birmingham City Police until the end of the Second World War.

Birmingham City Police officers marching to the Curzon Street Army Recruitment Office Nov 1915

Many officers resumed police duty only to find they were physically or mentally unfit for the work, subsequently being medically pensioned out of the force. Some allowances were made for officers to be able to do less stressful or demanding work or light duties. The Watch Committee was keen not to dispense of any man returning from the military for whom any work could be found. By April 1919 many men were highlighted as being unfit to carry out regular police duty and it is clear the force was doing everything it could do to not have the men medically pensioned off.

Other efforts were made to financially support the men returning from the Armed Forces, with attempts made to ensure they were not in an unfair position. On 3 April 1919 the Watch Committee announced that any men who had returned from military service who had been reduced in class before they left, would be reinstated into the class they would have been in, had no reduction taken place. It was also noted that in future, when men returned from military service they would immediately be placed in the class they would otherwise have been entitled to from length of service[xxxii].

These men, along with thousands of others returning from the front, were promised 'a land fit for heroes'. But what the officers found when they came back to Birmingham was poor quality housing, wages that had not risen in line with other occupations and a job that had become increasingly complex with wartime roles and responsibilities.

Sgt. A. SNELLING'S Squad, (Birmingham Police), Grenadier Guards, May, 1918.

Many Birmingham officers joined the Grenadier Guards in early 1918. Several strikers are included in this picture.

The National Union of Police and Prison Officers and the 1918 Strike

Small police unions had actually begun to appear across the country from around 1910, with police officers writing increasingly angry letters to the Police Review and getting more and more frustrated with their pay and working conditions. There wasn't really a suggestion of going on strike but a union seemed to offer an opportunity for their voices to be heard.[xxxiii]

The story of the strikes and the National Union of Police and Prison Officer's begins with a young Metropolitan police officer called John Syme. The Presbyterian Scot who joined the London force in 1894 was very different to the other officers (most of whom were ex-soldiers or young men from farms in the countryside) in the sense that he did not indulge in drinking, gambling or flirtations with young housemaids and instead lived a very clean and pure lifestyle. He was also very intelligent and knowledgeable about police procedure – which his comrades found very useful when they got stuck with their report writing.[xxxiv]

By 1909 he had been promoted to inspector and again he differed from his contemporaries due to his great patience and tolerance, not something which was experienced in abundance by the young men of the Metropolitan force from their superiors. John was very fair and knew when words of advice were most appropriate, when to give a warning and when to officially report a constable. That being said he was a stickler for discipline and did not tolerate officers drinking on duty or breaking the rules. However he was always prepared to forgive an honest mistake.[xxxv]

One particular incident led to John's eventual dismissal, the formation of the union and years of campaigning to clear his name and highlight corruption in the senior ranks of the force. It was a very simple case – two men, worse for wear from drink, had been trying to get into a house owned by one of the men (rather noisily). The man's wife refused him entry and the shouting and banging caused quite a disturbance, leading many neighbours to complain. Two officers attended and eventually arrested the men for attempting to enter the address 'without lawful excuse'. Upon arrival at the station, the men disclosed that they had indeed got lawful excuse to enter the property, as one was the owner and the other a lodger. Inspector Syme did the right thing and refused the charge – allowing the men to be on their way. Officers did not like having entries in the refused charge book, as the inevitable conclusion is that they had done something wrong (which they hadn't as the men had not disclosed all the information until they arrived at the station). Inspector Syme sympathised with the men and wrote an accompanying note with the entry, explaining the situation. The sub-divisional inspector criticised their actions and sent them before the acting superintendent. Inspector Syme again defended his men and was heavily criticised by the acting superintendent, who reported him to the assistant commissioner. To cut a long story short – Inspector Syme was transferred to another station and eventually dismissed, which began a long campaign against Commissioner Sir Edward Henry and the Metropolitan Police, trying to vindicate himself for the action he took and highlight the corrupt and improper actions of his senior officers, which he said was breeding discontent amongst the men. [xxxvi]

Syme joined forces with a couple of influential individuals including John Kempster – founder of the Police Review. Known as the 'policeman's friend', it was the most prominent voice to air (anonymously) officer grievances and complaints. Years of campaigning followed (including a number of convictions and prison sentences) and in October 1913, Syme created the Metropolitan Police Union, which soon became the National Union of Police and Prison Officers (NUPPO).

The aims of the union were said to be:

'To safeguard the police against official tyranny and injustice, to improve the conditions of the police service, to ensure equal chances of promotion, maintain just and efficient discipline, purge the service of corrupt and unworthy members and secure for the public honest and efficient police administration. Entrance fee one shilling – annual subscription one shilling.'[xxxvii]

Soon after the creation of the union the Great War began and the police service as a whole was challenged to carry out more duties with fewer officers, which no doubt contributed to the feeling of being underpaid and overworked.

The minimum rate of pay for officers in Birmingham in 1914 was 29s a week (the Metropolitan force was 30s). At the start of the war the pay was comparable to unskilled labourer rates and the police had the benefits of regular pay, holidays and a pension. Accommodation was often provided too which made the police quite an appealing occupation at that time.

Policing pay did not keep up with wartime inflation however – despite the authorities making some effort to bridge the gap with a war bonus – and by 1919 police officers could find themselves 10-20s worse off a week than bakers, train drivers and boot manufacturers.[xxxviii] In January 1919 the average weekly pay for officers returning from the Armed Forces was 51s a week compared to an average of 70s in other industries such as food production, manufacturing and transport services.

As well as issues with the pay and working conditions, schemes such as the 'charge allowance' aggrieved officers in the Metropolitan force and provided the 'seething discontent' which gave the union the perfect setting to recruit officers and gain momentum. The charge allowance was an additional payment made to a sub-divisional inspector if they achieved a certain amount of charges in their district – desperation to retain this allowance had apparently led some sub-inspectors to bully officers into making additional arrests and even force them to lie in court about circumstances of arrests, which led to perjury charges[xxxix].

By 1917 several officers within the Metropolitan Police had been dismissed or had their pay severely cut as punishment for attending union meetings or being members. Officers suspected of being members were interrogated and threatened with charges of insubordination, and Commissioner Henry went to great lengths to weed out any advocates of the union from his force (whilst still battling John Syme's very public vendetta against himself and senior members of the force). There were many raids on union meetings and one particular incident worthy of note concerns a meeting a Mareton Street. Of the 40 officers who were caught following the raid, 14 were sacked and the others had their pay heavily reduced. It was said that the unmarried officers held the doors shut in order that the married officers (due to their additional financial responsibilities) could escape out of the window and down the fire escape.[xl]

In May 1917 Syme had just been released from prison and the committee for the union determined that its affairs were in chaos and he could no longer be secretary – they wanted to distance themselves from his personal campaign and focus solely on improvements for the pay and working conditions for officers.

The new committee issued a revised set of rules including a 'no strike' provision. Ernest Harrison, a young constable sacked for participating in meetings who had delivered the message to Symes on behalf of the committee, was serious about the responsibilities of the union members. He also opposed the expanding links between the union and other unions. The number of senior members of various trade unions and M.P.s championing organised labour who supported the union and petitioned the Home Office for its recognition, were growing in number.[xli]

Between 1917 and 1918 there were many questions raised in Parliament about the police, liaison with the Home Office and trade union officials and the legitimacy of NUPPO. The Home Secretary defended the Commissioner who assured him that everything was under control and the men were satisfied with their lot. It was requested at Parliament that an enquiry was held into the grievances of police officers around the country but this was denied and M.P.s reassured that no such enquiry was necessary.

By this point talk had started of union members from across provincial forces (until this date the union had largely been London based) and PC Tommy Thiel (a Boer War veteran) had been appointed as the provincial organiser. Minimal progress had been made recruiting prison officers to NUPPO but by 1918 a second prison warder was recruited to the committee.[xlii]

In August 1918, PC Tommy Thiel was sacked for union activities, particularly relating to recruiting members in other forces, after a Manchester constable he had been liaising with turned all his union paperwork over to the Chief Constable, who promptly got in touch with Commissioner Henry. Now the Union had the opportunity they needed – they immediately made demands including:

➤ Reinstatement of PC Thiel
➤ That the weekly war bonus of 12/- be immediately increased to £1 for all officers, converted into permanent wages and made pensionable
➤ That a new war bonus of 12½ % of all wages and allowances be granted
➤ Complete official recognition of the National Union of Police and Prison Officers and its duly authorised officials

The union threatened that non-compliance with these demands by midnight on 29 August 1918 meant they would suspend several of their rules – including the crucial 'no strike' rule.[xliii]

The strike was well timed too, during the summer recess of Parliament. The Home Secretary Edward Cave was on holiday in Somerset, the Permanent Under-Secretary of State (Sir Edward Troup) refused to return from Berkshire for 12 hours and the Commissioner was in Ireland.[xliv] Edward Cave returned to London to deal with the escalating situation and the union letter was taken to the Home Office where he discussed it with Assistant Commissioner Frederick Wodehouse and Sir Ernley Blackwell, the Deputy Under-Secretary (Edward Troup returning a few hours later). The men did not take the threat seriously – Wodehouse assured them that the union membership numbers were low and that if a few troublesome members went on strike they would be firmly dealt with. The Home Secretary also decided to issue a statement saying the issue of police pay was under consideration, in order to placate officers considering striking.

No response was received to the demands by the specified deadline and the union called the men out on strike. To put the situation in context – an officer who went on strike and was dismissed, risked losing his pension and potentially being called up for military service whilst the Great War was still raging. They responded in their thousands – officials had seriously underestimated the discontent of the rank and file, and the reach of the union. Well over half of the Metropolitan force's strength of 12,000 officers went on strike, but it is unclear how many City of London officers participated, (a force with a strength of 1,200) with conflicting reports ranging from over 500[xlv] to nearly all of them[xlvi]. Whilst there was a huge amount of support for the strike in London, there were also many stories of officers being bullied into going out on strike by their colleagues, with initial non-strikers being vastly outnumbered – leading to the situation where close to the whole force left their posts. Special constables hurriedly drafted in were reportedly assaulted in some instances.

The event culminated in a march on Downing Street and Whitehall. Londoners were surprised to see columns of four officers marching with a solitary piper at their head[xlvii]. Armed troops were brought in to protect government buildings and those posted to Whitehall and Downing Street were apparently caught up in the overwhelming excitement of the situation and were reported to be fraternising with the strikes and saying they would disobey any order to disperse them[xlviii]. In the eventual sit-down discussion in the cabinet office - government officials including the Prime Minister (David Lloyd George), Home Secretary (George Cave), the Permanent Under-Secretary (Edward Troup) and former Home Secretary Winston Churchill (now Secretary of State for War) were present on one side of the table, and on the other side were NUPPO officials including ex-PC Tommy Thiel, chairman PC James Marston, honourary secretary PC John Crisp, PC John Zollner from the City of London Police and five other members of the executive committee - Field, Patterson, T Scott, Padfield and Simmons. Also there to broker a resolution were Charles Duncan MP (General Secretary of the Workers Union) and Duncan Carmichael – leader of the London Trades Council. The thousands of police officers outside were in good spirits: singing and waiting patiently for the positive news they hoped would come. They were indeed in a strong position.

Thousands of officers congregate on Downing Street – picture credit: The Sports and General Press Agency

City of London officers amongst the Metropolitan officers marching on Downing Street & Whitehall in August 1918

The Prime Minister had little choice – he offered the men an immediate increase in pay of 13s, the introduction of a child allowance, pensions for police widows, immediate reinstatement of Tommy Thiel and for the striking officers to be allowed to go back to work.

Commissioner Sir Edward Henry was deemed to be largely responsible and left the force the same day; Sir Cecil Frederick Neville Macready's appointment being announced that evening. In subsequent discussions the union officials negotiated the return of officers who had been dismissed for previous involvement with the union. The one point where the parties disagreed afterwards on what was resolved at the meeting – was the recognition of the union. The executive reported that the Prime Minister had agreed to recognise it after the war was over. The Home Office officials never accepted this and claimed they agreed only to some form of representation[xlix]. This was a major contributing factor in the subsequent 1919 strike.

Image of provincial organiser PC Tommy Thiel, acting honourary secretary PC John Crisp and NUPPO committee member T Scott in September 1918 in Police Review – *picture credit Daily Sketch* [l]

Lord Tenby (Home Secretary from 1954 to 1956) gave a personal recollection of 1918 to TA Critchley in his book *'A History of Police in England and Wales'*:

'My father, David Lloyd George, was at that time Prime Minister. Looking out of the window of 10 Downing Street, I saw a crowd of men outside, some wearing police uniform and others in civilian clothes. They seemed to appoint a small deputation and a few men came up and knocked at our door. The Prime Minister was told what was happening and was asked whether he would receive a deputation from the Police Union. He refused point blank to do so, as he did not recognise such a union. At the same time he expressed his willingness to receive a deputation of policemen. The strikers went and there were anxious talks among the crowd outside in Downing Street. Eventually the original deputation returned and the Prime Minister saw them and listened to what they had to say... Years later, one of my early tasks as Home Secretary was to receive, in my room at the Home Office, a deputation from the Police Federation. As we talked I was conscious of the startling contrast between these mature leaders of 70,000 police officers in England and Wales, discussing problems of common concern with the Home Secretary of the day, and the anxious, angry men who had come to see my father in Downing Street over 30 years earlier.' [li]

The immediate aftermath of the strike was the nationwide spread of NUPPO – previously confined to London with only small pockets of support elsewhere. New branches were being created all over the country, including under the disapproving eye of Birmingham Chief Constable Charles Haughton Rafter.

And what of ex-Inspector John Syme?

Reynolds and Judge finish the sad tale of former Inspector John Syme in *'The Night the Police Went on Strike'*. John's plight did not end with the re-instatement of the 1918 strikers nor with the creation of the Police Federation. The NUPPO Executive were openly critical of him in their newsletter and distanced themselves from his cause.

He was bitterly dismayed that no-one asked for him to be reinstated as part of the official deal made with the Home Office but unfortunately, many people kept their distance or did not support him openly because he was still determined to not only prove that he was a victim of injustice, but that corruption remained throughout the senior levels of the Metropolitan Police. He continued to publicly slander the Commissioner and on many occasions he made death threats against the King and Queen and the Prime Minister. No one really thought he would carry out the threats, but they attracted publicity to his plight and kept his case in the press. Unfortunately they also saw him imprisoned several times. Eventually he did receive some high profile support, with M.P.s raising his case in Parliament and asking for an enquiry. In 1921 the Police Review published the efforts of John's friend, John Penfold, to launch a testimonial fund. A total of £262 was raised - less than £44 being from serving officers of the Metropolitan Police. They did not seem to recognise him as the man who started all the action that eventually led to the Police Act 1919 and all the improvements they had benefited from. John actually only saw £132 of that, with the rest being swallowed up by administrative costs.

In 1921 John was certified 'insane' and sent to the workhouse asylum after trying to speak to the Prince of Wales, being released the next day. Prior to being sent to the asylum he was sent to prison for the 30th time. John had been a regular participant in the prison authorities 'cat and mouse' system whereby inmates went on hunger strike, were released in order to get better and then subsequently recalled to prison to complete their sentence.

In 1924 John was finally granted an enquiry – it lasted five days. Whilst the panel considered that he presented his case well (and he said himself he was pleased with how the enquiry had gone) they failed to acknowledge that anything unjust had been done to him. This had a devastating impact on John's already fragile mental health – he was again certified insane and sent to Broadmoor. In 1925 he was released and a group of M.P.s formed a committee to keep his case in front of Parliament.

In 1931 it was finally officially recognised that the actions leading to John's transfer were wrong, subsequently affecting his future career as a police officer, and he was granted a pension to recognise his fifteen years' service, including arrears dating back to his dismissal. John did not regard this as a complete success and continued to campaign for his complete vindication. He finally died in 1945 at the age of 73.

Ex-Inspector John Syme – ©Topfoto

The Desborough Committee and the Police Act 1919

The Desborough Committee (convened under Lord Desborough) were requested by Home Secretary Sir Edward Shortt early in 1919 to consider the recruitment, pay, working conditions, allowances and pensions of police officers across the country. Its official terms of reference were:

> 'To consider and report whether any and what changes should be made in the method of recruiting for, the conditions of service of, and the rates of pay, pensions and allowances of the police forces of England, Wales and Scotland.[lii]'

It is surprising that it took so long after the 1918 strike for the committee to be set up, but no doubt the urgency of the situation was expressed to the committee when it first sat. The rumblings of discontent were arising from the union once more – particularly as several months had now gone by since the armistice and there was still no talk of recognition of the union.

There were around 250 individual forces across England, Scotland and Wales at this time. The Committee accepted that they could not possibly see representatives from all of them (but were willing to consider any written evidence submitted). They requested interviews with Chief Constables from a variety of city, borough and county forces and officers at different ranks from a similar variety of forces. Newly appointed Metropolitan Commissioner Macready was one of those interviewed – he argued for a number of conditions for officers:

- A starting salary of 50s a week for constables, rising to a maximum of 60s a week after 20 years' service

- A standard rate of pay for police across the country, but with the Metropolitan Police being slightly higher

- A decent rent allowance

- Removal of the sick pay deductions (currently one shilling a day)

Sergeant Jack Hayes (the new general secretary of NUPPO) was called to give evidence and demanded even higher pay for constables (from 80s up to 100s) and also requested overtime payments instead of being granted time off. He was reported to be very diplomatic, intelligent and put his arguments across well. He later had a successful career as an M.P.

Sergeant Blackburn and PC Zollner from the City of London Police relayed tales of men applying to work on permanent night duty due to living in inadequate accommodation, getting into bed moments after their wife and children had gotten out. They also highlighted that officers needed to eat well for the physical activity of the role and likewise required good boots – all expenses that officers across the country were struggling to afford.[liii]

PC William Sinclair (a Birmingham officer who took part in the strike) gave evidence to the committee, stating 'We believe policemen have for years suffered in silence; they have had no medium through which they could voice their grievances excepting through a few friends in Parliament.[liv]

His Majesty's Inspectorate of Constabulary gave evidence that police work in 1919 was much more demanding than ever before, and required higher qualifications.[lv]

Sergeant George Miles (a representative of the men from Liverpool City Police) expressed a succinct and comprehensive view of the situation of police officers in 1919:

'In the past a policeman has been paid no more than an ordinary labourer; consequently, he has been respected and valued accordingly. He has been looked upon as one who, for a tip or a free drink, could be made to neglect his duty. Unfortunately, his continual fight against poverty has only too often made him susceptible to bribes and tips. There is no doubt we are now suffering from our lowly origin. There is no comparison between what is expected from the policemen of today and the policeman of old. Our predecessors were invariably big, illiterate men, from whom little was expected.' Nowadays a policeman *'must be as brave as a lion, as patient as Job, as wise as Solomon, as cunning as a fox, have the manners of a Chesterfield, the optimism of Mark Tapley, must be learned in criminal law and local by-laws, must be of strong moral character, able to resist all temptations, be prepared to act as a doctor, be a support to the weak and infirm, a terror to evil-doers, a friend and counsellor to all classes of the community, and a walking encyclopaedia.*[lvi]*'*

Manchester's Inspector Latham stated that *'the duties of a police officer [were] such as to demand a keener intelligence, better physique, sounder judgment, fearless courage and a higher moral character than are considered necessary in most other callings'*. Birmingham Sergeant Clowes concurred, stating that policemen should be ranked with the professions or highly skilled trades. They have to undertake *'continuous hours of study in order to make themselves proficient in their duties as constables owing to the increasing and complex nature of the legislation which is continually being introduced'*[lvii].

Many who gave evidence were asked about the benefits of a national police force, which would make consistent pay, training and promotion procedures easy to achieve, but would remove the local control and ability to promptly react to situations in specific areas and was thus a hugely unpopular idea and not included in the final recommendations.

During the review the committee considered the average pay of officers from different forces, with different variables such as length of service, marital status and number of children and compared this with the outgoings of police families of various sizes. This showed that in Birmingham a constable's basic weekly pay was between 43s and 53s with a war bonus of 12s and 2s 6d allowance for each child plus a rent allowance for married officers of 4s 2d – a total of 64s to 74s for married officers and 55s to 66s for single officers. It is worth noting that Birmingham pay for constables had only recently increased towards the end of 1918 (possibly a reaction to the strike and subsequent events in London) from a starting salary of 31s up to 44s with length of service.

Outgoings were also scrutinised to understand how far the pay would go in supporting families of different sizes in city, borough and county forces. Of the examples for eight families of city police constables, six had outgoings that were higher than their pay and allowances. One broke even and one had just short of two shillings spare at the end of the week.

The Desborough Committee published its first report as a white paper on 14 July 1919. It proposed:

- Standardised pay and conditions for police across the country
  - Constables were to start at £3 10s (70s), rising by 2s a year to £4 10s weekly pay
- A representative body for the police
- That a police department be set up within the Home Office
- Improved and more systematic training
- Abolition of police forces in non-county boroughs with less than 50,000 people
- A standardised discipline code and right of appeal
- Transfer of certain powers in borough forces from the Watch Committee to the chief constable

- Pension improvements
- Standardised arrangements for annual leave

The committee reported '*We are satisfied that a policeman has responsibilities and obligations which are peculiar to his calling and distinguish him from other public servants and municipal employees... the burden of individual discretion and responsibility placed upon a constable is much greater than that of any other public servant of subordinate rank.*'[lviii]

The report included a statement about the calibre of person required to be a police officer: '*not only must they be tall and physically strong, but must have a sound constitution*'. A man cannot make a good policeman unless his '*general intelligence, memory and powers of observation are distinctly above the average. His character should be unblemished: he should be humane and courteous and, generally, he should possess a combination of moral, mental and physical qualities not ordinarily required in other employments.*' The committee also set higher educational requirements and recommended standardised promotion procedures to discourage favouritism[lix]. It also acknowledged that training was deficient and recommended a universal system of one year's probation, including two months of instruction followed by one hour of instruction a day for the probationary period[lx].

The report's recommendations were at once put into motion in the Police Bill 1919 which created the Police Federation and banned members of the police from belonging to a union. There were also provisions for individuals attempting to cause disaffection within the police that included a prison sentence of up to two years. It went on to create the Police Council as a consultative body for future legislation. In addition, the Home Office pledged additional funds to cover 50% of expenditure by forces, instead of just pay and clothing which had previously been the case. This led to central government funding for policing to rise from £7m in 1914 to £18m in 1920[lxi]. The recommendations included backdating the pay award to 1 April, which meant officers would immediately receive four months back pay (a very clever move). Edward Shortt announced that this would form an immediate £10 back payment for all officers, whilst final calculations were worked out. This turned out to be very significant when the 1919 strike was announced. Another recommendation from the Police Act 1919 was that chief constables be appointed who had prior police experience. Prior to this date many had been appointed from the military, leading to a distinct lack of understanding of the role of constable and the experiences of officers. Due to the significant number of chief constables already serving with no prior police experience, it was many years before this became common practice[lxii].

The Police Bill was introduced into the House of Commons on 8 July 1919 and completed its passage there on 1 August, receiving Royal Assent on 17 August and becoming the Police Act 1919.

The second part of the Desborough report was published in 1920. There were provisions to improve leadership and reduce tension between rank and file officers and chief constables, with a requirement for newly appointed chief constables to have police experience (except in exceptional cases). Pay and allowances, along with pensions and medical care were carefully outlined to finally ensure standardisation across the forces. Watch Committees also lost the right to decide whether or not officers should be able to have their weekly rest day. There were improvements in training and education and a national promotion exam system was set up. Additional inspectors of constabulary were recruited to help ensure forces were adhering to the new regulations.[lxiii]

Policing Birmingham in 1919

By 1919 Sir Charles Haughton Rafter was celebrating 20 years as Chief Constable of the force. He had been complimented for many achievements including early introduction of blackouts during WWI (saving Birmingham from the Zeppelins), stamping out the Peaky Blinders (although other economic and social factors such as WWI also contributed) and the introduction of women police in Birmingham.

He had revamped the requirements of probationary constables before they were allowed to patrol the beat and implemented many new training methods and instruction classes. By 1919 Birmingham had a reputation for excellent training and efficiency with new constables spending per week:

- 12 hours in school
- 11 hours at drill
- Eight hours on patrol
- Six hours in court
- One hour at ambulance school
- Three evenings in structured study time
- Three hours a week at the gymnasium

As well as having the best training school in the country, Birmingham also had a reputation for the best police quarters[lxiv]. However this came at a cost – Rafter expected very high standards of the men and used police orders to give instructions for cleaning facilities and uniforms, and also included dormitory rule infractions in official disciplinary records (unlike other city forces).[lxv]

Rafter's strict regimes and draconian rule did not always earn him favour with the men, who sometimes found him hard to approach. One such example occurred in 1919 when constables complained that stray dogs being taken in at police stations did not have adequate food or kennels for the amount coming in. Frustrated at not being able to get Rafter to do anything about the problem, some of the men invited a local woman from a charity that looked after stray dogs to come and inspect the conditions. After hearing that the dogs relied upon scraps from the men for food she set about putting together a programme whereby she would take scraps donated from hotels and turn it into dog food, coming in regularly to feed the animals at different stations. She approached several superintendents who supported the idea but when Rafter heard about it, he claimed the dogs were perfectly well looked after and the force did not need the help. Clearly thinking about the reputational impact, he then enquired internally about the conditions in the kennels and after hearing they were inadequate, made sure that the situation was rectified[lxvi].

Prior to changes brought about by the Police Act 1919, Rafter relied more heavily on punishing men by stopping leave rather than imposing fines. Perhaps he realised the burden that additional fines would place on already struggling families, preferring instead to stop their leave and have them at work. Or perhaps he felt that punishments should include removal of benefits such as leave, with officers having to work harder as a result, which might make them think twice before making their next infraction[lxvii].

Birmingham City Police.

DUTIES OF RECRUITS.

HOURS DAILY.	MONDAY.	TUESDAY.	WEDNESDAY.	THURSDAY.	FRIDAY.	SATURDAY.
9.30 a.m. till 10.30 a.m.	Gymnasium.	Drill.	Gymnasium.	Drill.	Drill.	Gymnasium.
11.0 a.m. till 12 noon.	Court.	Court.	Court.	Court.	Court.	Court.
12 noon till 1 p.m.	School.	School.	School.	School.	School.	School.
1 p.m. till 2.30 p.m.	Dinner.	Dinner.	Dinner.	Dinner.	Dinner.	Dinner.
	Drill 2.30 p.m. to 3.15 p.m.	Drill 2.30 p.m. to 3.30 p.m.	Drill 2.30 p.m. to 3.15 p.m.	Fire Drill 2.30 p.m. to 3.30 p.m. Lingard Street Fire Station.	Drill 2.30 p.m. to 3.15 p.m.	
	School 3.30 p.m. to 4.30 p.m.	School 3.45 p.m. to 5 p.m.	School 3.30 p.m. to 4.30 p.m.	School 3.45 p.m. to 4.30 p.m.	School 3.30 p.m. to 4.30 p.m.	
	Patrol 6 p.m. to 10 p.m.	Evening for Home Study.	Evening for Home Study.	Patrol 6 p.m. to 10 p.m.	Evening for Home Study.	Patrol 6 p.m. to 10 p.m.

Council School Classes during the winter months from 7.30 till 9 p.m. on Monday, Tuesday, and Wednesday, take the place of Home Work and Patrol.

Ambulance Classes will be attended after Recruits are dismissed drill.

Recruits are required to devote their spare time to study.

They are expected to make themselves reasonably efficient within a reasonable time.

December, 1905.

Duties for new recruits from 1905, re-posted in Police orders 15 February 1919 page 524, with a note for superintendents to make suggestions for changes.

Birmingham City Police Senior Officers 1919

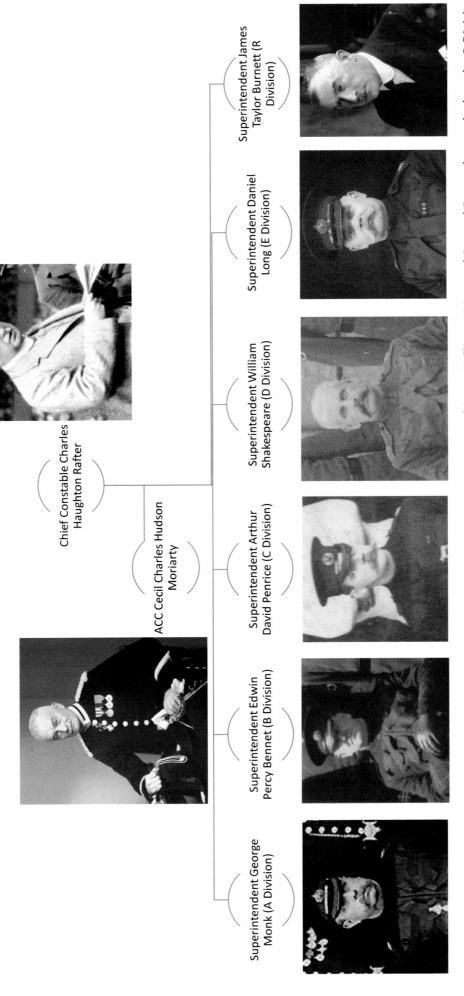

Chief Constable Charles Haughton Rafter

ACC Cecil Charles Hudson Moriarty

Superintendent George Monk (A Division)

Superintendent Edwin Percy Bennet (B Division)

Superintendent Arthur David Penrice (C Division)

Superintendent William Shakespeare (D Division)

Superintendent Daniel Long (E Division)

Superintendent James Taylor Burnett (R Division)

Supts William J May and Samuel Berry also worked on the R Division

In 1919 the force was divided into six divisions:

- A Division headquarters was Newton Street (cornering Corporation Street) and covered the City Centre including Digbeth and the Central Lock-up
- B Division headquarters was Ladywood and included Wellington Road, Harborne, Quinton, Selly Oak, Northfield, Bartley Green, Rednall, Longbridge, Stirchley, Kings Norton and West Heath
- C Division headquarters was over at Kenyon Street and included Handsworth, Bridge Street West, Holyhead Road, Lozells Road, Dudley Road and Wood Lane
- D Division headquarters were based at Victoria Road, Aston and included Duke Street, Erdington, Bloomsbury Street, Stetchford and part of Bordesley Green
- E Division headquarters was Moseley Street Police Station and included Balsall Heath, Coventry Road, part of Bordesley Green, Hay Mills, Sparkhill, Kings Heath, Acocks Green and Moseley.
- R Division was headquarters and included administrative roles and the Criminal Investigation Department.

In 1919 the establishment of the Birmingham City Police was 1431. The strength included a Chief Constable, an Assistant Chief Constable, eight superintendents, 58 inspectors, 148 sergeants and around 1,080 constables. Five of the superintendents covered the geographical divisions and three were allocated to the R Division.

1919 saw the majority of the officers who had joined the Armed Forces being demobilised and returning to Birmingham City Police. Most of them came between January and March but some continued to return later in the year.

An announcement was made in police orders in January 1919 reiterating the position that men who were re-joining were not only entitled to count their military service as approved service for pension purposes, but that they were entitled to claim any increases in pay that they would have had if they had never left the force. It was highlighted that many men returning were not aware of this and were therefore not claiming the increases they were entitled to.

Rafter and the Watch Committee had created a Representative Committee to address any grievances and complaints of the men. The committee had a wide remit, being able to make representation to the Watch Committee and the Chief Constable on issues of pay, allowances, working conditions, accommodation – everything but misconduct, which the committee had no authority to intervene in. This committee (and the first individuals nominated to sit on it) will be covered in more detail later in the book.

In May 1918 the force had implemented a significant pay rise (perhaps in anticipation of the Desborough Review findings) with pay for newly appointed constables going up from 27/- per week to 43/- per week, up to 53/- per week after 20 years' service (compared to 36/- per week on the previous scale). Basic pay for sergeants went up from 38/- per week to 56/- per week.

The 1919 Police Strike

Rather than having the effect of quelling all discontent, the 1918 strike seemed to have the opposite effect on police forces around the country with branches of NUPPO springing up everywhere. Bear in mind that officers outside of London had not seen the strikers bullying their colleagues into going on strike but instead, had seen that coming together as a group had been hugely successful and the police seemed to have an organisation that the government had listened to. NUPPO were of course saying that officials promised to recognise the union after the war which would have led many men to think they were joining a legitimate organisation.

Organised labour in Birmingham played a leading role in organising the Birmingham branch. Immediately after the 1918 strike the Birmingham Trades Council wrote to Duncan Carmichael asking for information[lxviii]. On 10 October it congratulated the Metropolitan Police on their success and pledged itself to give *'every assistance to the formation of a branch in Birmingham'*[lxix]. The Birmingham branch of NUPPO was subsequently formally inaugurated at a well-attended meeting at the Corn Exchange, held under the Trades Council's auspices and at the meeting of the council on 26 October, the new branches application for affiliation was *"heartily sanctioned"*.[lxx]

There was considerable support for the union in Birmingham and this was not confined to trade unions, but also middle-class conscientious objectors who had suffered indignities during WWI and believed formation of a police union would prevent reoccurrence of this. These included Unitarian minister Morgan Whiteman (a big supporter and fund raiser for the union) and the Labour party candidate Frederick Edmondson who said:

> *'The recent formation of a Police Union in Birmingham is likely to prove a benefit to the Public and to the Police. Winson Green Prison… will tell its own tale after the war is crowned by a just and humane peace; the experience of educated, refined and earnest "political prisoners" who have been confined as criminals within its walls will be of inestimable value for the future reform of our penal system.'*[lxxi]

Sir Charles Haughton Rafter had always forbidden his men to have anything to do with the union. Even after the Home Office stated that belonging to the union was no longer a disciplinary offence after the 1918 strike, Rafter still would not tolerate the organisation in Birmingham and issued orders to that effect. On 7 October 1918 in police orders it was stated:

> *'The Chief Constable has learned with extreme regret that certain persons have been approaching some members of the Police Force with a view to their joining a 'Police Union.'*

> *As a friend of the Force, and in the best interests of its Members, he strongly advised them not to have anything to do with this organisation. To become a member of it is also contrary to the Regulations of the Force.*

> *The Chief Constable thinks it right to inform Members of the Force what is being done by the Watch Committee and himself.*

> *Hitherto, it has been the rule when Members of the Force have had any proposal to make with regard to their pay, or other matter, to inform the Chief Constable of their desire to meet; when every facility for doing so was afforded to them; and their representations were afterwards carefully considered.*

> *With a view of systemising the method and to avoid special applications for such meetings being made from individual Members of the Force to hold such meetings, the Watch*

Committee are at present engaged in formulating a set of rules under which a Permanent Elective Committee will be set up within the Birmingham Police Force, which will be elected annually, by the Members of the Force; and which will be in a position to deal with matters which the meetings above referred to have considered; but in a more systematic and representative way. That is, all matters connected with the welfare of the Members of the Force, except matters of discipline. This committee will at all times be able to represent the views of the Force to the Chief Constable, or the Watch Committee. The details of this scheme will be issued at the earliest possible moment.

The Watch Committee are also engaged considering a new and improved scale of Police Pay, which will in due course receive the approval of the Home Secretary. The new scale will be retrospective, so that no time will be wasted.

The Chief Constable issues this Order with the object of re-assuring Members of the Force that their interests are being looked after; and with a view to removing any impression (which is a false impression); that they can obtain any benefit through becoming members of a 'Police Union'. This would not only be contrary to Police Regulations, but would be highly subversive of good Order and Discipline, in fact the two things cannot exist together in the same Force.

The recent disgraceful Strike of Police in the Metropolis, of which we are all ashamed, should act as a deterrent to Members of this Force, not to ally themselves in any way to an organisation which took part in such a disloyal occurrence.

It can do no good for any Policeman, but can do a great deal of harm to the Country.

In the meantime the Members of the Force can rest assured that the Chief Constable has their true interest at heart. [lxxii]

It is ironic that Rafter uses the 1918 strike as a deterrent when the union officials were no doubt using it as an example of the power the union wielded when they came together with sufficient force and demanded change. The chairman of the Birmingham branch of the union was Sergeant Edward Taylor – a seasoned officer with 23 years' service based at Kenyon Street Police Station.

By 18 October 1918 the Birmingham City Police Representative Committee was officially established for the men to air their grievances and for any issues to be brought before senior officers in a controlled and respectful manner. Police orders from 7 October, which discouraged the men from joining the union and introduced the idea of the committee, were followed by a pro forma for all superintendents to sign that indicated all the men on their division had seen the order and had the contents explained to them. After the committee was announced, within a couple of weeks elections were arranged at every station for the men to choose their representatives. One inspector, two sergeants and four constables were to be elected from each division with a total of 42 positions being available on the committee across the ranks of constable, sergeant and inspector. A special executive sub-committee of 12 individuals was also to be created to govern the main committee. The first officers elected to the board were as follows:

A Division

PC's 46 Raymont, 112 Hawkins, 71 W Sinclair and 192 W Booton (105 A Green received a joint number of votes with Sinclair and Booton but lost out in a subsequent deciding vote). Sergeants H Ward and P Hartley and Inspector Frankish.

PC's 41 Kelly, 118 Holmes, 84 Lake and 61 Bourne. Sergeants H Smith and F Shereston and Inspector Cook.

C Division

Constables 147 Jackson, 264 Warwood, 88 Mckie and 172 Godwin. Sergeants J Russell and E Taylor and Inspector Lomas.

D Division

Constables 97 Simons, 109 Bond, 98 Freckleton and 142 Nicholls. Sergeants Smith and Harris and Inspector Husband.

E Division

Constables 198 Walker, 8 Seedham, 115 George Ware and 161 Herbert Reeve (270 Albert Wilkinson and 147 John Whapples received an equal amount of votes as Ware and Reeve but lost out in a subsequent election between the men). Sergeants Doughty and Davies and Inspector Wasley.

R Division

Constables 118 Finemore, 115 Wright, 59 Eastwood and 85 Elderton. Sergeants Harris and Clowes and Inspector Hawkins.

Interestingly 11 of the men who received the most nominations (including the original tied votes) ended up being involved in the strike. They were clearly very determined to effect change within the force and were not afraid to take action. After the inaugural meeting of the committee was held, the executive sub-committee was nominated – it is of note that this included all three of the sergeants involved in the strike and two constables.

The board achieved improvements within the first year including the reinstatement of the weekly rest day, reducing restriction of the annual leave period (so leave didn't have to be taken in winter) and an increase in pay for special duty. Other requests were made but denied – including amending the split shift system to continuous shifts for the day duty men, an issue that had long bothered the Birmingham officers. This board clearly had some standing and was regularly mentioned at the Watch Committee and Judicial Sub-Committee, with Rafter agreeing to take actions and communication back to the board and vice versa. It had also been used as a vehicle for complaints to be registered and investigated regarding senior officer's treatment of constables – which the Judicial Sub-Committee were quick to point out was not within their remit:

> …'the Chief Constable be requested to point out to the Birmingham City Police Representative Committee in reply to the regulations approved by the Watch Committee for the establishment of their committee expressly excluded matters of police discipline, and that therefore it was not within their province to institute enquiries into the conduct of Superior officers and that in cases where the man feels that they have a grievance in any matter which is one of discipline their proper course is to lay the case before the Chief Constable, who will, in his turn, if he deems it advisable bring the matter to the notice of the Watch Committee[lxxiiilxxiv].

On 28 October 1918 the Watch Committee announced via police orders:

'Police Union

It having been brought to the notice of the Watch Committee that a movement has been started to organise a Police Union and that Members of the Birmingham Police Force have been approached to join such a Union; the Watch Committee desire to state that they view this action with great regret and wish to say that it meets with their strongest disapproval as being contrary to the Rules of the Force.

The Watch Committee have always been ready to receive and consider representations made to them by the Force in regard to any grievances or alleged cause of complaint affecting the interests of the men; and recently the Watch Committee have approved of a Representative Committee being appointed by the different ranks of the Force by which they can make known in a proper and constitutional manner any questions which they may desire to bring to the notice of the Police Authority.'

The union was not discouraged by the lack of formal recognition from senior officers in London and around the country and continued to press Parliament for national recognition as a formal union. Commissioner Macready met with the NUPPO executive committee on numerous occasions however after much bickering throughout 1919 the, at best professionally courteous, relationship broke down altogether and he refused to meet with them again.

In November 1918 there were complaints from Birmingham NUPPO men when it appeared they were passed over for a round of promotions[lxxv]. In December 1918 NUPPO issued its first magazine to give updates and information to its members across the country. Over 20 updates are given from provincial branches (police forces and prisons) and within the Birmingham update it states that Birmingham is set to be one of the largest in the country (presumably only London and Liverpool had higher membership) with members joining in their hundreds.

The NUPPO lapel badge owned by a Birmingham officer – part of the West Midlands Police Museum collection

There were further complaints in January 1919 when Rafter refused to allow members of the Birmingham branch of NUPPO to attend the union conference in London, which prompted several local trade union societies to petition the Watch Committee – complaining about the restrictions *'imposed upon the civic rights of the police in their capacity as citizens, demanding that the officers be allowed their basic civil rights'*. They also suggested that if the Watch Committee refused to withdraw the restrictions on the men, then the Home Office and Parliamentary Committee of the Trade Unions Congress be asked to get involved in the matter[lxxvi]. The Watch Committee refused to take action and instead referred the societies to the current Home Office discussions on recognition of the union, stating that it was not a matter for individual watch committees. Whilst the complaints of the societies were futile, it does demonstrate the visible local trade union support for the police union and the control Rafter had over his men.

Many members of the Birmingham City Police Representative Board were apparently active in the union but in April 1919, prior to electing a new board, the Honourable Secretary, Detective Sergeant William Clowes, announced:

'It should be clearly understood that the functions of the Representative Committee are not to promote strike (sic) and work in direct opposition to the Authorities, but to provide additional facilities for approaching the Authorities, and equating them with the real views and wishes of the members of the Force. In addition to forwarding requests similar to the above, this committee can also promote schemes and suggestions which will react to the comfort and general welfare of the Force, therefore it is important that each individual member should take a responsible and earnest part in the forthcoming election, so that the best possible results may be obtained for the furtherance of their own interests, for upon the capacity, level headedness, and moderation of each member of the Committee will depend the success, or otherwise, of the new Committee that is about to be formed.

No member should be elected, or allow himself to be elected, who is not willing to undertake the responsibility that is placed upon him, or object to the inconvenience and additional work he may be subjected to. [lxxvii]*'*

He went on to say the outgoing committee were recognised for being instrumental in obtaining the following concessions:

1. Weekly rest day restored with two consecutive rest days every 7th week
2. Annual leave restored and not to be taken during the months of December, January and February
3. Lost leave – payment for lost leave since August 1914
4. Special duty rates increased
5. Travelling allowances granted to members of A Division when travelling to court or other special duty, similar to what is allowed to members on other divisions
6. Uniform facilities for members of this committee to attend its meetings

In addition, other little matters which affected individual divisions had been immediately rectified when the attention of the Superintendent concerned had been drawn to them by members of the committee.

Sergeant Clowes finished by commenting that although the committee had only been in existence for under six months, the above record was put together as proof of valuable services it had rendered to members of the force during its tenure of office. When the nominations came in for the election of new members of the representative committee, these included 18 of the men later dismissed for participating in the strike, and 15 of these went on to be elected to the committee[lxxviii].

Rafter did give his representative board the chance to get involved in national discussions about police pay and conditions – allowing representatives to travel to London to give evidence before the Desborough Committee[lxxix].

There did seem to be a fair amount of support for the union in Birmingham, with membership numbers quoted as 400 a few weeks after the 1918 strike[lxxx] and by April 1919 police witnesses to the Desborough Committee claimed that 90% of the force were in the union.[lxxxi] The Birmingham Trades Council continued to be very vocal in its support of the union and gave considerable encouragement.[lxxxii]

It was clear that key members of the Birmingham Branch of NUPPO were getting themselves involved in matters that caused friction between themselves, Rafter and the Watch Committee. In May the Chairman of the Watch Committee (Alderman Sanders) referred to '*certain allegations which Sergeant Taylor had made at a public meeting held in Birmingham in furtherance of the suggested Police Union, with regard to the treatment meted out to returned disabled soldiers who were members of the Police Force, and reported that he had requested Sergeant Taylor to furnish the Committee with definite information in regard to such cases'*. Sergeant Doughty (the branch secretary) was also reported to the Watch Committee by Rafter for writing a letter to a subordinate member of the force, containing statements that in his opinion, amounted to undermining the discipline of the police.[lxxxiii] Legal advice was sought from the Acting Town Clerk and both sergeants were requested to respectfully appear before the Judicial Sub-Committee.

In May 1919 the union threatened another strike, going so far as to ballot its members. This time the main causes for concern were the dismissal of an active union member in the Metropolitan force (PC Spackman), an increase in pay and the lack of recognition of the union. The Watch Committee in Birmingham and Rafter issued further clarification on the situation to the officers in their force. This order stated that any striking officer would be dismissed and lose any service that counted towards their pension. It highlighted that the police did not fall under the Trades Dispute Act 1906 as they were not 'workmen' and that anyone on strike who interfered with an officer attempting to do his duty would be dealt with for obstruction of police (see below).

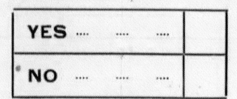

NATIONAL
UNION OF POLICE & PRISON OFFICERS.
Head Office: 191, Bishopsgate, London, E.C. 2.

BALLOT PAPER.
(Issued by Order of Executive Committee.)

Are you prepared to withdraw from duty in order to obtain—

Complete recognition of your Union?

Re-instatement of Ex-P.C. Spackman, and the reviewing of all cases of known victimisation?

An immediate increase of pay and pension for Police and Prison Officers, the Scale to be agreed upon between the Government and the E.C. of the Union; and total abolition of military control of the Police and Prison Services?

YES	....	....	....	
NO	....	....	....	

DIRECTIONS.

Place a cross—thus **X**—opposite " Yes " or " No," as the case may be. No mark other than one cross must be placed on the paper.

This paper to reach Branch Secretary or Chief Office by 12 noon Thursday, **May 29th, 1919.**

T.C.P.—3924

May 1919 NUPPO ballot paper – courtesy of the Working Class Movement Library

POLICE AND PRISON OFFICERS' UNION.

THREATENED POLICE STRIKE.

The Watch Committee have had under consideration the threatened declaration of a strike by the Executive of the Police and Prison Officers' Union, and have decided that any Officer or Man of the Birmingham City Police Force of whatever rank who participates therein and fails to report in the ordinary course of duty, or when called on, will be forthwith Dismissed from the Force.

They have also decided that such Officer or Man will under no circumstances be permitted to re-join the Birmingham City Police; and that Dismissal will result in the loss of all service counting towards pension.

The Watch Committee have the approval of the Government for this course.

It will be seen from the Home Secretary's reply to Mr. Wallace's question in the House of Commons on Wednesday last, a copy of which appeared in Police Orders yesterday, that the Government have definitely decided not to recognise the existing Police and Prison Officers' Union.

An Organisation will be set up by Authority within the Police Service to enable the men to protect their own interests. Particulars will be issued as soon as possible.

It will not be confined to a purely Local Organisation, but will include provision to enable the men to make their representations on a National basis on questions of Pay. &c., which effect the Police as a whole.

It is pointed out that the Trades Disputes Act, 1906, does not apply in the case of a Strike by the Police, as the Police are not "Workmen" within the definition of Section 5 (3) of the Act.

Any forcible prevention or interference with a Police Officer who is parading for Duty or is on Duty is an obstruction of the Police within the meaning of the Prevention of Crimes Act, 1885, and will be dealt with accordingly.

This notice is issued by the direction of the Watch Committee.

The Chief Constable feels assured that the large majority of the Birmingham City Police Force have no association with the organisation referred to, and he has the utmost confidence in the good sense and loyalty of the Police Force as a whole. He feels sure that the members of the Birmingham City Police Force will not take part in any movement such as described, but which seems to be in contemplation in connection with the Police Union which claims to have a membership in Birmingham.

By order,

CHARLES HAUGHTON RAFTER,

CHIEF CONSTABLE.

NUPPO themselves claimed 83% membership of the Birmingham force in May 1919 (with 96% of those favouring strike action).[lxxxiv] It was fortunate for the authorities that the strike did not go ahead at this time (it had insufficient support and the Executive Committee called it off), as the subsequent delay seemed to dissolve some of the pro-strike sentiment with a pay increase and working condition improvements promised imminently. As well as recognition, Sergeant William Doughty claimed the union also argued for 'withdrawal of militarist methods, and victimisation'.[lxxxv]

At the end of May 1919 the House of Commons was informed by Home Secretary Sir Edward Shortt that the Police and Prison Officers' Union was not to be formally recognised and it was acknowledged that there was still some unrest within the Metropolitan Police Force[lxxxvi].

In June the Home Office issued a recommended standard police pay scale. The Judicial Sub-Committee recommended that the Watch Committee adopt a similar scale for Birmingham which would see new constables starting on 70/- a week backdated to April – which took the form of an immediate interim £10 back payment for all officers serving in April, with final amounts to be confirmed later[lxxxvii]. Officers who joined after April would have an amount to be worked out based on the length of their service. Many of the officers who had several years' service and had recently returned from the Armed Forces were earning on average 50/- a week at this time so the pay increase was substantial.

At this time the Birmingham Representative Board also appeared before the Judicial Sub-Committee and made a number of requests, giving an interesting insight into what was bothering officers at the time. Included in this representation was a request about addressing the situation where many men (particularly those returning from service with the Armed Forces) were unable to live with their families due to a lack of police housing, poor pay for police reservists, exempting men with 20 years' service from much hated drill and to increase the amount of leave given to officers. The committee had actually highlighted a number of houses they believed should have been available for officers but had been let to other parties but the sub-committee put the record straight and said that all of the houses highlighted had been sold or were for sale[lxxxviii]. Regarding leave – the sub-committee at this time indicated that they thought the provisions were adequate but a year later leave provision was significantly increased from 9 to 14 days[lxxxix].

On 30 July 1919, the NUPPO executive met at the Union office and again posed the question – 'Do we strike?' Jack Hayes gave a report on the current situation and it was identified that the majority of the provincial forces were not going to support a strike. There were fears many of the London officers would not strike either. The union was arguably more frustrated with their lack of recognition now than with the pay and working conditions of officers across the country which was being openly addressed through the Desborough Committee and the Police Bill. The demands were thus: reinstatement of PC Spackman (who had been sacked for encouraging other officers to ignore the action to create a representative board and thus promote the union) and recognition of the union.

Whilst he felt it was futile, Jack Hayes wrote to Sir Lloyd George as requested by the executive, to ask for a meeting to consider recognition of the union before the Police Bill was passed into law. This was referred to the Home Secretary. When the executive went to see Prime Minister Lloyd George, he was not inclined to meet with them as the Metropolitan Commissioner Macready had told him the situation was in hand – so he brushed them aside[xc]. He was also well aware of the impending pay rise and imminent £10 payment per officer to be paid out within days.

When their pleas went unheard by the government and Lloyd George – the heavily divided committee made the decision to go on strike. They were also under the impression that they had significant trade union support that could bring the country to a halt – an impression that later turned out to be made on false promises. Their demands were that the provisions in the Police Bill regarding the prohibition of the union and creation of the Federation be removed, the union recognised, and key union officials reinstated. Jack Hayes issued the strike manifesto which was printed in full by the Daily Herald on 1 August 1919:

'You must act or lose your freedom forever. Your executive committee has, therefore, decided upon making use of the final argument and this statement should be accepted as official notification that members of the National Union of Police and Prison Officers withdraw their services immediately, such withdrawal to remain effective until the gross injustice imposed by the provisions of Section 1, 2 and 3 of the Police Bill are remedied, and full and frank recognition of your Union is conceded. The members of your executive committee have already withdrawn their services, and are prepared to sacrifice all for the cause, being assured that the members they represent will fight for justice and liberty, with determination second to none.'[xci]

This was not strictly true as a number of members of the executive had decided not to go on strike and many Metropolitan Police members of the union were horrified at the decision and remained on duty, severing their ties with the union.

Several key members of the union (involved in the previous successful strike) clearly saw the strike for the suicide mission that it was, and after tearing up their union cards, spent much time persuading the officers in their own stations not to go on strike. In London 308 men went on strike the first night (31 July into 1 August).[xcii]

London Strikers of 'B' division wait for news on 1 August 1919

During subsequent efforts by the union members to convince other officers that significantly higher numbers were actually on strike and reports in the media that the strike was a success, the total number of striking officers continued to grow.

Commissioner Macready ordered senior officers outside every sub-division headquarters to break up picket lines and dishearten the men, and ordered every sergeant, inspector and senior officer on duty to return to their station.

Violence broke out between striking and non-striking officers, with several of the latter being badly beaten up. Lunchtime on 1 August showed 546 Metropolitan officers were on strike, reaching 854 by the evening. Over the following five days, the figure rose to over 1,000 – with many joining the strike in its latter days. Possible reasons for this were several mixed (and false messages) being circulated by union members and the timing of the strike: during the holiday period, so many officers were just returning from leave on the Saturday and Sunday. [xciii]

After collecting their £10 back pay, a total of 58 City of London men went out on strike.

The London contingent received news from Liverpool that the majority of the force had gone out on strike, and whilst they were surely heartened at the news, they had to have realised that the vast majority of their own men had refused the call to action and the strike was doomed to fail. A total of 1,056 men had gone out on strike from the Metropolitan force[xciv].

But what was happening in Birmingham? Although the Watch Committee had discussed and approved the increase in police pay, this did not come into effect until later in August. Many officers though will likely have felt that the Birmingham Representative Board was already giving them a chance to air grievances and make representations to senior officers.

On 31 July with the Police Bill in all likelihood being passed into law and the strike imminent, Sergeant Taylor had sent two delegates to London. The two delegates were warders from Winson Green Prison (now HMP Birmingham). Whilst awaiting their colleagues' return, the union branch committee meeting was held on 1 August but the committee decided to await the news from London before making a decision. Sergeant Taylor returned to Kenyon Street at lunchtime and notified all the divisions that they were to go on duty as usual. A telegram was sent to the London NUPPO executive asking for instructions but none had been received (presumably by this point the NUPPO executive was already collapsing). That evening the committee held another meeting with members in conflict over what action to take.[xcv] Sergeant Taylor was apparently against striking, but he reminded those present that they had pledged their support for strike action if it was called, and it would be wrong to leave all the responsibility to the London officers. The majority present were cautious about committing to anything and the meeting was adjourned with no action decided. Sergeant Taylor made his way back to his station and had only just returned when the prison warders arrived back – they stated that Jack Hayes and the NUPPO executive wanted Birmingham to come out on strike. It was at this point, at 9:30pm, that Sergeant Taylor sent a message out to all divisions asking the men to come out on strike.[xcvi]

To put this request into context – all officers attending pay parades that day had received their £10 back pay (the equivalent of over £5,000 in 2019) and the evening papers had already started to indicate that the strike was nowhere near the same level as the previous one in 1918. Was it really worth risking their jobs and their pensions for a strike that was likely to fail?

It was reported that three of the eight men reporting for duty at Digbeth Street Police Station refused to go on duty. Only 62 men in total had gone on strike by 11:00am the next morning[xcvii]. The Birmingham Post stated *'The calling upon members of the Union to cease work does not seem to have been carried out in a very thorough manner'*[xcviii].

The Birmingham Post carried an interview with Sergeant Taylor, in which he stated (using NUPPO language) the Police Bill was an *'attempt to Prussianise the police force and deprive the men of the liberty they had enjoyed in pre-war days'*. He also criticised the rank system in the federation – stating that the *'forbidding of mass meetings would prevent the adequate or accurate representation of the men'*.[xcix]

Copy of the strike card of PC Thomas Fuller, endorsed by PC Charles Henry Thomas, Assistant Branch Secretary. With thanks to Joanna Silvester.

On 2 August an emergency meeting of the Watch Committee was held at Newton Street – Birmingham Police Headquarters. The Judicial Sub-Committee sat first and the Watch Committee sat immediately after. The press were frustrated as they were asked to leave for the sub-committee as matters were confidential, thinking they would be allowed back for the Watch Committee meeting. The next they knew of it both meetings had been completed. Councillor Hackett (the only Labour member of the six man sub-committee present) reportedly protested at the exclusion of the press[c].

Birmingham City Police Headquarters – on the corner of Newton Street and Steelhouse Lane

Rafter had faith that the majority of his men would not join the strike action – he declared to the committee that the situation was not serious enough to cancel rest days or annual leave.

The sub-committee (and subsequently the Watch Committee) determined that every man who had put himself on strike should be dismissed from the force with immediate effect. Police orders from 2 August were issued stating that *'The Watch Committee have today dismissed all men who are at present out on strike. Lists of names will be issued in Police Orders for the next watch.'*[ci]

Another order issued on 2 August lists 26 men from the E Division, 42 from the A Division and 21 from the C Division. A further three men were added who placed themselves on strike after the Watch Committee – all three from the C Division but one of them had been confused with an officer with the same surname. Arthur Jeffcoat was mistaken for Thomas Herbert Jeffcoat (who did go on strike) and C118 Edward Wilson was mistakenly recorded as C110 Edward Wilson. These errors were highlighted and amended the next day.

On Saturday afternoon the striking officers, boosted in numbers by trade union sympathisers and relatives, held a meeting in the Bull Ring and then marched through the streets. It is recorded that as they marched past Duke Street Police Station, Superintendent Shakespeare came out of his office to tell them they were all dismissed, at which they apparently cheered and threw their caps in the air.[cii]

Duke Street Police Station

Very little support was given by prison warders at Winson Green Prison – apparently Sergeant Taylor had suggested to Warder D'Arcy that 'it would be more humane to ensure that the warders stayed at work to feed the prisoners. Reynolds and Judge identify that six warders eventually went on strike, three of them later being evicted from their homes as they were provided as part of the employment package and belonged to the Prison Commissioners.[ciii]

Widespread support was expected by various trade unions – including the suggestion that trams would be stopped and gas/electricity halted. The secretary of the Birmingham Trades Council led credence to these suggestions at meetings he addressed on behalf of strikers, however none of it materialised.[civ]

A union meeting on Sunday 3 August in St. Jude's School was called an abrupt ending when the vicar appeared, totally unaware the hall was being used by the strikers, who he stated were bringing 'disgrace and discredit' upon the force.[cv] The meeting was chaired by another clergyman – Rev Morgan Whiteman, who was very supportive of the police union and often spoke on their behalf at meetings and raised money for them.[cvi] The meeting promptly reconvened in the Bull Ring, where various trade unions are said to have made promises for support which did not materialise.

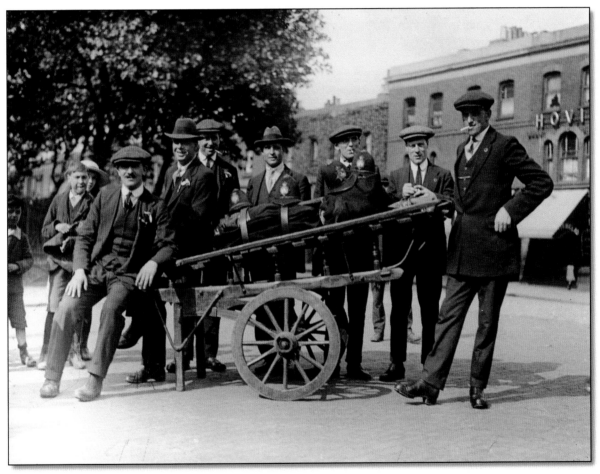

© Tower Hamlets Local History Library and Archives, photographer William Whiffin – Metropolitan police officers borrow a wheelbarrow to return their uniforms. PC Percy Perry is sitting on the end of the cart.

That day another order was issued with the names of eight further strikers from C Division, one from B division and eight from E Division who had gone on strike on 2 August. An additional name was given of PC E81 Teahan who had gone out on strike on 3 August. By 4 August 110 officers in Birmingham had gone on strike and Charles Rafter felt the need to issue further information about the circumstances via police orders, and to thank those who had remained loyal:

'In view of the unfortunate events of Friday night and Saturday the Chief Constable desires to convey to the members of the Police Force his admiration of the honourable manner in which the Force has acted during a period of great trial. They have been staunch and true to their honourable undertakings.

There was no strike and apparently no intention of a strike at half past 9 on Friday night, until certain Prison Wardens who were Officials of a Union, waylaid Ex Police Sergeant Taylor, who had been performing his section duty very well from 6 o'clock and who was going off duty at 10. These prison wardens directed Sergeant Taylor to call out a strike. They were overheard doing so and the Chief Constable has proof in his possession. Sergeant Taylor unfortunately yielded to these instructions and proceeded forthwith to call out certain members of the Police Force.

These prison wardens thereupon invaded the premises of the A. Division Police Stations and induced certain members of that Division to participate in this unfortunate movement.

Now the Chief Constable wants the members of the Police Force to take note of the following fact: The action of these Prison Wardens has led to 100 members of the Police Force being duped into going out on strike and being dismissed from the Police Force whilst they themselves have continued on duty in the Birmingham Prison.

They have taken very good care not to risk their own situations: but have made fools and catspaws of the members of the Police Force. Certain statements have appeared in the Press as to the number of the Birmingham Police who have taken part in this movement. It has been said that four hundred have done so. This is quite untrue. The correct number is 110. It has also been stated in the Press that members of the Police Force in uniform joined the procession of Police Strikers, making their number up to 200. This statement is also untrue.

The Chief Constable[cvii].

The Birmingham branch issued a leaflet setting out their case on 4 August: they made it clear that the strike was in protest to the Police Bill & for recognition of the union, not in support of greater improvement of pay and conditions. The leaflet stated the men were not consulted on the Police Bill and complained about the proposed Federation 'dividing the ranks' and rendering recommendations made on a general representative basis ineffective[cviii]. They also used the leaflet to highlight to the public and other unions concerns regarding clause three of the Police Bill which stated that imprisonment of up to two years could be given for calculated disaffection given to the service. It stated:

'This is not solely a policeman's fight but an effort to safeguard the elementary rights of citizenship and freedom'

'Our Union is about to be smashed, ruthlessly, once and for all. This Union is, up to now, a perfectly legal organisation; but if once the present Police Bill becomes law, you will witness the unprecedented occurrence of a properly constituted TRADE UNION BEING WIPED OUT By Act of Parliament! If that happens, a serious blow will have been struck at Trade Unionism in the country[cix].*'*

4 August orders went on to highlight that the press reports and union claims of 300-400 officers going on strike was quite untrue, with the true number being 110. They also dispelled the suggestion that officers in uniform had joined the procession of strikers.[cx]

A further order issued on 4 August added three men from the C Division to the list and four men from E Division. On 5 August another two names were added to the list – one from C Division and one from E Division. One name however is missing from most references to the strike in Birmingham, leading to the number of 119 officers being most commonly cited. Two days later, on 7 August, PC C297 George Arthur Wright is recorded as being dismissed for going out on strike. His record clearly states on 4 August that he was 'dismissed for participating in a police strike' on 2 August – so one of the early strikers that was identified two days later, and apparently missed out on the official lists contained within the police orders that have informed every subsequent publication referencing the strike in Birmingham.

One has to wonder if the relationship between the men and their senior offices on B and D divisions were much better than their colleagues on A, C and E divisions? Or perhaps communication to B and D divisions were slow initially, and when word got round it was clear that the strike was not going all that well?

It is rumoured that many men originally joined the strike action, but upon realising it was failing, quickly resumed their duty before they were recorded as being out on strike. Sergeant Taylor later complained about three such cases to the Chief Constable but he merely responded that the men were doing their duties satisfactorily.[cxi] These men would have had to be shielded by their senior officers and not reported. Perhaps some of the protective senior officers were on the B and D divisions? There would have been others still who were off duty in the first couple of days and when they returned to duty it was clear the strike had failed so they did not participate. What the true number of strikers was we will never know. One striker described it later to his family as a lottery as to who was dismissed[cxii].

Sergeant Taylor visited London to meet with the NUPPO executive on 9 August along with five other members of the Birmingham committee. During the previous week Tommy Thiel and Jack Hayes had been in regular contact and boosted the spirits of the Birmingham branch, so they were shocked to find out the true state of affairs concerning the split of the executive and the fact that half of them had remained on duty, particular as Hayes had told them the whole executive was on strike[cxiii].

After arriving back in Birmingham, Sergeant Taylor ordered a private meeting of the Birmingham union branch in the Barton Arms and sought out the police inspector and shorthand writer that had been ordered to attend every union meeting. He highlighted how they had been told lies by the executive members of the union and the officers informed the police officials that they would never have gone on strike if they had realised the true state of things. Sergeant Taylor made a plea on behalf of the striking officers: they regretted their actions and wished to be reinstated. The Chief Constable could be reassured of their loyalty in the future: '*We wish to go back honourably and unconditionally. We are not mutineers or criminals and I am convinced that we shall all be better policemen for our recent experience.*'[cxiv] Neither Rafter nor the Watch Committee could be swayed – this request and many that followed were ignored, and the men had to seek employment elsewhere.

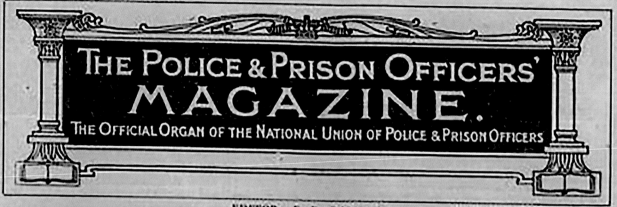

THE POLICE & PRISON OFFICERS' MAGAZINE.

THE OFFICIAL ORGAN OF THE NATIONAL UNION OF POLICE & PRISON OFFICERS

EDITOR: E. R. RAMSAY.

[Registered at the G.P.O. as a Newspaper

VOL. I., No. 33.   WEDNESDAY, OCTOBER 8, 1919.   ISSUED WEEKLY   Price 2d.

The Police Strike

TRADE UNIONISTS OF BRITAIN

This Fight is Your Fight.

The Government has Forced this Strike on the Police and Prison Officers.

Shortt has Slammed the Door. Lloyd George has Bolted it.

If the Government succeeds in Defeating Us, it will deal with You Next.

The Government is out to Smash the Trade Union Movement.

The Government tried to Reduce Your Wages.

By Reconstruction the Government means Restoration of pre-war Sweated Wages and Conditions.

The Press poured forth a Stream of Lies and Abuse about the Strikers.

If the Policemen Fail, Trade Unionism has Failed.

STAND BY YOUR BROTHERS!

All enquiries respecting advertisements should be addressed to Mr. S. F. Devitt, Advertisement Manager, Wardrobe Chambers, 165a Queen Victoria Street, London, E.C.4

Outside of London and Birmingham, the only other area affected by the strike was Merseyside – with officers from Liverpool, Bootle, Birkenhead and Wallasey going on strike.

Like in other forces the main gripe of the men was pay and conditions, but Liverpool also held many deep rooted issues of perceived favouritism, unfairness and bullying by senior officers. Liverpool police pay in spite of recent awards remained low and less than a man could earn as a labourer. Many officers still held a grudge that the rest days they had forfeited at the beginning of the war had not been compensated when officers from forces around them were paid. There was also a shortage of officers in the force that resulted in officers having to work additional hours daily, again without compensation. In addition, the system of promotion was seen as unfair by officers wishing to progress in the service. The Desborough Committee recommended the immediate payment of £10 to all officers and many forces had set to pay this out on the day the strike was to begin, no doubt to dissuade officers thinking of striking. After all, if pay was one of the main reasons for the strike then surely an immediate back payment should prevent it? Head Constable of Liverpool Francis Caldwell had not made the arrangements to do this at such a key time. There was said to be huge divisions between Francis Caldwell and his men, largely due to his letting senior officers run his divisions and keeping his distance. Liverpool men who reported to the Desborough Committee reported that he was not visible to the ordinary man and therefore did not have a true understanding of the mood of

the force. This is surprising as unlike many other chief officers, Francis had actually started his career as a constable.

The NUPPO branch in Liverpool was led by Sergeant Robert Tisseyman – an officer since 1894 he had but eight weeks to go until retirement and fully believed in the strike and its cause, eventually being weighed down by tremendous guilt at the fate of the men he had led out when they were not reinstated.

Picture and information from Liverpoolcitypolice.co.uk[cxv]

Two other notable individuals who led the strike action were PCs Holliday and Smithwick – both of whom sat on the national Executive of NUPPO. They attended a meeting of the executive on 28 July whereby much frustration was aired at the lack of support from Sir Lloyd George who had apparently promised them his door was open, should they find themselves in a similar situation to 1918. The meeting was heading towards a vote on the strike – but Holliday and Smithwick were so sure that the executive would call a strike, and so certain of the militancy of their members, that they left for Liverpool to 'call out the troops' before the vote had even been taken[cxvi].

T Holliday (left) and W B Smithwick (right) – from a 1919 NUPPO Executive picture courtesy of the Prison Officers Association

It could be argued that misinformation coming from *The Herald* about events in London led to more Liverpool officers striking. They eagerly awaited news from the morning papers on 1 August and *The Herald* had significantly inflated the numbers and the success of the strike back in London during the first day[cxvii]. Hundreds of the Liverpool men joined the strike action immediately.

Trade union leaders like Walter Citrine tried without success to persuade Liverpool workers to strike in support of the police. It is hardly surprising that this was not forthcoming as police and organised labour particularly in the dock areas had clashed violently over the years during disputes with many a dock worker feeling a blow from an officer's truncheon.

It was said the two most significant factors in the Liverpool situation, therefore, were the fondness for violence of the population of the docks and the very low morale of the force[cxviii].

Despite Macready contacting the Liverpool officials assuring them that the strike was a failure in London the Liverpool Watch Committee were better placed to assess the mood of the force and had little reason to think that their remaining officers would not strike. It was all very well for Macready to enforce 'the sack and no reinstatement' in London where a small proportion of the force had struck than in Liverpool where the recipe for civil unrest had been mixed and hung in the air.

The Lord Mayor, Alderman John Ritchie, visited Hatton Garden's parade room to address the officers that had not gone on strike (mainly new recruits and young in service officers it must be said) and told them how the city was depending on their loyalty – it needed them to protect it. The Watch Committee decided to try and reason with the hundreds of men on strike. In what must be seen as a generous offer the committee announced that every striker had until 8pm that evening to return to duty. This offer was made perhaps in hope that word of the strike's failure for the most part may encourage the men to reconsider their actions. Two sergeants and 50 constables took up the offer and returned to duty. Had the deadline been extended to ensure more men had received the message - the number may have been greater as this was a time when word of mouth was the main way to pass messages and many men who had struck were not at home when the messenger called. PC 'Shiny' Salt was one of the first to hear of the offer and as station keeper on G Division, he was in plain clothes and therefore took the opportunity to take a list of his fellow officers and head out of the station, trying to reach as many as possible to help them save their jobs, much to his inspector's scepticism[cxix]. One such constable who took the warning was Joseph Smith, who later become Chief Constable of Liverpool City Police[cxx]. The men that did return would be badly needed in the rioting that followed and the move may have been considered as shrewd by some but Macready only saw this as a sign of weakness.

Approximately half of Liverpool's 2,000 officers struck very quickly. The available officers were deployed in most likely trouble spots the first night of the strike and no doubt the mobs were a little confused as they thought the police were in strike yet here was a show of force. The resulting breakdown in law and order saw Sandon Dock an early target of an alcohol fuelled mob, determined to break into the bulging warehouses in the dock. They were met by a group of hastily gathered officers numbering just 11 and mostly new recruits. When the dockyard gates were forced by a mob 30 times their number the police charged, the matter was settled and the mob dispersed. The first victory was to the police and the first of many prisoners were taken to the cells. There were other incidents this first night including an attack on Sturla's department store. By the time the officers arrived the mob had already finished the process of systematically looting and destroying property. Despite these incidents the Liverpool City Police had got off lightly as word of the true number of officers that had struck was not well known. Francis Caldwell knew this was just the beginning and the likely location of disorder would be in London Road and Scotland Road, the two main thoroughfares to the dock areas with their warehouses an easy target without the police to protect them.

The following morning the Lord Mayor made a direct appeal for not only as many special constables as possible to be on duty Saturday night but also as many citizens who were willing to assist in keeping law and order to come forward. Mr Caldwell would have taken some comfort that the neighbouring force in Birkenhead had voted against the strike on 1 August but as the nervous hours passed bad news was to follow. Perhaps it was the 200 or so striking Liverpool officers marching to Birkenhead that influenced the smaller force, when 60 men (nearly a quarter of the force) went on strike and this was to increase to half the total force with looting following immediately. A total of 114 of the 225 men that made up the Birkenhead force went on strike.

Further bad news was to follow when the Bootle force went out on strike and out of a total of 110 men, only 16 reported for duty. Liverpool officers then travelled to Wallasey, a force of 120 men, and tried to speak to officers there to convince them to join the strike. Several Wallasey officers were initially displeased at how they had received news of the strike - after receiving a telegram from London stating the strike had been cancelled, they had decided initially not to strike, only to later find out about it through the papers. Chief Officer Mr Barry refused to allow the Liverpool officers to talk to his men, but stated they could come back tomorrow and address the whole force provided that he could address them first. Therefore on Sunday 3 August, Mr Barry gave a speech to his officers reminding them that the action was unlawful and any officer who joined it would be dismissed and lose all pension contributions. He pointed out the hardship their wives and children would suffer as a result. The Liverpool officers then addressed the Wallasey force and took a vote on the strike with only one officer voting to strike. Constable Edward F Jones was dismissed on 14 August for being involved in union activities and joining the strike. He remained the only officer to partake in the strike action from the force. With Liverpool, Bootle and Birkenhead all joining in the strike – Wallasey was therefore the only working police force in those parts. Violence had broken out when a uniformed Wallasey constable was attacked in Seacombe by Liverpool strikers who came across on the ferry, until three women who had witnessed the assault came to his rescue. Mr Barry recommended to his men that they go home and get changed into plain clothes – which worked a treat when 400 or so officers came from Liverpool to goad the uniformed Wallasey officers and could not find any. After trying and failing to identify where the officers lived, the Liverpool strikers gave up and returned to Liverpool[cxxi].

Military support was requested over the Mersey back in Liverpool. The exact number of soldiers drafted in is unknown but there were several hundred from the Welch Fusiliers and also 700 men from the Leicestershire and Notts & Derby Regiments. Four tanks also appeared on the streets of Liverpool.

In an unusual move a request was made for the Navy to be deployed on the Mersey and after some initial reluctance battleships HMS *Valient*, HMS *Venomous* and HMS *Whitley* were despatched, but it would take two days for them to reach Liverpool. Some questioned if this was really required but the argument was that these ships could move at will up and down the Mersey and deploy troops very quickly on the docks where and when they were required.

When NUPPO strikers decided to march through Liverpool this increased the confidence of local criminals that there were no officers left to police the streets – the striking officers were joined by supportive members of the public, leading to a total number of round 1,600 – much higher than the actual number of strikers, leading to comments in some quarters that nearly the whole force was out.

Thus the scene was now set and as the warm summer evening came to an end officers predicted the likely flashpoint areas and began to position themselves. The army were only to be called in as a last resort. Nobody really wanted armed troops with fixed bayonets dealing with mobs; the thought of a nervous or frightened soldier unused to mob violence starting to shoot up the area was a frightening prospect. Tension mounted as the shadows turned into darkness and at closing time for the pubs the mobs poured out and the predicted rioting ensued. The decision was made earlier than hoped to call on the army to assist as the thin blue line was at breaking point. The police aided by the soldiers battled mobs throughout the night but were unable to prevent extensive damage and looting in the docks area.

As Sunday began the rioters who hadn't been arrested, dispersed and rested as did the police in preparation for the following night. As these rioters emerged from their beds it was an early start at the public houses. With the police officers resting only the army were seen in smaller numbers guarding the attacked premises from further looting. As the day wore on one such rioter by the name of Cuthbert Thomas Howlett was particularly vocal and was soon encouraging the mob, stating that there was no need to wait and they should start the process of systematically looting again. A mob led by Howlett attacked and looted several liquor bottlings stores, taking vast amounts of alcohol – much consumed immediately by the crowd. Shortly after the mob attacked Burke's Bonded Warehouse in neighbouring Love Lane, they attracted the attention of the Sherwood Foresters (Notts and Derby Regiment) officers who made short work of arresting some of the looters. Howlett led the mob towards the truck perhaps in an attempt to free the men and took a hold of Lance Corporal Seymour and began dragging him. Seymour must have been terrified at the prospect of losing his rifle to the drunken man and the carnage that would have followed. The slightly built Lance Corporal Seymour was no match for the drunken Howlett and the loaded riffle carried by Seymour was discharged in the struggle: Howlett fell dying and the discouraged mob dispersed. He died 12 hours later in hospital but this was only a temporary reprieve as mobs gathered later that day and the rioting began again[cxxii]. The troops with their bayonets fixed had no hesitation in prodding the rioter to make him disperse and the rifle butt was also used to great effect. In addition, police truncheons were used in large numbers that night. There was better co-ordination between the police and the army: any rioter who evaded the army and double backed to continue their violent crimes found the police were then unexpectedly appearing to deal with them. It was 3am the following morning when things quietened down enough for the police to withdraw and leave the peacekeeping to the army.

Striking officer PC Morley was so appalled by rioters that he arrested two men for breaking and entering shops on 3 August.[cxxiii]

One notable incident occurred when the strikers descended upon Tue-brook Bridewell (a custody block) and the inspector sent his men out the back door and over the back wall to get away from them, much to the amusement of local children who saw them go[cxxiv].

By Bank Holiday Monday the total number of people arrested and appearing at court in Liverpool stood at 350 and there were nearly 100 more from Birkenhead, but even more were to follow. In London Road alone over 200 premises had been broken into and most of them stripped bare. Some buildings had been gutted in just a 600 yard stretch of the road but the defenders had protected most of the city from the same treatment by containing the riot.

Arrest of looters in Liverpool

On this Monday no doubt the authorities were preparing for the trouble ahead and planning their tactics and deployment but there were now two things acting in favour of the police and army. Firstly the weather had broken and the rain had started, which at times was very heavy. Secondly: destroyers HMS Venomous and HMS Whitley had arrived in the Mersey and were moored alongside the pier head preparing to land 'blue Jackets' to protect the docks. This was followed later in the morning by the battleship HMS Valiant seen approaching through the mist and rain. Crowds had gathered to look at the spectacle including, it has been said, some strikers. Things were settling down in the dock area, the rioting was over.

A total of 954 men went on strike and were dismissed in Liverpool. In the aftermath of the strike, Liverpool were so keen to fill the gaps left by the dismissed men that they employed police pensioners on a large scale and rushed other new recruits onto the street without giving them sufficient training. In all the chaos, one striker from Bootle was hired in the Liverpool force, serving eight years before his record from his previous force came to light. He was immediately dismissed.[cxxv]

The Chief Constable and the Watch Committee in Liverpool rewarded those who had remained on duty financially with up to four week's extra pay, and even those who had initially gone on strike but returned to duty received one week's extra pay.

NUPPO denounced the rioting – stating it was 'conduct calculated to discredit the strike, which will form a pretext for the purpose of calling upon the use of the Military interference[cxxvi]' but found it had lost a lot of public support as a result of the riots.

A collection was started in Liverpool for the men who remained loyal. Francis Caldwell refused to allow his men to take the money therefore instead a baton with a silver ring referencing the riots was given to all of them. It is said that sergeant's chevrons were broadened with silver wire and inspector's flat caps were decorated with a silver band instead of the traditional black one – a tradition that still exists today in Merseyside Police.

Picture and info courtesy of Liverpoolcitypolice.co.uk, the online museum of the Liverpool Police

A total of 2,400 men went on strike across the country in 1919 – out of the union's supposed membership of 50,000. Many former union members responded to the action for striking by burning their union membership cards – they felt the pay increase had answered their demands for better pay and recognition[cxxvii]. The only officers allowed to re-join were the 52 Liverpool officers who took advantage of the Watch Committee's ultimatum before it was too late. Despite multiple requests before their chief constables, watch committees and Parliament (including support from Labour and union officials) – with the exception of one Birkenhead officer who joined the Royal Irish Constabulary and the Bootle officer mentioned above – it was previously thought none of those officers ever wore a police uniform again.[cxxviii]

We are fortunate at the time of publication of this book to have access to the 1939 register, which gives occupations and voluntary emergency services roles of individuals living in Britain at the start of World War II. From this register (and additional online research) we have gleaned that one Birmingham officer re-joined the force as a special constable. Frank Howes is recorded as a special constable living in Birmingham in September 1939. No trace could be found of Frank amongst the Birmingham City Police special constable registers, so perhaps he was volunteering with Warwickshire or Staffordshire. Another officer was also to wear a police uniform again: Frederick Husselbee joined Staffordshire County Police as a First Police Reserve, an occupation recorded in the 1939 register. It is not known exactly when the men joined their respective forces nor how long they served. It is also not known if they declared their involvement in the strike action – perhaps 20 years after the strike it was no longer relevant to the authorities to know and they did not ask? One would imagine the former officers did not voluntarily offer the information.

Frederick Husselbee

The NUPPO membership card of Liverpool officer PC G Martin is held by the West Midlands Police Museum (see below), after being donated by PC Martin's daughter. His story is rather interesting, in that shortly before the strike he was seriously injured in a fire and was hospitalised. The day before the strike he was visited in the hospital by the police surgeon and asked about his views on the proposed strike. He said that he would support the majority of his colleagues. The doctor reported Martin fit for duty, even though he couldn't even get out of bed. He was unable to parade for duty the next day and was promptly sacked for going on strike!

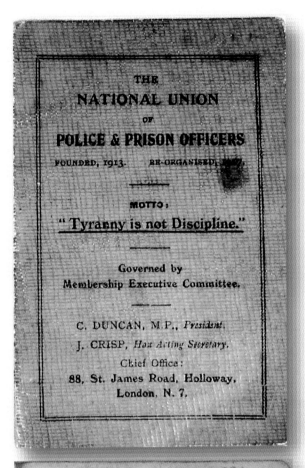

THE

NATIONAL UNION
OF
POLICE & PRISON OFFICERS

FOUNDED, 1913.   RE-ORGANISED, 1917.

MOTTO:

"Tyranny is not Discipline."

Governed by
Membership Executive Committee.

C. DUNCAN, M.P., *President.*

J. CRISP, *Hon Acting Secretary.*

Chief Office:
88, St. James Road, Holloway,
London, N. 7.

G. Martin   L. Poole.

(331)

Member's Card No. 8920 B

ENTRANCE FEE, **1/-**

MEMBER'S SUBSCRIPTION, **2/-** per quarter.

Payable in the first month of each quarter.

Your next Subscription is due on:

1918.

	Date received.	Amount.	Sig.	Arrears.
January				
April				
July				
October	11	3/-	JWH	

1919.

	Date received.	Amount.	Sig.	Arrears.
January	1	3/-	JWH	
April				
July				
October				

1591·734

OBJECTS.

To secure to the Members fair play and justice.

To improve the conditions of the Police and Prison Services.

To ensure to each man equal chances for promotion or special appointments.

To maintain just and efficient discipline.

To secure to the Public an honest and efficient administration.

1920.

	Date received.	Amount.	Sig.	Arrears.
January				
April				
July				
October				

1921.

	Date received.	Amount.	Sig.	Arrears.
January				
April				
July				
October				

Membership.

Open to members of any Police Force or Constabulary; to Officers of the Prison Service; and to Dock and Railway Police.

Notes of Importance.

What is really needful is for Police and Prison Officers to enrol at once, and recognition will soon be obtained.

Recognise the Union and the Union will be recognised.

Every member secure another one. Only thus will you win the day.

We are out to win and we are going to win.

Unite and the victory will be accomplished.

Your opportunity has come.

Quit ye like Men.
Be Strong.

Unity is Strength.

C.P.—4171

Following the Call to Action – the Birmingham Strikers

Friday 1 August 1919

Sergeant C5 Edward Charles Taylor

Edward Charles Taylor was born on 2 February 1875 in Bricklehampton, Worcester to parents George and Susan. In the 1881 census George gave his occupation as an agricultural Labourer, Edward is shown as six years old and the eldest of three children. By the 1891 census Edward is the eldest of six children, aged 16, however his mother 'Susan' is not shown at the address, having stayed with an aunt and uncle in Stoke the day the census was taken. Edward has now taken up the same trade as his father, perhaps working together. We know that Edward was to move out of the agricultural business as he is shown as being employed by a railway company from October 1893 when he became a porter in Worcester. He was to stay for three years before resigning and joining Birmingham City Police on 7 September 1896, when he was given the warrant number 6724.

It is likely that Edward moved initially into single quarters when he joined the police but he married Annie Maria Sheller in Bordesley in 1898 and at that time presumably set up home with her. Throughout his career he was to receive a total of 19 awards, receiving his first on 11 October 1898 when he was awarded a gratuity of £2.2.0 and complimented for courageous conduct in stopping a runaway horse in the High Street and also for vigilance and for tact in arresting thieves in Barford Street. By 1901 we have our first address for Edward as a married man as the census shows him living in Suffolk Street, Birmingham together with Annie and one year old son Percy. Also shown at the address is Maria Sheller the mother of Annie. As aforementioned, as a constable Edward lent his uniform to Sir Lloyd George MP so he could escape a riot at the Town Hall in 1901.

Throughout 1902 he was to receive two more awards when on 22 March 1902 he was awarded a gratuity of one guinea and complimented for zeal, vigilance and ability in three important cases leading to the conviction of thieves. This was followed on 24 September when Edward was awarded £1.1.0 for courageous conduct when he again stopped a runaway horse. It was 25 November 1903 when he received his next award and for that he was given his 1st stripe of merit and complimented in police orders for zeal and alertness in the arrest of thieves. On 13 December 1905 he was again awarded a guinea and complimented for courageous conduct when stopping a third runaway horse.

Clearly a bit of a thief taker, on 24 July 1907 Edward was awarded a guinea for alertness leading to the arrest of thieves. On 23 February 1910 he was awarded the 2nd stripe of merit for good police duty in a case of robbery in a brothel and also in a case of shoplifting and for general good duty. On 17 May 1911 he was awarded a gratuity of one guinea and complimented for good duty in the arrest of warehouse breakers loitering and arresting a thief from description. On 21 June 1911 Edward was promoted to sergeant.

In the 1911 census Edward and Annie are shown as living in Wrentham Street, Birmingham together with six children of their own with the youngest (Grace) only four months old. There are two boarders shown as living with the family, one of them was Police Constable William Sinclair whom the reader may note was a fellow striker. On 30 January 1912 Edward was complimented for the arrest of thieves in two cases at assizes. On 11 June 1912 he was further complimented, firstly for the arrest of a man stealing brass goods and secondly for a man arrested for a stabbing. On 16 April 1913 he was awarded a gratuity of one guinea and complimented for rendering first aid. This April also saw a complaint from a fellow officer (PC Albert Malcolm) who alleged that Edward had accused him of being drunk and striking him on the jaw. He also alleged that Edward had brought him a 'considerable distance' off his beat before telling him to return and he would hear no more of it. We will never know what conversations took place concerning this but no action was taken against Edward and the comment 'Explained' has been entered on his record. On 16 July 1913 he was awarded a gratuity of a guinea and complimented for services at a fire: rescuing a person from a burning building.

Edward was clearly a religious man as he is pictured in the Bible Class Institute and Mission around 1913 (sitting next to his old lodger William Sinclair). On 1 March 1915 there is a further complaint recorded against Edward when he instructed an officer (PC Ernest Buckley) to execute a commitment warrant at an unreasonable time (night). For this he was required to pay £1 in compensation presumable to the owner. On 2 February 1916 he was again awarded a guinea and complimented for prompt action when he discovered a fire and rescued horses from a burning building.

On 2 May 1917 he was awarded a 2nd stripe of merit (officers had to start again upon promotion to sergeant and it may be that the first stripe as sergeant was not recorded on his record) and complimented for good police duty in six cases at petty sessions, two cases of first aid and stopping yet another runaway horse. On 2 January 1918 Edward was awarded a special pay rise and complimented for good police duty in a number of cases and for skill in rendering first aid to a person choking. On 2 October that year he received his biggest gratuity yet when he was awarded five guineas and complimented for obtaining information which led to the arrest and conviction of thieves stealing and receiving rubber tyres, resulting in £1,200 (worth over £35,000 in 2019) of motor tyres being recovered, also for good police duty in nine cases at petty sessions and rendering first aid to two people, one with a smashed hand and one with a dislocated knee.

On 20 January 1919 Edward received a third complaint. Following a burglary at Messrs Ames, Stokes, Stevens & Co a Mr Bembridge complained that he had unnecessarily been fetched from his home at midnight and been asked impertinent and suggestive questions concerning the offence on 4 January. The summary page is simply endorsed 'not proven' – clearly Edward's version of events was satisfactory to senior officers. On 23 June 1919 Edward received his final award. He was awarded a gratuity of three guineas and complimented for the arrest of thieves. He also assisted another officer in a case of safe robbery and yet another in rendering first aid to a person with a fractured femur and a case of asphyxiation.

Bible Class Police Institute & Mission

The final entry on the summary for Edward is when he was reported by Superintendent Arthur Penrice for inciting men to leave their duty and going out on a police strike and declaring about 10pm 1 August 1919 that they were on strike.

Being the local branch chair of the union cost Edward dearly. By all accounts he had not wanted to call the strike but when instructed to do so he did. He had demonstrated time and time again over 23 years to be an exceptional officer who was just a few years away from retirement but lost everything. He had the longest service and lost the most pension contributions; had he remained his record would undoubtedly have been marked 'Service Exemplary'.

Little is known about Edward after he was dismissed but on the voters lists from the 1920s he is shown as living at 54 Ludgate Hill, Birmingham.

In 1920 Edward had been successful in his election campaign and was serving on Birmingham Council as a Labour councillor for St Paul's ward. It has not been possible to locate Edward and wife Annie in the 1939 register so perhaps they had died by this time or were out of the country. Edward is recorded in the 1939 register living with son Roland (spelt Rowland) and daughter Nancy in Bristol, with his occupation showing as coal manager.

PC A210 Alfred William Bragg

Alfred William Bragg was born in Woolwich in June 1889. In the 1891 census he is living with parents Alfred and Eliza and his three-year-old sister Ethel in Plumstead, Kent. His father is a machinist. In the 1901 census there are six children at the address (including Alfred) and two visitors.

Alfred joined the Army in January 1907. On his attestation papers he stated he was currently serving with the militia. He lied about his age to make himself 18 (he was actually 17). Alfred became Private 8360 serving with the 1st and 3rd Battalions Prince of Wales's Own (West Yorkshire) Regiment. He appeared on the 1911 census whilst serving and seemed to forget how old he said he was as he stated his age as 24 (he would have been almost 21).

He left the Army in 1913 and joined the Birmingham City Police in December of that year. His service with the police was to be very short as he was recalled to the Forces in August 1914 and spent much of the next three years in France. His character was recorded as 'honest and reliable' with a 'cheerful disposition'. It was noted that he had a promise of employment within the Birmingham Constabulary. During his military service Alfred was wounded eight times including a gunshot wound (GSW) to his left leg and one to his right foot. Whilst serving with the military Alfred married Lillian Lawley in 1915, but she sadly died in 1919.

He wrote to senior officials shortly before he left the Army, requesting that he be allowed to leave and return to his prior occupation with the Birmingham City Police – stating the work there was of more importance than what he had found himself doing in the Forces of late. Alfred earned the Victory Medal and British War Medal during his service and was given a silver badge (for wounds) upon leaving.

Alfred was discharged on 21 January 1919 and returned immediately to the Birmingham police. The next and final entry on his record is when he was reported by Superintendent George Monk for being absent from duty on Friday 1 August and was dismissed.

In 1923 Alfred married Sarah Ann and the couple lived together in Harvey Road, Birmingham. The 1939 register showed his occupation as carpenter and joiner. Alfred died in 1968 aged 78.

PC A204 John Clansey

John Clansey was born in January 1893 in West Bromwich to William and Mary Ann Clansey. In the 1901 census he was the middle child of five. His father's occupation was shown as coach smith. In the 1911 census John's occupation was recorded as 'spring eye roller'. There are seven younger siblings and one older sibling at the address with him and his parents.

In May 1914 John joined the Birmingham City Police with warrant number 8489. He joined the Armed Forces in November 1915, returning in January 1919. This picture shows him in a group of Birmingham police officers marching to Curzon Street recruitment office to sign up in November 1915.

He was reported by Superintendent George Monk for being absent from duty and participating in a police strike on 1 August 1919 and was dismissed.

In 1920 John married Vera Jenkinson in Birmingham. In the 1939 register John had left Birmingham and was working in Sheffield as an 'eye roller laminated spring'. He is one of only a few former officers to leave Birmingham. John died in 1982 at the age of 89 in Nottinghamshire.

PC A211 Fred Bruce Crouch

Fred was born in September 1891 to Frederick and Florence Crouch in Northamptonshire. In the 1901 census he was living with his parents, two older brothers, a younger brother and two younger sisters in St. Giles, Northampton. The family also had a boarder. His father was a shoe finisher and his brother (at 13-years-old) was already a shoe maker. By 1911 Fred and his other older brother had joined the family trade – his older brother being a clicker and he a pressman. The family also had one further daughter.

In August 1914 Fred joined Birmingham City Police under warrant number 8687. He married Florence Mabel Coles in 1915 but the couple had no children. In May 1917 he was complimented and awarded a guinea for courageous conduct in stopping a runaway horse. After being attested in December 1915, in April 1918 Fred was called up to the Grenadier Guards as private (guardsman) 32810. He returned to the Birmingham police in January 1919. The last entry on Fred's record was being dismissed for participating in a police strike on 1 August after being reported by Superintendent George Monk.

After leaving the police Fred returned to Northampton where he ran a grocers, which was recorded as his occupation on the 1939 register, living with Florence. *We are grateful to Tim Joyce, great nephew of Frederick, for sharing information and the picture of Frederick after he left the police.*

PC A143 Horace Dowell

Horace was born in 1890 in Rowley Regis, Staffordshire, to William and Elizabeth Dowell. In the 1891 census Horace was the youngest of five children, with his father and eldest brother working as labourers. In 1901, still living in Rowley Regis, William and his eldest son William junior were working as stone quarrymen. The majority of men in their street had found work at the quarry in various different roles. Horace's 15-year-old sister was working as an apprentice dressmaker and at 10 – Horace was at school.

In 1911 Horace was the only one of his siblings still living with his parents, and they had taken in a married couple and their one-year-old son as boarders. Horace was also working in the quarry as a labourer.

In May 1913 Horace joined Birmingham City Police with warrant number 8300. He was complimented and awarded a guinea for vigilance in the arrest of a warehouse breaker in December 1913, quite early in his career. In July 1915 he was complimented and awarded a guinea for courageous conduct in stopping a runaway horse, and in May 1917 Horace was mobilised and left the police to join the Armed Forces, having originally been attested in December 1915 and joining the Army Reserve. He served with the Royal Garrison Artillery as Gunner 159421. In October 1918 Horace was admitted to hospital suffering with severe influenza and his next of kin were informed. He made a full recovery and returned to the forces, shortly after qualifying as a signaller. He returned to France before being demobilised in February 1919 – returning to the police the same month.

The next entry on Horace's record is when he was reported for being absent from duty on 1 August and participating in a police strike, for which he was reported by Superintendent George Monk and dismissed.

At some point Horace moved back to Rowley Regis – in 1939 he was living with his wife and two daughters, with his occupation showing as 'sawyer (wood)'. Horace died in 1952 aged 62.

With thanks to Horace's nephew Jonathan Timmins for providing his police picture and additional information.

PC A180 Henry Allan Field

Henry Allan Field was born in July 1885 to William and Ellen Field in Lydbrook, Gloucestershire. In the 1891 census Henry had two younger brothers and his father's occupation was railway signalman. The family also had a boarder living with them. By the 1901 census William and Ellen had two more sons and Henry was working as a carpenter's apprentice. In 1904 Henry married Laura Amy Davies.

In July 1906 Henry joined the Birmingham City Police with warrant number 7525. He was subject of a complaint in November 1909 by the Carpenters and Joiners Association for working as a carpenter during 1909 whilst also working as a constable, thereby depriving another carpenter of work. This complaint was not proven and no further action was taken. If the allegation was indeed true it perhaps hints at the economical struggles of police officers at this time.

In January 1910 Henry was complimented for vigilance in the arrest of till robbers and awarded a guinea. Later that year in September Henry was again complimented for vigilance and awarded a guinea, this time for the arrest of slot meter thieves. In July 1911 he was complimented for skill in rendering first aid. In June 1913 Henry was awarded the 1st stripe of merit for arrest of a shop breaker and recovery of goods worth £28.10s. In February 1916 he was again complimented and rewarded with a guinea for vigilance in arresting warehouse breakers.

In June 1919 Henry showed bravery and vigilance at a fire in Fazeley Street and was again awarded a guinea. Without one punishment on his record up to this point, but several compliments and awards for excellent police work and skills, Henry went out on strike on 1 August and was reported by Superintendent George Monk and dismissed.

The 1939 register shows Henry and Laura living with two daughters and having two other individuals living at their address. His occupation was carpenter and joiner. Henry died in 1979 aged 93.

PC C271 Herbert Godwin

Herbert was born in April 1886 in Burton-on-Trent to parents Charles and Rosa. Charles' occupation was a cooper and Herbert was one of five children in the 1891 census. In the 1901 census Charles and Herbert's older brother Fred were working as coopers, and Herbert's occupation was shown as cooper & labourer. In 1908 Herbert married Lily Blanche Smith and the couple went on to have five children.

In 1911 Herbert was living with his wife and two children and a married couple who were boarding with them. His occupation was cask smeller – an important job in a brewery! Herbert's older brother William was a policeman in Wolverhampton Borough Police and later became a chief inspector.

In January 1912 Herbert joined Birmingham City Police with warrant number 8154 and he and his wife moved to Hockley, as he found he was unable to be a police constable in Burton-on-Trent. His record is fairly uneventful until February 1919 when he was awarded the certificate of merit from the Royal Humane Society for using artificial respiration. In June 1919 Herbert was awarded a gratuity for the arrest of youths smashing windows and also for his first aid skills (again using artificial respiration).

Herbert was stationed at Kenyon Street and would therefore have known Sergeant Edward Taylor, the branch leader who called the strike. Herbert was part of a group spreading the word and encouraging others to strike at the very beginning, trying to drum up support from their colleagues for the union.

It states on his record that he was reported by Superintendent Arthur Penrice for inciting men to leave their police duty and going on strike at 10pm on 1 August.

In 1922 Herbert was working as a boiler trimmer at the coal fired Nechells Power Station and also spent time at Summer Lane Power Station. In the 1939 register Herbert was living with Lily and two of their children and his occupation was stated as 'wiring and fitting of electric cookers'.

Herbert retired in 1951 and died in Birmingham in 1964 aged 78.

With thanks to Herbert's granddaughter Lesley for information about Herbert and the picture of him and Lily.

PC A142 Horace Goode

Horace was born in 1889 in Leicestershire to Frederick and Lucy. In the 1891 census he is the youngest of five children and Frederick's occupation is recorded as goods porter. By the 1901 census Frederick is sadly recorded as a widower and only three of his children are still living with him.

In February 1911 Horace joined Birmingham City Police with warrant number 7854. In April that year he was boarding with Police Constable Theophilus John Turner and his family, along with another boarder who worked for the Birmingham City Gas Department. He had married Jane Lawrence in 1909 but she was living with her brother-in-law, sister, their child and her own one-year-old daughter Nellie in Little Bowden, Market Harborough in 1911. The police force would instruct their officers where they could reside, in single quarters, pre-approved accommodation or police houses provided by the force for which the officer would pay rent. Potentially Horace and Jane had been waiting for a suitable house to become available, or maybe Jane hadn't yet wanted to leave Leicestershire?

In July 1915 Horace was complimented and awarded two guineas for vigilance in tracing thieves from footprint evidence and rendering first aid in a case of varicose veins.

Horace left the police in April 1918 to join the Armed Forces as Lance Corporal 42198 in 3rd Battalion Somerset Light Infantry. Horace returned to the police in January 1919. In June 1919 Horace was complimented and awarded a guinea for demonstrating courageous conduct in stopping a runaway horse.

The final entry on his record is dated 2 August and relates to Horace going out on strike on 1 August, for which he was reported by Superintendent George Monk and dismissed.

In the 1939 register he was working as a meat market attendant and was living alone, although it states he was married. His wife Jane was staying with one of their three children in Market Harborough. Horace died in 1958 aged 68.

PC A105 Arthur James Green

Arthur Green's birth was registered between December 1885 and February 1886. He was born in Nottingham to parents George and Sophia. In the 1891 census Arthur is the youngest of four children and his father is a stationary engine driver. The 1911 census shows Arthur living as a boarder at a lodgings house in Nottingham. His occupation is recorded as insurance agent.

In July 1911 Arthur joined the Birmingham City Police with warrant number 7877. His record states his former occupation was police constable (which must have been either before or after the 1911 census) and he is 6' 1 ½". His police career is fairly uneventful, until February 1916 when he was awarded a guinea for skill in rendering first aid to a burns victim.

The final entry in his record is dated 2 August 1919 when Superintendent George Monk reported him to for participating in a police strike on 1 August 1919, for which he was dismissed.

PC A34 William Alfred Green

William was born towards the end of 1884 in Melton Mowbray, Leicester to parents John and Sarah. In the 1891 census John's occupation is agricultural labourer and William is one of three children. He joined the Birmingham City Police on 22 March 1909, aged 24, with warrant number 7739. His record states he was English and 6' 3". In the 1911 census he is living at Moor Street Police Station.

The first entry of note on William's record is from January 1912 when he was reported by Inspector Cartwright for being drunk when coming off duty at 1:35am on 24 December. For this he was suspended until 1 January (perhaps Christmas made this last longer than it would have otherwise?) and reinstated, with his punishment being two days leave stopped. Ironically this meant he could

spend Christmas at home before getting his punishment.

This blip on his record didn't stop William progressing through the classes – reaching 2nd class constable by March 1914.

The next time William comes to notice is in October 1916 when Sergeant Barret reported him for being absent from his special protection duty (armed) for six minutes from 9:19pm until 9:25pm on the 25th August. He was then seen coming from an entry leading to a local pub. Certain locations around the city had been allocated as special protection duty during the War, should the Zeppelins drop bombs on the city. For this he was 'censured' by the Judicial Sub-Committee.

The final entry on William's record comes on 2 August 1919 when he was reported by Superintendent George Monk for being absent from duty on 1 August and participating in a police strike, for which he was dismissed.

PC A112 Arthur James Hawkins

Arthur was born in Birmingham in 1884 to parents Arthur and Ruth. In the 1891 census Arthur is the eldest of two children and Ruth's mother is also living with the family. Arthur senior's occupation is warehouseman. In the 1901 census Arthur is working as a carpenter alongside his father with his occupation showing as 'carpenter's son'. In 1908 Arthur married Dorothy Agnes Mason.

In July 1906 Arthur joined Birmingham City Police with warrant number 7526. There are no compliments or misconduct incidents on his record, simply good police service leading to increases in pay each year. In the 1911 census Arthur is living with Dorothy and their two children. The family also have a boarder at the address.

The final entry is from 2 August when Superintendent George Monk reported Arthur for being absent from duty on 1 August and participating in the police strike, for which he was dismissed.

Arthur and Dorothy remained in Birmingham and Arthur died in 1929, aged 44.

PC A82 Edward Thomas Hunt

Edward Hunt was born in 1886 in Alcester, Warwickshire to George and Mary Ann Hunt. In the 1891 census Edward is the youngest of five children and his father's occupation is recorded as agricultural labourer. By 1901 Edward is one of only two of the siblings left at home, but they are joined by his sister's husband and daughter. He is now working as a ploughboy, with the family living at Rose Hall in Oversley, Warwickshire. His father and brother-in-law also have agricultural occupations of cowman and groom/gardener.

Edward joined Birmingham City Police in February 1911 with warrant number 7853, with his previous occupation recorded as farm hand. Within his first year in February 1912, Edward was complimented and awarded a guinea for the arrest of a thief loitering at night. He married Martha Stanley in July 1912.

In July 1916 Edward was awarded a guinea and complimented for his courageous conduct in stopping a runaway horse. The final entry on his otherwise unblemished record comes on 2 August 1919 when Edward was reported by Superintendent George Monk for being absent from duty on 1 August and participating in a police strike, for which he was dismissed.

In the 1939 register Edward's occupation is shown as aero policeman and he is living with Martha and their daughter Ivy.

PC A126 Alfred Ernest Leath

Alfred Leath was born on 10 July 1894 in Wharton, Leominster to parents Edwin and Harriet. By 1901 he was the youngest of five sons with the family still living in Wharton. His father Edwin was a farm labourer at the time. In 1911 we know that the family were living in Marlbrook, Leominster. At this time Edwin was a widower working as a farm waggoner and Alfred (now 16) was working as an assistant gamekeeper.

On 22 February 1915 Alfred joined Birmingham City Police and was given the warrant number 8587, but on 15 November that year he resigned to join HM Forces, becoming Corporal 2690 Leath of the Military Foot Police. Very little has survived of his service records but he was awarded both the British War Medal and Victory Medal for his service to his country.

On 21 March 1919 Alfred re-joined Birmingham City police and the final entry on his service record followed on 2 August 1919 when he was reported by Superintendent George Monk for being absent from duty on Friday 1 August 1919 and participating in a police strike.

In 1920 Alfred was living at 3 Court, 19 Weaman Street in Birmingham and went on to marry Sarah Wall in 1923. By 1939 both Alfred and Sarah are living at Avenue Lodge, Birmingham Road, Walsall. Alfred by this time was a mental health nurse and was also registered as an Air Raid Precaution (ARP) worker. In 1949 Alfred was residing in Great Barr, Birmingham and remained a mental health nurse. Alfred died in 1966 aged 72.

PC A176 Charles Henry Lickorish

Charles Lickorish was born on 5 February 1884 in Kimberley, Nottinghamshire to parents John and Martha. Charles was the middle of three boys in 1891 and the family were living in Sneinton, Nottingham. John was a railway signalman by trade.

By 1901 the family were still living in Nottinghamshire but had moved to Sherwood Street. Charles at this point was the eldest of three children in the house. He was 17 years old and an apprentice carpenter.

On 20 March 1906 Charles joined Birmingham City Police and was given the warrant number 7548. It would have been normal practice for him to have moved into single quarters upon joining. On 26 July 1909 he was awarded a gratuity of a guinea and complimented for courageous conduct in stopping a runaway horse. In the 1911 census he was in single quarters in Moor Street together with 18 other police officers. On 15 December 1912 Charles married Nellie Daisy Olive Hopkins at St Andrews Church Birmingham. The couple lived at 176 St Andrews Road, Birmingham.

On 2 July 1917 Charles received a complaint when a tram conductress complained that Charles had refused to take a stray dog from off a tramcar two weeks prior. For this matter he was cautioned by the Judicial Sub-Committee.

The final entry on his record dated 2 August 1919 was when he was reported by Superintendent George Monk for being absent from duty on Friday 1 August 1919 and for participating in a police strike, for which he was dismissed.

In 1939 Charles had moved back to Nottingham with Nellie, living in Kerrick Road. Charles had gone back to his old trade as a carpenter/shop fitter and he is also shown as a journeyman. He died in Nottingham in 1972 aged 88 years.

PC A39 Frank Jarman

Frank Jarman was born in April 1887 in Letchworth, Herts to parents George and Sarah. In the 1891 census the family are living in Cambridge. George was working as an agricultural labourer and Frank was the eldest of two children. By 1901 Frank was the eldest of seven children. George was working as a horse-keeper on a farm and Frank was showing as a farm labourer.

In October 1905 Frank enlisted in the Royal Navy as Gunner 11585 (Royal Marine Artillery). Once his time was up he became a bricklayer before joining the Birmingham City Police in November 1912. Still on the reserve list he was called up to the Reserve Fleet in August 1914. Frank married Amy Elizabeth Howells in 1915. He returned in March 1919 a week after completing service with the Royal Navy, earning himself a 1914 Star, Victory Medal and British War Medal. The final entry on his record comes when he was reported by Superintendent George Monk for being absent from duty and participating in a police strike on 1 August 1919, for which he was dismissed.

The 1939 register shows Frank living with his wife Amy and working as a millwrights mate engineer, having returned to Letchworth. He died in 1960 aged 73.

PC A171 Ernest William Pittam

Ernest was born in Bicester, Oxfordshire in 1889, the second of six children of John and Mary Pittam. John was an agricultural worker/cowman. By 1911 Ernest was working as a general labourer and in January 1912 he joined Birmingham City Police with the warrant number 8156. In December 1915 he joined the Armed Forces and was posted to the Army Reserve, being mobilised in April 1918. Ernest had married Emily Stevens in January 1916 and the couple had two daughters who died during infancy. Their son Stanley Ernest was born in September 1918. He became Private 25775 in the Coldstream Guards. In November 1918 he was promoted to lance corporal and in February 1919 he returned to the Birmingham City Police with a new warrant number of 8841.

The final entry on Ernest's record is from 2 August when he was reported by Superintendent George Monk for being absent from police duty on 1 August and participating in a police strike, for which he was dismissed.

During the 1930s the Birmingham Trade Directory indicates Ernest was running a coffee house. By the 1939 register he was working as a window cleaner. His wife Emily is showing as a shop keeper in a coffee house. Ernest died in 1958 aged 69.

PC A27 Albert James Pout

Albert was born on New Year's Eve 1896 to parents Arthur and Eliza in Kent. The 1901 census shows the family living with Eliza's 84-year-old father in his cottage in Blean, Kent. Albert was the middle child of three and his father's occupation was shown as gardener. By 1911 the family were living in their own house, Albert's father and brother were shown as domestic gardeners and Albert was recorded as an assistant florist. Interestingly his brother Arthur shows on both census records as being born at the Tower of London, which must relate to his father (an army pensioner) being stationed at the army barracks there around the time of his birth. It must be quite a rare birthplace!

Albert served in the First World War as Gunner 121083 Pout of the Royal Field Artillery, receiving the British War Medal and the Victory Medal. He was formerly a sapper with the Royal Engineers.

On 28 April 1919 Albert joined Birmingham City Police and was given warrant number 8964. He was 22 years of age and single, likely going straight into single men's quarters. There are no other entries on his record other than to say he was reported by Superintendent George Monk for being absent from duty on 1 August 1919 and participating in a police strike, for which he was dismissed.

With only a few days over three month's service, Albert must have either found the work, pay and conditions really not to his liking or simply got caught up in the sentiment of the other strikers and joined his colleagues in protesting. He had by far the shortest service out of any of the strikers.

Albert died in 1981 in Grimsby, aged 84.

PC A196 Francis Thomas Edward Price

Francis was born in August 1889 in Wolverhampton to parents Mary and George. In the 1901 census George was working as a milk seller and Francis was the third eldest of seven children. The family were living in Wolverhampton.

Francis was employed by a railway company from January 1907 working initially as an engine cleaner, then a shunter and sub fireman. In January 1910 he left to 'better his position' although he had no offer of employment elsewhere. We don't know what he did in the meantime, other than featuring on the April 1911 census as an unemployed railway worker living in Wolverhampton in his Aunt's boarding house, but in October 1911 Francis joined Birmingham City Police, being given warrant number 7901. In June 1912 he received his only compliment and award of a guinea for courageous conduct in stopping a runaway horse.

In December 1915 Francis was attested to the Army and immediately joined the reserves, being called up for service in April 1918. In January 1916 he married Mary Ethel Taylor. When Francis joined the Army he became Private 25773 Francis Thomas Edward Price of the Coldstream Guards.

Francis had no misconduct entries on his record until 2 August when he was reported by Superintendent George Monk for being absent from duty and participating in a police strike on 1 August 1919, for which he was dismissed.

In the 1939 register Francis and Mary were living with three children in Birmingham and his occupation was show as gas worker. He died in 1951 aged 62.

PC A113 William Turner Wise

William Wise was born on 19 February 1890 to parents William and Mercy. In the 1891 census William is shown as the youngest of four children living in Harley Street, Bath. His father gave his occupation as a baker. Also shown as living at the address is William senior's sister-in-law 'Bertha' who is shown as being a baker's assistant which gives us the first indication that this was a family business. By the time of the 1901 census the family still live in Harley Street. At this time William senior, Bertha and also the eldest son (Albert - now 20 years old) are shown as bakers. By the time of the 1911 census the family are still living in Harley Street and William junior (now 21 years old) is also shown as 'assisting in the business' which was presumably the family baking business.

On 13 April 1912 William married Emma Selina Gertrude Chappell in the county of Bath. At some point the couple moved to Trenville Avenue, Mosely and they were living there when William joined

Birmingham City Police on 6 March 1915. He was given the warrant number 8610 and his short service was uneventful; he resigned from the police to join His Majesties Forces on 4 March 1917 where he served in the Military Mounted Police. William's police service record later shows that he re-joined Birmingham City on 13 June 1919 and was given a new warrant number of 9025. Most officers finished their military service and returned to the police in January or February, there is no explanation why the process took so long for William.

The last entry on his record, dated 2 August 1919, states he was reported by Superintendent George Monk for being absent form duty on Friday 1 August and participating in a police strike.

In the 1939 register both William and Emma are living at Cateswell Road, Birmingham. There is a record of a death for William Turner Wise on the 27 October 1953 aged 63 years.

Saturday 2 August 1919

PC A79 Jack Allen

Jack was born in Ansley, Warwickshire, on 3 June 1887. His baptism record records his parents as Hannah and John Allen (a collier) although it would appear John was also known as Jack, as he appears on the 1891 census. Living in 'Number 3, New Building' in Ansley, Jack (Snr) is a coal miner, living with wife Hannah and children Tom (11), Edward (9), Sarah (7) and Jack (3). A lodger (Tom Allbrighton, another miner) also resides at the address.

Jack joined Birmingham City Police on 3 August 1909, giving his former occupation as miner. Initially a constable in the 5th class he was paid 25/- a week. Given the warrant number 7751 he was attached to the A Division (city centre). On 18 October 1911 Jack was awarded a gratuity of one guinea for 'courageous conduct' in stopping a runaway horse.

In the 1911 census Jack is living at Moseley Street Police Station with 22 other constables. Also living at the premises is Superintendent Joseph Clarke along with his wife and seven children.

In April 1913 Jack once again demonstrated extreme courage in stopping a runaway horse and was once again commended by the Watch Committee.

In 1914 Jack married Edith Agnes Russell. The couple had three children: Stanley John (born in 1914), Elsie Sarah (born in 1917) and Grace Marjorie (born in 1928). Interestingly Edith's three sisters also married police officers who had been based at Moseley Street Police Station. Her oldest sister Nellie Lavinia Russell married Thomas Mooney (a fellow striker), the third oldest sister Beatrice Alice Russell married Henry (Harry) Paragreen who sadly died during the Spanish flu epidemic in 1918, and later married William Woodyatt, both of whom had been based at Moseley Street. The youngest daughter Elsie Margaret Doris (known as Mollie) married William Henry Robinson – another officer from Moseley Street Police Station. William Robinson had been in the army from 1909 to 1919 and joined the Birmingham City Police in August 1919 – after the strike. So between them four sisters had married five Birmingham police officers!

Jack's third compliment (and one guinea gratuity) comes when he made an arrest whilst off duty of someone breaking into premises.

> On 29 April 1918 Jack enlisted in the Army as private 172888 in the Machine Gun Corps. Records suggest that he did not serve overseas after completing his training. He served for a short time and then re-joined the police on 27 January 1919 – his wages had risen up to 57/- a week and his new warrant number was 8741. Interestingly Jack appears on the 1919 absent voter's list which shows him as Corporal 133517 in the Machine Gun Corps. This is because the register was actually taken in 1918, before he returned to Birmingham.

Jack went on strike on 2 August 1919 and was reported by Superintendent George Monk and dismissed.

After being dismissed from the police force Jack set up his own coal haulage business at 29 Mona Road, Small Heath and he and his wife Edith also ran a shop at 209 St Andrew's Road, Small Heath, very close to Birmingham City Football Club. On the 1939 register Jack describes himself as a coal dealer master and is living with wife Edith, and daughters Elsie Sarah and Grace Marjorie. Jack died at home on 6 September 1942, at 21 Wichnor Road, Solihull, aged only 55 years. He was buried at Brandwood End Cemetery, Kings Heath, Birmingham.

We are very grateful to Jack's family (particularly Stan Russell, great-grandson of Edith's parents Harry and Mary Russell and his second cousin Miriam Watkins, whose mother Joan was the daughter of PC Harry Paragreen) for pictures and details about him and his family.

PC E128 Thomas William Baggott

Born in 1888 in West Bromwich, which at that time was in Staffordshire, in the 1891 census two-year-old Thomas is living with his parents Joseph and Selina, four older brothers, three older sisters and one younger sister, at 198 Spon Lane. His father's occupation is coal dealer.

By the 1901 census, the family have moved to 15 Arthur Street. Joseph is now retired, Selina sadly died in 1892 and Thomas's younger sister Florence is also missing from the address. 12-year-old Thomas is there with only two older brothers and two older sisters.

In the 1911 census Thomas is now the head of his household at 3 Francis Street, West Bromwich. He is married to Sarah Ann Baggott with a daughter Violet (11 months) and also living at the address is Sarah's sister who undertakes domestic duties in the household.

The following year on 9 December 1912 Thomas joined Birmingham City Police with warrant number 8784.

He is promoted to the 4th class in 1913 and receives a small pay rise each year up to 36/- per week in 1917. Thomas is complimented in police orders and given a gratuity of one guinea in January 1918 for skill in rendering first aid for a broken leg. By April 1918 he left the police force to join the Armed Forces – the 5th (Reserve) Battalion Grenadier Guards. His service record shows he had three further children – Lillian, Dorothy and Thomas William. We know he had one further son – James Henry.

Thomas was de-mobilised and re-joined the Birmingham Police on 3 February 1919. Nothing further is mentioned in his record until he joined the strike on 2 August 1919, was reported by Superintendent Daniel Long and dismissed.

In 1939 Thomas's occupation is shown as a carpenter. His granddaughter Rose said he was a glass blower before being a police constable and then became a cabinet maker.

Thomas died on 6 April 1978 aged 89.

With thanks to Thomas's granddaughter Rose for the information and picture of Thomas

PC C113 Joseph Bailey

Joseph was born on 20 January 1884 to Robert and Elizabeth Bailey. In the 1891 census he is living at 206 Canal Side in Walsall Wood with his father's occupation showing as miner. At the address are his mother, father, two older brothers and an older sister. In 1901 only one other brother is still living with him and his parents, at another address in Walsall Wood. 17-year-old Joseph and older brother Thomas are both showing as coal miners alongside their father.

In 1909 Joseph married Elsie Maud Smith and the couple had a daughter (also Elsie Maud) in 1910.

Joseph joined Birmingham City Police on 21 April 1908, warrant number 7692, collar number C113 and when promoted to 4th class in April 1909 was paid 27/- a week. He was complimented in July 1909 for good police duty in connection with the arrest of individuals for warehouse breaking. He was complimented again and awarded a guinea in October 1909 for courageous conduct in stopping a runaway horse.

Joseph must have served in the army prior to joining the police, as at the outbreak of war in 1914 he was immediately recalled to re-join his regiment. He served as Private 13819 Joseph Bailey, South Staffordshire Regiment. During the Great War he would have served with the 8th (Service) Battalion which entered France on 14 July 1915 and took part in many battles including Delville Wood on the Somme 1916 and Ypres 1917. The battalion was broken up in early 1918 and he would have moved to another unit. Joseph was discharged from the Army on 26 January 1919. He re-joined the Birmingham Police on 3 February 1919 with his pay now at 57/- a week.

The next and final entry on his record is being reported by Superintendent Penrice for being absent from duty and participating in a police strike on 2 August 1919.

In 1939 Joseph is living with Elsie and John Powell in Waldron's Moor – his occupation is chocolate concher and John is an apprentice concher. Elsie is too young to have been Joseph's wife of the same name and born sixteen years before his daughter Elsie, so his relationship to them is unclear.

Moseley Street Police Station, where many of the striking officers were based and had lived in at some time – in 2019 being used as a male hostel. ©Richard Law[cxxix]

PC C180 George William Barker

George was born in 1888 in Elveden, Suffolk. In the 1891 census he is living with his parents John (a groom) and Emily, five older sisters, one older brother and one younger brother, in Brandon Road, Elveden.

In 1901 the family are still living at Brandon Road and John is now a general labourer. Seven of the children are still living at home with John and Emily. In 1911 only one sibling remains with George and their parents – his 28-year-old sister Elizabeth is a domestic housemaid and George is a decorator. John is still a general labourer. His sister Louisa's daughter Dorothy is living with her grandparents and aunt and uncle so perhaps she had fallen on hard times.

George joined Birmingham City Police on 6 June 1914, warrant number 8500, collar number C180, with his wages being 27/- a week. Each year George's wages were increased slightly and there are no commendations or misconduct entries on his record. In April 1915 he married Beatrice Olivia Hope and the couple went on to have two daughters. In December 1915 George joined the military as a reservist and he was called to the colours to serve with the Grenadier Guards in April 1918 as private 33017, re-joining the police upon de-mobilisation in January 1919 with warrant number 8633 (he was given back his old collar number).

Seven months later on 2 August George was reported by Superintendent Penrice for participating in a police strike and was dismissed.

In the 1939 register George's occupation is a painter and glazier. He is living with 20-year-old daughter Iris and 16-year-old daughter Gwendoline Beatrice.

George died on 27 June 1957 – living in Tamworth. His effects went to his daughter Gwendoline Beatrice.

PC A174 John Bayley

Born in 1883 in Aldbrough, Yorkshire, in the 1891 census John is living with father George (a wheelwright), mother Hannah, one older brother and a younger brother and sister in the village of Lelley in Holderness, East Riding.

In the 1901 census John is the eldest of the siblings living at home with his parents and he now has three younger sisters and two younger brothers. John's occupation is recorded as wheelwright along with his father. The family are living in a cottage in the village of Garton, Holderness, East Riding.

In January 1905 John joined the Hull City Police. He is recorded as being fair with blue eyes and 6'0" and half an inch tall. His record is brief and there is only one entry of interest – John was reprimanded by the Chief Constable in August 1906 for 'failing to find a smoke room window on his beat insecure'. He resigned on 13 March 1907[cxxx].

John joined Birmingham City Police in March 1907 with warrant number 7581 and collar number A174. He was appointed in March 1908 and signed an entry in the ledger to say that he would not claim his service with Hull towards his superannuation as per the Police Act 1890. The next entry on his record shows that he was reprimanded for giving unsatisfactory evidence against William Baskerville who was charged with being disorderly, before the Magistrates in July 1907. The punishment for this was that his leave was stopped until further notice. His record shows that leave was reinstated at the beginning of January 1908. In the 1911 census John is living with 31 other constables at Duke Street Police Station.

There are no further black marks on John's record – his work seems to have been satisfactory as he received pay increases and moved up the classes until being reported by Superintendent Monk for participating in a police strike on 2 August 1919 when he was dismissed.

In 1920 John married Lilian I Hayes. In 1939 John and Lilian are living on Woodlands Park Road in Birmingham and his occupation is shown as warehouseman.

John died in 1959 in Birmingham aged 76.

PC E119 Thomas Beardsall

Thomas Beardsall was born in 1889 in Blackburn and in the 1891 census is living with his father James (a railway goods porter), mother Isabella, two older brothers and uncle at 12 John Street in Blackburn. 10 years later and Thomas's father is now a railway goods checker and Thomas has a younger brother. The family are now living at 32 John Street.

By the 1911 census Thomas had married Lydia Turner and the couple were living with her parents and siblings, along with their 11-month-old son, in Blackburn. Thomas is a grocer's assistant and Lydia is a cleaner.

In March 1914 Thomas joined the Birmingham City Police with warrant number 8461 and became PC E119. There is not one blemish on his record, with indications of good performance by his yearly pay increases and rise through the classes.

He served with HM Forces from April 1918 to January 1919 in the Grenadier Guards (after registering as a reservist in December 1915) and the final entry after he re-joined the Birmingham police was that he was dismissed for participating in a police strike on 2 August. Walter went on to have three daughters with Lydia during the 1920s but sadly died in July 1930 – when his youngest child was only four years old.

PC C256 Alfred Belcher

Alfred Belcher was born in Wigan in December 1883 to James and Elizabeth Belcher. James' occupation is shown as a coach smith in the 1891 census.

Alfred joined Birmingham City Police in 1903, shortly before his 20th birthday. He is given warrant number 7329 and collar number C256. By June 1904 Alfred is commended and rewarded with a guinea for 'alertness in detecting two men house breaking, leading to their arrest and conviction.'

In 1909 he married Margaret Amelia Hammond and in the 1911 census the couple have a three month old daughter – Mary Marguerite Belcher. Margaret sadly died in 1914 aged only 34.

In April 1910 Alfred was commended and again rewarded with a guinea for his actions in rendering first aid to a man and horse who had been burnt by sulphuric acid. Clearly having a knack for medical care, in February 1916 Alfred rendered first aid to an individual with a fractured clavicle and was awarded another guinea.

In 1916 Alfred married Ada Silver and had a second child – Thomas – in 1922, but tragically he became a widower for the second time when she died in 1936.

In June 1919 Alfred was awarded the 1st stripe of merit for courageous conduct in stopping a runaway horse. Generally officers are awarded a guinea for this action so to be awarded a stripe of merit must have taken very brave action.

Sadly the next and final entry on his record is regarding the police strike – which Alfred took part in on 2 August 1919 and was immediately dismissed.

Alfred married a third time in 1938 to Christina E Halloran. In the 1939 register Alfred is living with Christina and his occupation is recorded as grocery warehouseman.

PC C74 George William Bingle

George was born in Bismore, Gloucestershire, in 1884 to George and Emily Bingle. In 1891 George had three younger sisters, his father's occupation is umbrella stick maker and the family are living in Stroud.

By 1901 George has another younger sister and a younger brother. George is also now a stick worker along with his father.

George joined the Birmingham City Police on 29 September 1904 with warrant number 7397 and collar number C74. His record contains a similar number of misconduct entries as it does recognition for bravery and good work. The first black mark on his record comes in February 1906 when a 14-year-old girl made a complaint of assault against him. An investigation took place and George was proved innocent of the allegation.

The next month George was complimented for vigilance in the arrest of shop breakers at night, leading to their conviction. In February 1909 George was complimented and awarded a guinea for vigilance in stopping a runaway horse. In March 1911 he was disciplined for not parading at Kenyon Street Police Station at 5:45am as per his sergeant's instructions and instead turning up at Bridge Street West Police Station. His leave was stopped for one day as punishment.

In April 1911 George was awarded a guinea and complimented for skill in rendering first aid to an individual with a 'spiked arm'. In February 1912 George was reprimanded again for being absent from his beat for 1 hour and 50 minutes, when he was found in a house on Summer Lane at 4am.

The 1911 census shows George living at Bridge Street West Police Station with five other constables.

In September 1912 he was awarded the first stripe of merit for vigilance in the arrest of metal stealers and recovery of the metal. In October 1913 George was promoted to the first long service class – for officers who had nine years' service and were performing satisfactorily. In 1916 George married May Smith.

In June 1919 George was again awarded a gratuity for rendering first aid in the form of artificial respiration. The next entry is when he was reported for being absent from duty by Superintendent Arthur Penrice on Saturday 2nd August and dismissed.

In the 1920s George is living with May in Barnt Green Road in Birmingham. He died in 1934 aged 50.

PC E107 George Blackham

George was born in February 1881 in Handsworth (which was then part of Staffordshire) – one of the few strikers who was born locally. George's mother must have died when he was very young as his father has a different wife in the 1881 census (where two month old George first appears) to 1891. In 1891 at the family address in Aston Manor George had an older sister, a younger sister and two younger brothers. The family must have been well off as also living at their address was a servant and a nurse. George's father Walter is an accountant.

In 1902 George joined Birmingham City Police as constable E107 with warrant number 7202.

In 1904 George married Florence May Mayon and in the 1911 census the couple are living with their five-year-old daughter Florence Georgina.

In January 1907 George is complimented for vigilance in the arrest of thieves at night. The following April he was given a guinea for prompt action in putting out a fire. In June 1913 he was awarded a further guinea for arresting a man in possession of stolen brass and also for skill in rendering first aid for someone who had been poisoned. In July 1915 George was awarded another guinea for courageous conduct in stopping a runaway horse.

On 2 August 1919 George took part in the strike and was reported by Superintendent Danny Long for being absent from duty and participating in the strike and was dismissed.

In 1939 George is living with Florence and is working as a caretaker. He died in 1944 aged 63.

PC A192 William Frederick Booton

William was born in July 1886 in Rock, Worcestershire, to William and Eliza. William senior worked as a farm labourer. William junior joined the Birmingham City Police in July 1908 with warrant number 7704. In the census of 1911 he is living at Moseley Street Police Station along with several other strike officers.

In August 1911 William is complimented and awarded a guinea for courageous conduct in stopping a runaway horse. In May 1915 he married Mabel Green and the couple had two children – Alec William Edgar in 1918 and Donald in 1926.

In July 1915 William was complimented and awarded a guinea for skill in rendering first aid. In May 1917 William was awarded the first stripe of merit for arrests in connection with bicycle thieves and rendering first aid.

In January and May 1918 William was commended on two more occasions - first for rendering first aid and secondly for an arrest in connection with an indecent assault on a girl.

By September 1918 William is earning 51/- a week. The next entry on his record is that he was reported by Superintendent George Monk for being absent from duty on 2 August 1919 and was dismissed.

In 1921 William is registered as a shop keeper in Sun Street West, Birmingham. Tragedy struck in 1937 when his oldest son Alec, who was working as an assistant teacher, was killed whilst cycling adjacent to a lorry when the lorry suddenly turned left. In 1939 William is living with Mabel and Donald and his occupation is showing as foreman and clerk.

During World War II William was an air raid warden. During the night of 19 November 1940, during the heaviest air raid Birmingham suffered during the war, William was killed at St. Paul's School.

PC E152 Francis Frederick Bruton

Francis was born in December 1888 to Albert and Ellen Bruton in Gloucestershire. In the 1891 census the family are living in Kingswood in Gloucester. Francis has two older sisters and an older brother and his father's occupation is elastic maker. In the 1901 census Francis is now showing as Frank. The family remains in Kingswood, his older brother is still residing at the family home and one sister has returned to the address as a widow, along with her three-year-old son. In 1911, again in Kingswood, Francis is the only son remaining at the address with Albert and Ellen and the family also have a boarder.

Francis married in June 1914 to Grace Ellen Cox and the couple had a son in August 1915. He joined the Birmingham Police in December 1914 with warrant number 8657. He is complimented in December 1915 when he was awarded a guinea for skill in rendering first aid.

Francis signed up with the Armed Forces in 1915, being attested in December and immediately transferring to the reserves. At this time he was living at 2 Park Place, Salop Street, Birmingham. Francis was called to the colours in April 1918, joining the Grenadier Guards as Guardsman 33221. Francis transferred to the reserves in January 1919 and re-joined the police. The final entry on his record is when Superintendent Daniel Long reported him for being absent from duty on Saturday 2 August 1919 when he was dismissed.

During the 1930s Francis was still living at Park Place with Grace Ellen and in the 1939 register his occupation is showing as foreman. Francis died in March 1948 aged 59.

PC C225 Charles Wilfred Bullock

Charles was born in November 1883 to Eberson and Elizabeth Bullock in Birmingham. In the 1891 census Eberson is a silversmith and the family have seven children including Charles who is the youngest but one. They are living at 8 Court, 3 House on Great Colmore Street, Birmingham. In 1901 Eberson is still a silversmith and the family have managed to get out of the slum housing of the Birmingham courts – they are now living in Fallows Road, Aston. Charles is now 17 and it is stated that he has 'no occupation'. It was unusual for a young person who has finished school not to have a job

to generate income to support the family.

Charles joined the Metropolitan Police in July 1909, leaving in September 1909 to join Staffordshire Constabulary. The 1911 census shows him living at Perry Barr Police Station on Canterbury Road, Handsworth (pictured), at that time part of Staffordshire Police, along with four other constables. A separate page records an Inspector Hall and his wife, along with two visitors (all shown at the Police Office, Perry Barr) and on a third page is a prisoner in the cells!

Charles transferred again in November 1911 to Birmingham as part of the expansion of the Birmingham area (and subsequently police force) when Handsworth became part of the city.

In June 1914 Charles was complimented and awarded the 1st stripe of merit for courageous conduct in stopping a runaway horse. In November 1914 he was complained of by an attendance officer at a school for failing to assist in obtaining the name and address of a boy found working at a butchers at 10:35pm on a Saturday night. In 1917 Charles received two further black marks to his record – once for being drunk on duty in uniform at Lozells Road Police Station at 2am on 15 January and once for being off his special duty post and found gossiping at the adjoining post on a Sunday afternoon in April.

In June 1919 Charles redeemed himself – being awarded a guinea for courageous conduct in stopping a runaway horse. The last entry is from Saturday 2 August where Charles was reported by Superintendent Arthur Penrice for being absent from duty and participating in a police strike, whereby he was dismissed from the force.

The 1939 register shows Charles living with Elizabeth and both are working as fish fryers although it is recorded that Charles is the owner of the establishment.

Charles died in 1963 aged 79.

PC E33 John Burke

John was born in 1876 in Wakefield, Yorkshire (making him the third eldest participant in the strike, after First Police Reserve Edwin Foster and Sergeant Edward Taylor - born in 1874 and 1875 respectively) to Mary and Daniel Burke.

In 1890 John found himself in Wakefield Prison after being convicted of damaging strawberry plants and being given a choice between a seven day prison sentence or an 11/- fine. The 1891 census shows John living in Wakefield with four brothers and a sister, along with his mother and uncle – the census records his father as being away.

At 18 years of age in 1894 John was again convicted – this time of trespassing at a railway station and sentenced to 14 days imprisonment (or a £1.1.6 fine). It would seem the military saved John from getting deeper into a life of crime – in 1895 he enlisted in the Yorkshire Light Infantry with regimental number 5063.

John joined the Birmingham City Police in February 1902 with warrant number 7143. In March 1911 he was cautioned for being absent from his day duty for one hour 40 minutes. He was in trouble again in October 1911 for allowing a prisoner to escape. For this he was demoted from the 1st long service class to the standard 1st class – which meant a reduction in salary of 1/ per week. It was another year until he was reinstated, in October 1912. In August 1914 John was again reprimanded for being drunk whilst parading for duty at Sparkhill Police Station. He was initially suspended, and then reinstated with a final caution.

In November 1914 John was temporarily transferred to the Army base at Budbrook Barracks as a drill instructor. This did not go smoothly initially as he was reported by the inspector in charge of the detachment for not reporting to his supervising officer when completing his duty and for returning to the barracks in a drunken state at 11:50pm on Friday 27 November. By November 1915 John returned to the Birmingham force.

John went out on strike on 2 August and was reported by Superintendent Daniel Long and dismissed. It is believed John died in 1932 aged 56.

PC E123 Alfred Cartwright

Alfred Cartwright was born in December 1882 in Quarry Bank, Staffordshire, to Eli and Lucy Cartwright. The 1891 census shows Alfred living with three older brothers at the family house in Kingswinford. In the 1901 census Alfred is living in Quarry Bank still with his 20-year-old brother and their parents and both Alfred and his father are shown as general labourers.

Alfred married Elizabeth Daisy Cox in 1905 in Stourbridge and the couple had three children. He joined the Birmingham City Police in December 1905 with warrant number 7495.

This picture is from a group picture of Birmingham officers, believed to have been taken during one of the strikes that the police assisted with. The collar number is hard to make out and it is difficult to tell if the prefix is R or E but if the full number is E123 then it will be Alfred.

Alfred was cautioned in April 1907 for leaving his night duty before being relieved and in May 1908 was complimented for 'good services' at a fire in Deritend. In November 1908 he was complained of for going to an address and making highly improper remarks to the two female residents whilst the male householder was away at a convalescent home. In October 1910 Alfred received recognition from the Royal Humane Society for rescuing an individual from a canal and a year later he was awarded the 1st stripe of merit for performing artificial respiration on another individual rescued from the canal for an hour and 40 minutes.

The 1911 census shows Alfred living with wife Daisy and their three children in a back-to-back in Birmingham. Later that year Alfred received another black mark on his record for being drunk on duty in Lawley Street at 2:20am on 10 July. He was suspended for a day and had his leave stopped. He was back in the good books the following year – receiving the 2nd stripe of merit for giving artificial respiration. By September 1914 Alfred was in trouble again – fined 2/ for being found asleep during night duty at 2:45am. In May 1918 and again in June 1919 he was awarded a guinea for courageous conduct in stopping a runaway horse.

The last entry on his record is of course being dismissed for participating in a police strike, after being reported by Superintendent Daniel Long on 2 August 1919.

The 1939 register shows Alfred living in Sheldon with his occupation being city parks gardener.

Alfred died in 1954 in Birmingham aged 71.

PC E168 Alfred Comley

Alfred was born in 1891 in Oldland, Bristol, to Alfred and Ellen Comley. In the 1901 census Alfred is living with his parents, older sister and younger brother. His father's occupation is coal miner. In 1911 Alfred married Florence Louisa Gray and in the 1911 census the couple are living in Bristol together. Alfred's occupation is coal trammer and the couple went on to have two children before Florence sadly died in 1913.

Alfred joined Birmingham City Police on 24 September 1913. His first compliment comes in December 1914 when he received recognition for rendering first aid to an individual with a fractured leg. He was awarded a guinea for his efforts.

In 1915 Alfred married Minnie Stokes and went on to have two children with her. In April 1917 he was in trouble for turning up 20 minutes late for first day watch at Hay Mills Police Station and was fined 1s.

Alfred was recognised again in May 1917 for courageous conduct in stopping a runaway horse and was once more rewarded with a guinea.

In April 1918 he joined the Armed Forces, serving with the Grenadier Guards under regiment number 33229. Alfred re-joined the force in February 1919. He received another black mark to his record in June 1919 for *using obscene language to two members of the force whilst off duty on Coventry Road at 10:05pm*. For this he was fined 1s.

The final entry on his record is being reported by Superintendent Daniel Long for going on strike on 2 August 1919 for which he was dismissed.

In the 1939 register Minnie is living with her widowed mother, two of her children and a married couple slightly older than her children. The record states Minnie is married rather than widowed but Alfred is not on the record, possibly staying elsewhere at the time.

PC E224 Harry Somerville D'Northwood

Harry Sommerville D'Northwood was born in Colwell, Ledbury in 1883. In the 1901 Census he is shown as residing at 25 Gladstone Road Widnes, Lancashire as a boarder, giving his occupation as a general labourer. He joined Worcestershire Police on 15 December 1903 and married Lucy May Keen in 1907.

His police records show that he was awarded £1.0.0 in July 1909 for a *'smart arrest'*. On 9 November 1911 he transferred to Birmingham City Police as part of the Greater Birmingham Expansion when Kings Norton and Northfield became part of the city. He was given warrant number 8001. In the 1911 census we learn that he is living with his wife Lucy May at 773 Warwick Road, Tyseley and two daughters. The couple would later have two further daughters.

The final entry on his police record shows that he was reported by Superintendent Daniel Long and dismissed for participating in a police strike on 2 August 1919.

The 1939 register shows that all family members are still living at the same address. Harry is shown as a gas plant operator.

Harry died on 1 October 1956, aged 73.

PC C270 Arthur Davies

Arthur was born in 1880 in All Saints, Hereford, to James and Mary. In 1881 James is working as a labourer and Arthur is living with his parents, three step-brothers and a step-sister. By 1891 the family are still in Hereford and James is now a yardman. Arthur's step-siblings have moved out and he is with his parents and a 71-year-old boarder.

In 1901, three of Arthur's step-siblings have moved back into the family home – aged, 33, 30 and 29. The eldest is widowed and the other two show as single. Arthur is now working as a railway engine fireman and his father is now a corporation carter.

Arthur joined Birmingham City Police in February 1902 with warrant number 7141. He receives his first recognition for prompt action upon discovering a house fire, rescuing the individuals inside and extinguishing the fire. For this he was awarded one guinea – which goes to show how dangerous runaway horses were considered, with one guinea normally being the reward for action in those cases. In 1910 Arthur is rewarded again for prompt action at a fire, allowed to retain 5/- sent to him as a reward and awarded a guinea by the Watch Committee.

Arthur married his wife Lily in 1904 and in the 1911 census, he is living with Lily and their children Lilian Mary (aged five) and George (one month) in Vicarage Road, Harborne.

In July 1913 Arthur was complimented in police orders - this time for courageous action in stopping a runaway horse, and awarded one guinea, and again in December 1914 for rendering first aid for a fractured arm. Arthur demonstrated his first aid skills once again in May 1918 in a case of poisoning, for which he was awarded another guinea.

The next entry on Arthur's record is being reported by Superintendent Arthur Penrice for being absent from duty and participating in a police strike on 2 August 1919, for which he was dismissed.

Sergeant E3 David Davies

David Davies was born in 1878 in Carmarthenshire. In 1901 he is boarding with a family in Aston and working as a carpenter. He joined the Birmingham City Police in September 1902 with warrant number 7193. No misconduct or compliments are recorded for the first ten years and the only entry of note on his record is his promotion to sergeant in December 1913.

David married Amy Baker in 1908 – his deceased father is recorded on the wedding certificate as previously being a farmer. In the 1911 census he is living with Amy in Harborne. In February 1916 David was awarded a guinea for rendering first aid in two separate cases – one for a case of poisoning and one for an internal haemorrhage. In January 1918 he was complimented again and awarded a guinea for courageous conduct in stopping a runaway horse.

The final entry on his record is when he was reported by Superintendent Daniel Long for being absent from duty on 2 August and participating in a police strike.

In June 1920 David was the Labour candidate for the Erdington South Ward. Presumably he was not elected as throughout 1921 David was campaigning for election in the Balsall Heath area.

PC C220 George Edmund Davies

George was born around 1891 and joined the Birmingham Police in May 1913 aged 22, with warrant number 8307. Within five months he was in trouble for being drunk on his night duty beat on Brearley Street at 1:20am. For this he was briefly suspended and had one days leave stopped. In June 1914 he was complimented and awarded a guinea for skill in rendering first aid in a case of varicose veins. Officers often had to stop and offer first aid when varicose veins burst, which could be quite serious if the bleeding could not be stopped.

In February 1916 George was again complimented and awarded a guinea – this time for courageous action in stopping a runaway horse.

The final entry is from 4 August when George was reported by Superintendent Arthur Penrice for being absent from duty and participating in a police strike on 2 August, for which he was dismissed.

There is a George E Davies living in Birmingham and working for Cadburys as a chocolate concher on the 1939 register which is highly likely to be the former constable. There is also a George E Davies who died in Birmingham in 1958 aged 67.

PC A25 George Dexter

George Dexter was born around 1884 and when he joined the Birmingham Police in 1913 with warrant number 8277, his previous occupation is shown as labourer, with some Army service. In October 1913 he was awarded a guinea and complimented in police orders for skill in rendering first aid in a case of varicose veins. In March 1914 George was in trouble for absenting himself from an evening police class and being late for night duty the same day, for which he was cautioned. He was called up for service with the Army Reserve in August 1914, re-joining the police in February 1919. He was dismissed from the police for participating in a police strike on 2 August after being reported by Superintendent George Monk.

There is a George Dexter born in 1883 living in Birmingham on the 1939 register. His occupation is labourer (emery worker) and he is single, living with a married couple in their 20s. There is also a George Dexter who died in Birmingham in 1942, aged 59, both of which are likely to be the former constable.

Sergeant E30 William Henry Doughty

William was born in July 1875 in Bangalore, India to James and Margaret Doughty. In 1889 (aged 14) William enlisted with the 4th Hussars with regimental number 2722. In 1902 he married Maud Alice Taylor whilst living in Farnham and the couple went on to have three boys together.

William joined Birmingham City Police in June 1904 with warrant number 7369. With five months' service he received his first compliment and award of one guinea for 'vigilance in three good cases at sessions'.

It is unusual for an officer to be recognised for good work so early in service, particularly for an element of good police work like this, so William had clearly taken to police work. He was promoted to sergeant in December 1912 as a gymnastics instructor.

This picture from 1907 shows William Henry Doughty with the Birmingham City Police Gymnasium Class.

In September 1914 William was lent to the Army as a drill instructor for seven months until April 1915. His previous Army experience no doubt proving useful.

With not one blemish on his record, William joined the strike on 2 August and was dismissed after being reported by Superintendent Daniel Long.

Remaining in Birmingham, William and his family lived in Sparkhill and in 1939 his occupation is showing as 'book keeper, guns BSA'. William died in 1951 in Solihull aged 75.

PC C198 Gilbert Dove

Gilbert Dove was born in 1886 in Reigate, Surrey, to John and Mary Dove. In the 1901 census Gilbert is the middle child of five and John's occupation is shown as boot maker. In 1910 he married Caroline Cook and in 1911 the couple are living in Surrey. Gilbert's occupation is railway shunter. Gilbert and Caroline went on to have three sons.

In October 1911 Gilbert joined Birmingham City Police with warrant number 7925. In May 1917 he was awarded a guinea for skill in rendering first aid when he resuscitated a young boy. The following month the Royal Humane Society awarded him a certificate for his actions.

Another officer with an unblemished record – Gilbert took part in the strike on 2 August 1919 and was dismissed once reported by Superintendent Arthur Penrice.

In the 1939 register Gilbert is living with Caroline at 44 Duke Street, Birmingham and his occupation is recorded as motor driver, with light and heavy licenses. At this time the Birmingham Police garages were also based at Duke Street so Gilbert must have seen police vehicles coming in and out all the time.

In 1964 Gilbert died, aged 77, in Surrey.

PC C279 John Early

There is insufficient information held by the museum on John Early to be able to identify anything about his early life or family. Likely of Irish descent, John joined the force in February 1912, aged 26 and single, with warrant number 8188.

In June 1913 John found himself in trouble after being found drunk whilst on strike duty at Holyhead Road Police Station. He was suspended and when reinstated had his leave stopped – losing one day.

John remained with the force during the Great War, with no further misconduct nor any commendations on his record. The final entry relates to him joining the strike on Saturday 2 August, being reported by Superintendent Arthur Penrice and dismissed.

PC A206 Austin Evans

Austin was born in 1890 in Buckland, Gloucestershire to Henry and Joyce Evans. In the 1891 census he is living with his parents and two older sisters, lodging at a house in Buckland. Henry's occupation is general labourer. In 1891 the family are now in their own house, with three more children. Henry is working as an agricultural labourer. By 1911, Austin is also working as a labourer and his 14-year-old brother is working on a farm.

In October 1913 Austin joined the Birmingham City Police with warrant number 8388. There are no instances of misconduct or compliments documented on his record. He left the force to join the Armed Forces in April 1918 after being attested and joining the Army Reserves in December 1915, as private 33237 in the Grenadier Guards. Austin married Ellen Gibbens in June 1918 and spent seven days in hospital in August 1918 with scabies. He re-joined the police in January 1919.

The final entry on Austin's record is being reported by Superintendent George Monk and dismissed for participating in a police strike on 2 August 1919.

PC A66 William Ewart Farmer

William was born in Kidderminster in May 1893 to William and Edith Farmer. In the 1901 census he was their only child and William senior's occupation was recorded as manager of a boat shop.

By the 1911 census William is the eldest of five children, with two younger brothers and two younger sisters and was then working as a grocery shop assistant. The family were still living in Kidderminster.

In March 1914 William joined Birmingham City Police with warrant number 8445. His record shows that he was 5 feet 11½ inches tall. In March 1917 William was called up to the Army as gunner 136194 in the Royal Garrison Artillery after initially signing up in December 1915.

William married Esther Mary Rogers in 1917 and the couple had a son in 1918. He re-joined the police in February 1919 and in June 1919 was awarded a guinea and complimented for the arrest of thieves loitering at night. The final entry on his record is when he was reported by Superintendent George Monk for being absent from duty and participating in a police strike on 2 August, for which he was dismissed.

In 1920 William wrote to the Army asking for reference papers stating he had applied for a job and specific forms had been asked for. In the 1939 register William and Ethel are living with their 13-year-old daughter in Stratford-on-Avon. His occupation is shown as wholesale tea salesman and he is also recorded as an ARP (air raid precaution) warden. There is a William E Farmer who died in 1968 aged 74 who is likely to be the former officer.

PC EM58 Edwin Frederick Foster

Edwin Foster was the only member of the First Police Reserve to go out on strike with the regular officers. The First Police Reserve were created following a Home Office circular in 1911 which urged the creation of a reserve of men consisting of police pensioners and other trained men who could be called up for service during periods of emergency and temporarily added to the force as paid constables. This is in addition to the Second Police Reserve – what we now call the Special Constabulary, a list of fit men ready to be called up in an emergency to act as special constables.

There is an Edwin Frederick Foster born towards the end of 1874 in Aston who is likely to be the former officer. He joined the force on 12 September 1914 with warrant number 274, declaring that he had no police or military service. Edwin was posted to the E division with a collar number identifying him as a member of the police reserve – EM58.

He is listed with the officers reported on 2 August as going out on strike on that day or the previous day.

There is an Edwin F Foster living in Birmingham on the 1939 register with his wife Elizabeth and at least three of their children, along with members of the Harvey family. He is stated as being incapacitated and retired. Elizabeth is working as a charwoman. Edwin died in Birmingham in 1942 aged 67.

PC A91 John French

John was born in March 1891 in Northamptonshire to Emma and Francis French. In the 1891 census John is the youngest of four children and his father's occupation is agricultural labourer. In the 1901 census the family have one more child and John's father and eldest brother are working at a horse dealers as grooms. In 1911 only two of John's siblings are still at home with their parents and John's occupation is showing as shoe machine operative. In November 1911 John married Emma Mary Green but she sadly died in 1913.

In March 1914 John joined the Birmingham City Police with warrant number 8457. His height is shown as 6 feet 2 inches. On 8 April 1918 John was cautioned for failing to remain at his special duty post (armed). On 22 April John left the police to join the Armed Forces, having registered with the reserves in December 1915. He served in the Grenadier Guards as a lance corporal in the 1st Provost Battalion. In November 1918 he missed parade and was demoted to private. In February 1919 John returned to the police.

In May 1919 John was cautioned for failing to proceed to a collision between two motor vehicles. On 2 August he failed to report for duty and was reported by Superintendent George Monk for participating in a police strike. He was dismissed the force.

In 1921 John married Agnes M Edginton in Solihull and one daughter is shown as living with them in Solihull in the 1939 register. John's occupation at that time was a cinema foreman. In 1971 John died, aged 80.

PC E271 William Ewart Gardner

William was born to George and Emily Gardner in Gloucester in January 1895. In the 1901 census he is one of seven children and his father's occupation is railway engine driver. In 1911 (aged 16) William is working as a market gardener on his own account.

On 7 December 1914 William joined the Birmingham City Police with warrant number 8566. In March 1917 he was called up to the Armed Forces after joining the reserves in December 1915. Shortly after this he was awarded a guinea and a certificate from the Society for the Protection of Life from Fire for rescuing a woman from a burning building, which presumably occurred prior to him leaving the force. He joined the Coldstream Guards. His service records show he was hospitalised three times – with tonsillitis and twice with a fever. He returned to the force slightly later than many of his colleagues in July 1919. William was reported by Superintendent Daniel Long for being absent from duty and participating in a police strike on 2 August 1919 for which he was dismissed.

In 1927 William married Blanche E Hodges and in 1939 the couple were living together in Cheltenham with two daughters. William's occupation was farming and market gardening (own account) and his wife was assisting him with their poultry farm.

PC A41 Algy Leonard Giles

Algy was born in December 1888 in Hampshire to Charles and Lydia Giles. In the 1891 census he is living with his parents and sister in his grandfather's house. His grandfather's occupation is shown as farmer and although his father's occupation is not recorded, it is likely he also helped out on the farm.

In the 1901 census Charles and Lydia have their own house – just as well as they have seven children by this point! Charles is now working for himself as a blacksmith. In the 1911 census the family have moved from Hampshire to Suffolk. As well as the seven children living with them, Charles and Lydia have four other children who have now left the family home and have also taken two children in as boarders aged four and 11. Charles is now working as a farmer and Algy (the eldest child at 22) is also working on his father's farm.

Algy married Ethel M Hills in 1913 and on 17 December 1913 Algy joined the Birmingham City Police with warrant number 8426. His occupation was recorded as farm hand and he was 5' 10 ½". There are no compliments or awards on his record but equally there are no misconduct reports so Algy kept himself out of trouble and did what was required. He left the police to join the Armed Forces in April 1918 although his regiment has not been identified. Algy returned to the police in January 1919.

The final entry on Algy's record is from 2 August when he was reported by Superintendent George Monk for participating in a police strike, for which he was dismissed.

Algy stayed in Birmingham initially, but by the 1939 register we can see he has taken his family back to Suffolk and they are living on Hill Farm. Algy is working as a dairy farmer and his son Raymond is working as a tractor driver on the farm. He had four children with Ethel and the younger two are still living with them on the farm.

Algy died aged 85 in 1973.

PC A163 John Thomas Griffin

We believe that our John Thomas Griffin was born in September 1891 in Kinver, Stafford, to John and Mary Griffin. This John Thomas Griffin is working in Cadburys in 1939 and we know our police strikers were welcomed there. In 1911 the family are living near Littleton, Evesham with John senior working as a farm bailiff and his son John working as a waggoner.

John joined Birmingham City Police on 19 May 1913 with warrant number 8315. His early career was uneventful, until May 1917 when he was awarded a guinea and complimented for rendering first aid in the case of a severed artery.

Later that month on 17 May 1917, John left the police to join the Army – returning in February 1919. The final entry on his record is when he was reported by Superintendent George Monk for being absent from duty and participating in a police strike on 2 August 1919, for which he was dismissed.

As aforementioned there is a John Thomas Griffin working as a patrolman at the Cadbury Chocolate Works in the 1939 register and it is highly likely that this is the former officer, as we know Cadburys were forthcoming in offering jobs to the police strikers. Also on this record is his wife Martha G Griffin.

PC C233 Reginald Alfred Homan Harding

Reginald was born in July 1892 in Kempsey, Worcestershire, to parents Alfred and Julia. In the 1901 census he is the oldest of three children and his father's occupation is baker and sub-postmaster.

In September 1913 Reginald joined the Birmingham City Police with warrant number 8643. There are two compliments on his record – one in May 1917 for stopping a runaway horse and one in January 1918 for the arrest of a man stealing brass. He was awarded a guinea on each occasion.

Enlisting in December 1915, Reginald was called up to the Armed Forces in April 1918, serving as Private (Guardsman) 33262 Harding in the Grenadier Guards. He joined 1st (Provost) Battalion {police} 13th Company. In 1916 Reginald married Susan Grey.

Reginald re-joined the police in January 1919 and the final entry on his record is for participating in a police strike on 2 August 1919, for which he was dismissed.

In 1939 he is still living in Birmingham, now with Laura Harding, and working as an accounts collector. Reginald died in 1946 aged 54.

PC A19 Alfred Harris

Alfred was born around 1888 – it hasn't been possible to establish many details of his early life but on his marriage to Nellie Rice in 1916 his father William's occupation is recorded as boatman.

Alfred joined Worcestershire County Police in 1908 and upon the Birmingham expansion in 1911, transferred to Birmingham City Police with warrant number 8008. In July 1912 Alfred was in trouble for fighting with a fellow constable in the station yard at Sparkhill Police Station. He was found to be guilty of *'slightly improper conduct'* (!) and his punishment was transfer to the A Division.

He immediately fared better – being complimented and awarded a guinea for courageous conduct in stopping a runaway horse in September 1912. This was not to last though, as in March 1913 Alfred was reported by his sergeant for being drunk on duty in Suffolk Street at 1:20am. For this his promotion pay scale was deferred and he was severely cautioned.

In November 1915 Alfred resigned to join HM Armed Forces. He became Private 18201 Harris in the Coldstream Guards and served until March 1917, when he was issued a silver war badge after being discharged for DAH. This relates to 'disorderly action of the heart' – often relating to stress or fatigue and sometimes known as soldier's heart.

After re-joining the Birmingham police, there are no further compliments or misconduct reports until 2 August when Alfred is reported by Superintendent George Monk for being absent from duty and participating in a police strike.

The 1939 register shows Alfred living with Nellie and working as a works policeman.

PC A68 Frederick James Hayward

It hasn't been possible to confirm details of Frederick's early life, but we know he joined Birmingham City Police in April 1912 and was given warrant number 8215. His record shows he previously worked in the mines and was 5'10¾" tall. He was single and 21 years of age, so born around 1890/1891.

Frederick's record does not get off to a good start – he was reported for being absent from night duty in March 1913 when he was found drunk in bed in his quarters at Duke Street Police Station at 10:25pm. He was suspended for five days and had one day's leave stopped as a result. Later that year in October Frederick was complimented and awarded a guinea for skill in rendering first aid, in a case where he used artificial respiration.

In January 1917 Frederick finds himself in trouble again – this time for being found drunk off duty whilst in plain clothes in the Bull Ring at 9:30pm on 9 January. He was briefly suspended and fined one day's pay. This demonstrates how tightly controlled the officers' lives were, even out of uniform in their own time. Three months later Frederick is again reprimanded – this time for being absent from his night beat for two hours, between 1:45am and 3:45am. For this his pay was reduced by 2s a week. It is not a surprise that shortly after all of these misconduct reports Frederick signs up to join the Armed Forces, leaving the force in June 1917 and returning in February 1919.

The final entry on Frederick's record is when he was reported by Superintendent George Monk for being absent from duty and participating in a police strike on 2 August 1919, for which he was dismissed.

PC E189 Harry Henderson

Harry was born in January 1890. It hasn't been possible to confirm any details about his early life, but we know he joined Birmingham City Police in May 1913 with warrant number 8324. He married Gertrude Hannah Beale in 1915.

His service seems to have been quite uneventful, with no incidents of note until April 1918 when he was called up for service with the Armed Forces, after enlisting in December 1915. Harry's first son was born in October 1918.

Harry joined the Grenadier Guards as Guardsman 33266 Henderson in the 5th Reserve Battalion, returning to the police in February 1919. The next and final entry on his record is when he was reported by Superintendent Daniel Long for being absent from duty on 2 August 1919 and participating in a police strike, for which he was dismissed.

In the 1939 register Harry is living with Gertrude and their two sons and is working in metal work as an internal grinder (heavy works).

PC C272 Charles John Hill

Charles was born in Saltley, Birmingham in March 1876 to parents Samuel and Jane and was the second youngest of four children. Samuel's occupation was recorded as labourer. By the 1891 census Charles (aged 15) is working as a green grocer and Samuel is showing as a lifter at a local works.

In 1900 Charles married Flora Elizabeth Sutton in Stafford. In the 1901 census the couple are living in Aston Park.

Charles joined Birmingham City Police in May 1901 with warrant number 7075. His career got off to a good start – Charles was awarded the 1st stripe of merit for good police duty in arresting a burglar in March 1903. Two months later he had one days leave stopped for gossiping for three minutes (!) whilst on duty at 9:15pm. In June 1904 Charles is again in trouble for leaving his night duty post at 2:05am and telling falsehoods to his inspector. His leave was stopped until further notice.

After almost nine years without incident, Charles fell afoul of his superiors once more in February 1913 for being drunk whilst on duty at 9:20pm. He was suspended for five days and had one day's leave stopped. In December 1913 Charles was complimented and awarded a guinea for courageous conduct in stopping a runaway horse. In March 1914 Charles was back in trouble – this time for parading for duty whilst drunk at Ladywood Police Station. His leave was again stopped for one day and this time he was transferred to the C Division (having originally been posted to the B Division).

In June 1914 Charles was once again the subject of a misconduct report after absenting himself from his beat and being found at his home under the influence of drink. He was again suspended and this time dropped two classes which led to a 2s reduction in pay per week. It is interesting that at this point he was not dismissed – either the impending war was making the Watch Committee hold on to its resources, or perhaps Charles was really a good officer and there were extenuating circumstances behind his alcohol issues that helped him hold on to his job. In July 1915 his reduction in pay was lifted and Charles was not in trouble again until the events of August 1919. He went out on strike on 2 August and was reported by Superintendent Arthur Penrice and was dismissed.

In the 1939 register Charles is living with Flora and working as a night watchman. He died in 1954 aged 77.

With thanks to Charles' great granddaughter Mary-Jo Smith for his picture.

PC E159 John Hind

John was born in April 1882 in Wigton, Cumberland to parents Charles and Ellen Hind. In the 1891 census he is one of five sons and his father worked as a blacksmith. In the 1901 census John is 18 and is living and working on a farm in Westward, Cumberland.

In 1906 John married Margaret Jane Allison and the couple had a total of five children.

They moved to Birmingham for better work prospects and left their eldest daughter Evelyn Blanche in Cumberland with her grandparents. John joined Birmingham City Police in October 1907 with warrant number 7641. In December 1910 he was awarded a guinea and complimented in police orders for vigilance at night in the arrest of a warehousebreaker.

In the 1911 census John and Margaret are living with their children aged 3 and 1 at Wellington Place, Camp Hill, Birmingham. He was recognised for good work again in February 1912 with the arrest of a thief loitering at night, which earned him another guinea and compliment in police orders. The rest of John's career is fairly uneventful, with natural progression through the classes through good work and length of service.

The final entry on his record is from 2 August 1919 when he was reported by Superintendent Daniel Long for being absent from duty and participating in a police strike, for which he was dismissed.

John and Margaret were expecting another baby at the time of the strike, so he risked quite a lot by joining his fellow union members. He worked in security for a while and then in the 1939 register his occupation is shown as 'tube labourer and bencher'. He is living with Margaret in Lily Road, Birmingham. John died in 1971 aged 88.

With thanks to John's granddaughter Karen for providing the additional information and photograph. Karen also served with the police, being a West Midlands Police staff member from 1974 to 1983.

PC A95 John Hodgkiss

John was born in Walsall in 1885 to parents James and Martha. In the 1891 census he is the second youngest of five children and his father's occupation is coal miner. By the 1901 census John is also working in the colliery. John was involved in an accident in the colliery in January 1905 when a fall of rock cut his arms and head, necessitating his removal to hospital.

John joined Birmingham City Police in January 1906 with warrant number 7503. He was recognised early in his career when complimented in police orders for *'promptitude and intelligence in the arrest of a person who snatched a watch and chain'* in November 1906. This was closely followed with a reward of a guinea for courageous conduct in stopping a runaway horse in March 1907 and again in December 1907. In 1907 John married Emma Littley in Aston and the couple went on to have seven children.

In April 1908 John was complained of by an individual who stated he shuffled him out of a queue and called him an 'old fool' but the Judicial Sub-Committee decided the complaint had no foundation and that was the end of the matter. In September 1908 he was complimented for assistance rendered at a fire in Barwick Street.

In October 1908 John was in trouble for being found drinking whilst on duty at 10:40pm in the Rose and Crown PH on Moor Street. For this matter his leave was stopped until further notice. The next entry of significance is when John was complimented for arrest of a thief in January 1912.

This was closely followed in March 1912 by a claim from a lady who stated that John assaulted her in her house. For this the Watch Committee censured him and reduced him two classes down to 4th class constable. He was complimented again shortly after in June 1912 for courageous conduct in stopping a runaway horse, for which he was awarded a guinea. Nine months later he was reinstated as a 2nd class constable. In 1915 tragedy struck when Special Constable George Croydon was found unconscious by his special protection duty post at Moor Street Train Station. John was also working on the line and when he shouted to George and received no response he proceeded up the line until he came across the body of his colleague. George was transported to the General Hospital where he died shortly after.

In May 1917 John was again complimented and awarded a guinea for arrest of a warehousebreaker.

The final entry on his record is when he was reported on 2 August 1919 by Superintendent George Monk for being absent from duty and participating in a police strike, for which he was dismissed.

In 1937 John died, aged 52. The 1939 register shows his widow Emma living with two of their children.

With thanks to John's grandson Michael Hodgkiss for information and the photograph. Michael was also a police officer serving with West Midlands Police from 1975 to 2006.

PC A142 Charles Holman

Charles was born about 1880 in Bewdley, Worcestershire to Thomas and Mary Ann Holman. In the 1881 census Thomas is working as a boot and shoe maker and Charles is the youngest of five children. By the 1901 census Charles is working as a general labourer and his father has died. Mary Ann is shown as living off her own means.

In July 1901 Charles joined Birmingham City Police with warrant number 7083. In 1901 he married Edith Lloyd in Kidderminster. Charles got into trouble for seeing in the New Year with a drink in 1903 which unfortunately saw him reprimanded for being drunk whilst on duty; losing him two days' pay and leading to his leave being stopped indefinitely. Later that month he was again in trouble for spending 20 minutes in a coffee house (!) whilst on duty, which saw his leave stopped once more.

By May 1906 Charles was finally being complimented – for the arrest of a person whilst picking pockets, which led to a conviction. In December 1906 Charles was again complimented and awarded a guinea for vigilance in the arrest of a thief. In April 1909 he was complimented and awarded a guinea for courageous conduct in stopping a runaway horse. In 1911 Charles and Edith are living in Balsall Heath and have five children.

The final entry on Charles' record is from 2 August 1919 when he was reported by Superintendent George Monk for being absent from police duty and participating in a police strike, for which he was dismissed.

PC C190 Frank Howes

Frank was born in December 1888 in Quarrendon, Aylesbury, Buckinghamshire to parents Joseph and Sarah. Joseph worked as an agricultural labourer and in the 1891 census Frank is the youngest of four children. By 1911 Frank and his younger sister are the only two children still living with their parents. Joseph was by that time working as a shepherd and Frank a domestic groom.

Frank joined Birmingham City Police in October 1911, aged 22, with warrant number 7898. In the 1912 electoral roll he is living at Kenyon Street Police Station.

In March 1914 a complaint was made against Frank that he had damaged the front door of a dwelling house at 11:40pm one evening – however the Judicial Sub-Committee decided the complaint was unproven. In June 1919 Frank was again in trouble after being found by his inspector off his night duty beat, in the tram depot smoking and reading a newspaper at 12:10am!

The final entry on Frank's record is from 4 August when he was reported by Superintendent Arthur Penrice for being absent from duty on 2 August and participating in a police strike, for which he was dismissed.

In the 1939 register Frank is living in Birmingham with his occupation shown as a works policeman and also volunteering as a special constable, which could be the only case of its kind for a 1919 striker to re-join the police as a special constable. No trace could be found of him in the Birmingham special constable registers so it is not clear which police force he was serving with – potentially Warwickshire or Staffordshire. There is also a death record for a Frank Howes, aged 54, in Birmingham in 1943.

PC A76 Frederick William Husselbee

Frederick was born in October 1886 in Penkridge, Staffordshire to parents John and Hannah. In the

1891 census Frederick is one of three siblings living with their parents and cousin. The family are living in Bednall and John's occupation is recorded as blacksmith. In the 1901 census 14-year-old Frederick is now working alongside his father as an apprentice. He has another sister and also at the address are his grandmother and three cousins.

In 1908 Frederick married Sarah Ann Reader in Stone and in 1911 the couple are living together in Huntington, Staffordshire. His occupation is blacksmith striker. On 9 December 1912 he joined the Birmingham City Police with warrant number 8265.

In February 1916 Frederick was awarded a guinea and complimented for courageous conduct in stopping a runaway horse.

The only other incident of note on his record is when he was reported by Inspector Cartwright in March 1919 for being absent from his night duty beat and being seen coming out of the Digbeth Institute at 5:20am on 22 March. For this he was reduced by 1/- a week.

The final entry on Frederick's record is dated 2 August 1919 when he was reported by Superintendent George Monk for being absent from duty and participating in a police strike, for which he was dismissed.

In the 1939 register Frederick is living with Sarah in Cannock and his occupation is recorded as crane driver. Interestingly he is shown as a member of the First Police Reserve (likely within the Staffordshire force) – making him potentially one of only two of the Birmingham strikers to have been able to regain positions in police forces. Frederick died in 1956 aged 69.

PC C95 Horace Victor Hussell

Horace was born in September 1885 in Birmingham, to parents Sarah and James. In the 1891 census James is working as an engine fitter and Horace is the youngest of four children. The family also have a servant living with them in their house in Ladywood. By 1901 only two of the children are left in the family home, there is no servant, James is running his own tobacconist shop and 15-year-old Horace is shown as a scholar.

In 1905 Horace married Florence Ada Bills and the couple had one child by the time he joined Birmingham City Police in March 1908, with warrant number 7679. In April 1910 he received his first and only compliment for his investigation of an 'unnatural offence case' and was rewarded with a guinea.

The 1911 census shows Horace living with Ada and their two children in The Crescent, Cambridge Street, which was a partially completed regency style terrace, started in 1795 and finally demolished in the 1960s. It was based on the structure of the road of the same name (later named Royal Crescent) in Bath. Different wars and other economic struggles prevented its completion. The building must have been very impressive for Horace has indicated his dwelling had 11 rooms (excluding bathrooms, landing, lobby, scullery etc.). If this is correct it must have been hard to afford on a policeman's salary, so perhaps money was coming in from elsewhere or he or his wife had inherited some money from family?

Plan of The Crescent by Francis Jukes, from the design of John Rawstone[cxxxi]

Later in 1911 Horace received his first and only complaint – by a member of the public stating that he had been striking him about the face and kicking his body. The Judicial Sub-Committee must have thought there was something in it as they censured Horace. From September 1914 to April 1915 he was lent to the Army as a drill instructor. Following this in May 1915 Horace left the force to join HM Forces, becoming Sapper 92869 Hussell of Q Company, Royal Engineers. He served overseas and become a Company Quartermaster Sergeant. He received a silver wound badge due to sickness at the end of his service, returning to the force in December 1918 with a new warrant number of 9088. Horace received the British War Medal and the Victory Medal for his service. The final entry of note on Horace's record is when he was reported by Superintendent Arthur Penrice for being absent from police duty on 2 August 1919 and participating in a police strike, for which he was dismissed.

The family remained in Birmingham and in 1939 Horace, Florence and their daughter Gwendoline are living at the School House, King Edward's Grammar School, Stratford Road. Gwendoline is married and there is another person living at the address, too young to be revealed when the register was released in 2015 – perhaps Gwendoline's child?

Horace died in 1965 in Lichfield, Staffordshire, aged 79, shortly before his 80th birthday.

PC C47 Arthur Ingram

Arthur was born in 1879 in Shenstone, Staffordshire to parents William and Ann. In the 1881 census William's occupation is recorded as farm labourer and Arthur is the second youngest of five children. In 1891 William is now a coal miner and Arthur is the second eldest of six children at the address. In 1899 Arthur enlisted in the Grenadier Guards with service number 1886.

In September 1903 Arthur joined Birmingham City Police with warrant number 7310. During 1905 he married Amelia Catherine Weaver. In March 1906 he was in trouble for the first time when reported for being in a 'cakehouse' from 3am until 4:10am whilst on night duty. For this his leave was stopped until further notice by Rafter.

In December 1910 Arthur received his first compliment and award of one guinea for his activity in the arrest of two warehousebreakers in a jeweller's premises at 5:30am on 21 December, leading to their conviction. The 1911 census shows Arthur and Amelia living with their three children in Wellesley Street, Aston.

In January 1916 he was in trouble again – this time reported by Superintendent Arthur Penrice for being found asleep in a hut whilst on special protection duty under arms, at 5:20am on 30 December. For this matter his wages were reduced from 37/- per week to 36/- until April 1917. In April 1918 Arthur's wife made a complaint to the force that he had assaulted her in their home. Superintendent George Monk reported Arthur for the matter but it would seem there was insufficient evidence as the case was dismissed. In May 1918 Arthur received his second compliment and award of a guinea – this time for skill in rendering first aid in a case of burns.

The final entry on Arthur's record is of course him being reported by Superintendent Arthur Penrice for being absent from duty on 2 August 1919 and participating in a police strike, for which he was dismissed.

There is an Arthur Ingram who died in 1923 in Shipston on Stour, Warwickshire which is likely to be the former officer.

PC C147 Henry Jackson

Henry was born in March 1876 to parents William and Mary in Ashby-de-la-Zouche, Leicestershire. In the 1891 census, William is working as an agricultural labourer and Henry is the eldest of four children.

The family are still living in Ashby-de-la-Zouche. In 1901 Henry is working as a railway porter and living as a boarder with a family in Duddeston, Aston.

In November 1901 Henry joined Birmingham City Police and was given the warrant number 7132. In March 1905 he was in trouble for not assisting a fellow constable in removing prisoners from the cells to the prison van and for 'stating an untruth in the orderly room'. For this matter Henry's leave was stopped for two months. Henry redeemed himself quickly with an award of a guinea and a compliment for courageous conduct in stopping a runaway horse in April 1905. In January 1906 he was complimented and again awarded a guinea for intelligence and activity leading to the arrest and conviction of a highway robber.

Around 1909 Henry married Minnie and in the 1911 census the couple are living together with their son Henri.

In July 1911 Henry was again complimented and awarded the first stripe of merit for courageous conduct in stopping a runaway horse. In February 1912 Henry received two further compliments and was awarded two guineas for skill in rendering first aid to a burns victim and for stopping another runaway horse.

Henry continued to progress through the classes to the 1st long service class. In October 1918 he received his final compliment and award of a guinea for rendering first aid to an individual with a broken leg. The final entry on his record is when he was reported by Superintendent Arthur Penrice for being absent from duty and participating in a police strike, for which he was dismissed.

In the 1939 register Henry is living with Minnie and their daughter Ruth, along with another child too young to be identified when the register was released. His occupation is shown as works fireman.

Henry died in June 1958 aged 82.

PC C243 Thomas Herbert Jeffcott

Thomas was born in July 1893 in Nuneaton to parents Thomas and Alice. In the 1901 census Thomas snr is working as a stone quarryman and Thomas junior is the second eldest of four children. A visitor is also present at the address. By the 1911 census, 18-year-old Thomas and his younger brother are also quarrymen and there are four other children at the address.

In March 1914 Thomas joined Birmingham City Police and was given warrant number 8449. In 1915 he married Laura Olorenshaw. There are no commendations or misconduct entries on his record for his relatively short service with the police. The only entry of significance indicates he was reported by Superintendent Arthur Penrice for being absent from police duty and participating in a police strike on 2 August 1919, for which he was dismissed.

In 1939 Thomas is living with Laura and three children – his occupation is shown as coal dealer. He died in 1946 aged 53.

PC E43 Robert Jones

Robert was born in July 1893 to parents Evan and Ellen, in Ffestiniog Wales. In 1901 the family are still living in Capel Gwyn, Ffestiniog and Robert is the eldest of four children. His father is employed as a slate quarryman. By the 1911 census Robert is the eldest of five children.

Brummagem magazine issue 192 from March 2017 (produced by Birmingham historian Carl Chinn) featured an article written about Robert which gave a lot of information about him. We are informed

that he had been working in Maenofferen Quarry since the age of around 13. The family initially believed Robert had joined South Wales Police and were very concerned about this as South Wales was a 'rough place' in those times. It was later learned that he had in fact joined Birmingham City Police. Before joining he needed testimonials. The first of these he obtained from his school teacher Mr Thomas Jones who wrote *"Mr Robert Jones asks me for a testimonial and as I know him from boyhood and have always cherished a high opinion of him as a perfectly sober, steady young man, it gives me great pleasure to do so. He is a healthy, clean, wholesome fellow of an agreeable disposition and well brought up. I have no doubt he will be quite a bright, sane, active and obliging officer. He has my cordial recommendation."*

He had a second similar glowing reference from a Mr Griffith Jones who was the quarry manager at Maenofferen where Robert had worked for the last eight years. Robert joined Birmingham City Police on 8 February 1915 and was given the warrant number 8585.

Later that year on 15 November he resigned from the service to join HM Forces and became Private 2183 Jones of the 6th Company Welch Guards. We know that he went over to France twice and fought in the battle of the Somme before returning home later with frost bite. During his service at home he was at the Tower of London guarding Sir Roger Casement, the Irish spy. On 13 July 1916 Robert returned to France and became a Lewis gunner and remained there until 16 March 1917. On 28

March 1918 Robert was on 48 hours leave in England when he returned to Ffestiniog to marry Ellen Williams. But within a few days he had returned to France. We also know from the article that he was wounded in the face at some point and on 25 February 1919 was officially discharged and immediately re-joined Birmingham City Police.

The final entry on his police service record is dated 2 August 1919 when he was reported by Superintendent Daniel Long for being absent from duty on Saturday 2 August 1919 and for participating in a police strike, for which he was dismissed.

In 1920 Robert's first child Eluned was born and the family moved to Birmingham, living initially in lodgings and then into 2 Back of 27 Parker Street Birmingham, one of the famous Birmingham back-to-backs. Like many other dismissed officers

Robert secured employment with Cadburys. By 1925 the family were living at 12 Blackthorn Road, Bournville and the following year his second child Gordon was born. Both Robert and Ellen became regular church goers. The Welsh chapel was a big part of Robert's life and he was a deacon with the Welsh Wesleyans. He would often travel into Birmingham and other parts of the Midlands to preach.

In 1939 Robert was still working for Cadbury as a chocolate concher and living at Blackthorn Road with Ellen and one of their children.

PC E204 Thomas Frederick Jones

Thomas Jones was born on 21 December 1886 in Fownhope Herefordshire to parents Thomas and Laura. In 1891 the family were living in a cottage on Common Hill, Fownhope. Thomas was the eldest of two children and his father was a stone mason by trade. In 1901 we know the family were still living in Common Hill. At this time Thomas (who also used his middle name on occasion) was now the eldest of five children and working as a cowman on a farm aged just 14.

Thomas's family have told us that on 16 September 1907 Thomas left the family home with the intention of joining Worcester City Police but on arriving at Deansway, Worcester found that the height requirement was six feet two inches and he was only six feet one and a half so therefore could not be accepted. He was advised to go to Worcestershire County Constabulary at Hindlip Hall as he would meet their height requirements. He did this and was accepted and posted to Selly Oak Police Station which also had the facility for single men's quarters on site. In the 1911 census he was living with five other officers in single men's quarters at Kings Heath Police Station. On 9 November 1911 as part of the Birmingham expansion when several parts of Worcestershire (including Selly Oak and Kings Heath) became part of Birmingham, he entered service with Birmingham City Police and was given the warrant number 7962.

On 18 July 1912 he was disciplined for the first of several times when it was reported that he was found asleep on the lawn in front of 77 Institute Road, Kings Heath. For this matter he had one days leave stopped by Rafter. The following year on 9 October it was reported that he had been drunk when coming off duty on 7 October. He was again stopped one day's leave for this matter. The following month he was disciplined a third time when it was reported that he was absent from his beat for two hours on 22 November and yet again had one days leave stopped by Rafter. The year 1914 passed quietly enough for Thomas but on 1 February 1915 once again he was reported for a discipline matter when Sergeant Watson reported him for being drunk when on duty. For this matter he was reduced in pay one shilling per week and given a final caution by the Judicial Sub-Committee. On 6 December 1916 it was reported that he was drunk when reporting off duty at Edward Road Police Station at 9.55pm on Friday 3 November 1916 and also had left his day duty beats 17, 18 and 19 before being relieved. For this matter the Judicial Sub-Committee reprimanded him and again reduced him in pay two shillings. At some point before 1916, stories passed down through the family tell that Thomas was beaten up and left for dead by a gang of Peaky Blinders, leading him to suffer with sinus problems for the rest of his life.

In 1916 Thomas married Helena Richmond and the couple had their first child in March 1917 when Ethel Maud was born. The family lived by this time at 13 Balsall Road, Birmingham. We know from his family that Thomas and Helena attended several Union meetings and Helena was very unhappy with the pay and conditions, such as shift patterns, which she considered awful.

The final entry on Thomas's service record is dated 2 August 1919 when he was reported by Superintendent Daniel Long for being absent from duty on Saturday 2 August 1919 and for participating in a police strike, for which he was dismissed.

Following the dismissal George Cadbury took on some of the sacked men and Thomas worked at the Cadbury Plant initially. Family history handed down was that the first thing Thomas did following the sack was to shave off his moustache and let his hair grow. In the 1939 register Thomas and Helena are living with their three daughters. Their eldest is working at Cadbury's as a chocolate box maker and Thomas has declared his occupation as fitter's mate.

Thomas Frederick Jones died on 29 December 1961. His home address was 42 Fordhouse lane, Stirchley, Birmingham. He left £423 and 14s to his widow Helena Annie Jones. He is buried in St Nicholas Church Yard, Kings Norton.

Thomas's grandson Geoffrey Reading also became a policeman – joining Birmingham City Police in the early 1960s and later West Midlands Police following the 1974 amalgamation. We are grateful to Geoffrey for sharing pictures and information about Thomas.

PC E49 Joseph Lesley

Joseph Lesley was born on 10 May 1883 in Lincoln to parents William and Jane. In 1891 he was one of eight children and the family were living in Turner Street Lincoln. His father was a blacksmith by trade. By 1901 the family still lived in Turner Street but Joseph was now one of only four children at the address. Now aged 18 years, Joseph was working as a druggist porter.

In July 1906 Joseph joined Birmingham City Police and was given the warrant number 7530. His career started off promisingly enough when on 13 June 1907 he was complimented for a good case of rendering first aid. The following month on 24 July he was awarded a gratuity of a guinea for the prompt and efficient manner in which he acted in the case of a larceny. Unfortunately this was followed closely by several incidents of discipline. The first was reported on 8 August 1907 when it was reported that he was loitering in an entry in Kingston Street for 30 minutes the previous week. For this Joseph had his leave stopped until 17 October 1907. The second incident was the following year when on 14 September he was reported for being absent from his day duty post in Snow Hill for 15 minutes, and was found in the Metropole Theatre. For this he had one day's leave stopped. The next discipline entry is dated 30 December 1909 when it was reported that he was drunk whilst on duty in Summer Lane for which he had his leave stopped for two days. On 17 February 1910 Joseph was complimented for his first aid skills for a second time in a case of poisoning. On 27 April 1911 he was reported for disobeying an order for not showing PC Bennet how to work his night duty beat when ordered to by Sergeant Wright. For this matter the Chief Constable severely cautioned him.

In 1911 Joseph is one of six police officers living in single quarters at Bridge Street West Police Station. Of note two of the other officers were PC's Lewis Shaw and George Bingle who also took part in the strike. In 1912 Joseph married Alice Morgan. Alice was widowed after her husband Walter Morgan died early in 1912. Alice had one child by the name of Alice Leah Morgan who had been born in 1901 and presumably lived with Joseph and his wife. On 23 November 1911 there was further discipline when he was reported for loitering on a portion of his beat and leaving his beat before being relieved at 10am on Sunday 12 November. For this matter he was stopped one days leave. Joseph ended 1911 without further discipline but a few months later on 3 February he was suspended for being drunk. For this incident he had two days leave stopped and received a final warning.

Perhaps this final warning was what Joseph needed as for the next seven years his record was very good and included a gratuity of one guinea awarded to him for a third incident of first aid rendered to somebody with a fractured leg.

The final entry for Joseph on his personnel record is dated 2 August 1919 when he was reported by Superintendent Daniel Long for being absent from duty on Saturday 2 August 1919 and for participating in a police strike.

In 1939 Joseph was living with Alice in Cartland Road, Birmingham. Joseph at this time worked in the stores of the cocoa chocolate works in Bournville as a labourer. We also know from the family that Joseph was sadly to lose his wife as she died sometime in the first half of 1951 but Joseph remarried later that year to Elizabeth Waldron, herself a widow. We also know from the family that Joseph died on 3 April 1954 in Birmingham aged 70 years.

With thanks to Ian Cann (whose great great aunt was Joseph's sister) for providing additional information.

PC C124 William Malone

William Malone was born in Cooleen, Kilkenny, Ireland on 12 April 1877 to parents James and Charlotte. He joined Birmingham City Police as a single man on 1 February 1902 and was given the warrant number 7136.

On 23 January 1905, Superintendent Jones (fire brigade) reported William for not sending an alarm of fire which had happened on 8 January. The Judicial Sub-Committee deemed that no blame should be attached to him for the incident and it appears no further action was taken. In 1905 William married Harriet Mary Fitzhugh. In 1911 the couple were living at 180 Shenstone Road, Birmingham together with two children.

During his service William was to receive two awards and one misconduct report. The first award is recorded on 13 October 1913 when he was awarded a gratuity of one guinea and complimented for rendering first aid to a person with varicose veins. On 11 March 1916 he was reported for neglect of duty for failing to report a case under the lighting order (Defence of the Realm Regulation) by allowing a light to cast a distinct illumination from a window in Willow Avenue the previous Tuesday. In wartime this was a serious matter as the threat from German Zeppelins was very real. He was stopped one day's leave by the Chief Constable for this matter. A few years later on 16 June 1919 he received his second award. Again this was for rendering first aid, this time to a person with a fractured leg.

The final entry on his service record is dated 2 August 1919 when he was reported by Superintendent Arthur Penrice for being absent from duty on Saturday 2 August 1919 and participating in a police strike, for which he was dismissed.

The family continue to live in Shenstone Road and in 1939 William is shown as a 'checker of goods, out of business'. He had also registered as an air raid precaution (ARP) officer in a first aid post in Dudley Road, Birmingham.

William died in Birmingham in 1958, he was 81 years old.

PC A148 Joseph Philip Marlow

Joseph Marlow was born in the district of Uppingham, Hallerton, Leicestershire on 6 December 1875 to parents Joseph and Sarah. The family lived in Hallerton and in 1881 Joseph was the youngest of two children and his father was a general labourer. In 1891 the family were living in Hunts Lane, Hallerton and Joseph preferred to use his middle name of Philip. He was an agricultural labourer like his father. At the start of 1901 we know that Joseph was still living with his family and working as a domestic labourer but it is clear that he wanted a change as on 15 July 1901 he joined Birmingham City Police and was given the warrant number 7085.

Joseph married Edith Cursley in 1904 and by 1906 the couple had their first child. On 8 April 1907 Joseph was disciplined for not making the effort to secure the arrest of two men and one woman who had broken into a shop. For this matter he was censured for inefficiency. By 1911 the family were living at 230 St Benedicts Road, Small Heath, Birmingham. In 1915 the couple had their second child.

The final entry on Joseph's service record is dated 2 August 1919 and informs us that he was reported by Superintendent George Monk for being absent from duty on Saturday 2 August 1919 and for participating in a police strike. He was dismissed.

The family moved to another house in St Benedicts Road and in the 1939 register Joseph is once again working as a labourer. Based on age and place of residence it is highly likely that Joseph died the following year in 1940 aged 64 years old.

PC E266 Joseph Marsh

It has not been possible to confirm details of Joseph's early life but we do know that he joined Birmingham City Police on 4 December 1914 and was given the warrant number 8556. Upon joining we know that he was aged 20 and single.

The following year on 15 November 1915 he resigned to join HM forces. We also know that Joseph was living in single quarters at Moseley Street Police Station when he enlisted into the Royal Garrison Artillery (RGA) as Corporal 69681 Marsh in the 1st Battery AA Section (anti-aircraft).

This picture shows Joseph in the Birmingham City Police Gymnastics Class 1915.

Joseph was to re-join Birmingham City Police on 10 February 1919 and was given the new warrant number 8861. The final entry on his police service record informs us that he was reported on 2 August 1919 by Superintendent Daniel Long for being absent from duty on 2 August 1919 and for participating in a police strike, for which he was dismissed.

PC C63 Joseph Turner Marsh

Joseph Marsh was born around 1881 in Coopers Bank near Dudley to parents Joseph and Sarah. The family lived in a cottage on Coopers Bank Road. He was one of seven children and his father gave his occupation as a coal miner. By 1901 we know the family still lived at the same address but Sarah was by then a widow and Joseph had followed in his father's footsteps, becoming a coal miner. On 30 September 1901 Joseph married Kate Cavell at St Edmunds in Dudley, Worcestershire.

It is apparent the life of a coal miner was not for Joseph as he joined Birmingham City Police on 19 December 1905 and was given the warrant number 7499. On 30 September 1908 he was awarded a guinea for skill in rendering first aid to an individual with a broken thigh and he was awarded the 1st stripe of merit the following month for rendering first aid to a boy with a wounded abdomen.

The first two years of Joseph's service had gone well but this was not to last. On 7 January 1909 it was reported that he had been on licensed premises for the purposes of obtaining drink whilst on night duty on 19 December for which he had his leave stopped for two days. This was followed on 29 July

1909 when it was reported that he had shouted at his sergeant and caused a crowd to assemble, and had also been insolent to his sergeant when being spoken to about been absent from his beat a few days earlier. For this second matter he was stopped one days leave.

Things looked up slightly for Joseph when on 23 February 1910 he was awarded a guinea and complimented for vigilance in the arrest of two slot meter thieves. On 29 June 1910 he received a complaint from Annie Beech of the Red Cow Public House for assaulting her 12-year-old son by striking him on the face and then assaulting her, by striking her on the arm and chest with his fist after she remonstrated with him.

There are no other details but he was reduced by one class and transferred from the A to C Division. In 1911 we know that

Joseph and Kate were living at 53 Nelson Street, Birmingham. At that time the couple had five children of their own.

The final entry on his record is dated 2 August 1919 when he was reported by Superintendent Arthur Penrice for being absent from duty on Saturday 2 August and for participating in a police strike for which he was dismissed.

Sadly within a year of being dismissed Joseph died aged only 38 years.

With thanks to Joseph's great granddaughter Sally Hughes for providing a picture of him.

PC E126 John George Mattock

John Mattock was born in Leicester on 26 October 1879 to parents George and Kate. In the 1881 census he was the only child living with his parents in George Street, Leicestershire. His father stated he was a hand labourer. By 1891 the family have moved to Main Street, Fleckney in Leicestershire. At this time we know that John is the eldest of six children and that despite only being only 11 years old he is by this time a farm labourer. There were further moves and additions to John's family: in 1901 the family were living in Gladstone Street, Leicestershire and with three more additions to the family John is now the eldest of 10 children and is employed as a framework knitter.

John joined Birmingham City Police on 29 February 1904 and was given the warrant number 7343. He married Minnie Spencer in 1907 in Kings Norton and the couple lived at 121 Vincent Street, Balsall Heath. Throughout his 15 years of service he did not receive any awards but was promoted to 1st class constable in 1911.

The final entry on his record is dated 2 August 1919 when he was reported by Superintendent Daniel Long for being absent from duty on Saturday 2 August 1919 and for participating in a police strike, for which he was dismissed.

The family continued to live at the Vincent Street address until 1930 when they moved to 26 Lofthouse Cresent, Birmingham. Sadly in 1932 Minnie died at the age of 57 years. John later married Emily Rose Ballard and the couple also lived in Lofthouse Cresent. In 1939 we know that there are just the two of them living at the address and John is employed as a stocker/loader coco chocolate worker – another striker given employment by Cadbury's.

John died in 1955 aged 75 in Birmingham.

PC E233 George Frederick Milburn

George Milburn was born on 11 February 1889 in Birmingham to parents Charles and Elizabeth. In the 1891 census the family lived at 94 Clifton Road in the Parish of Kings Norton - then part of Worcestershire. George is shown as one of four children and his father gave his occupation as a general labourer. By the time of the 1901 census the family are living at 176 Grange Road, Kings Norton. There were several additions to the family as George is shown as one of seven children and there is also a boarder living at the address. This house still stands today and is only a small terraced house so must have been a little crowded in there.

By the time of the 1911 census George (now 22 years old) is living at Hay Mills Police Station. He had joined Worcestershire Police on 4 February 1911 however he is shown as 'received from Worcester' into the Birmingham City Police on 9 November 1911 and was given the warrant number 8075. In 1912 he has a polling address of Coventry Road Police station. On 13 September 1913 George married Kate Small in Yardley Parish Church.

Throughout what would be eight years' service George received just one award. Recorded on 5 July 1915 he was awarded a gratuity of two guineas and complimented for his prompt action in connection with a burst steam pipe at night in a council school. The aid he rendered prevented an explosion. He had also displayed his skill in first aid in a case of suffocation.

The final entry on his service record is dated 4 August 1919 when he was reported by Superintendent Daniel Long for being absent from duty on Saturday 2 August 1919 and for participating in a police strike, for which he was dismissed.

In the 1939 register we find George and Kate living with four daughters in Hay Mills. At the time of the census he gave his occupation as a journeyman painter. George Frederick Milburn died on 29 December 1953 aged 64.

PC C188 Thomas Mooney

Thomas Mooney was born in Skipton, Yorkshire on 7 March 1881 to parents John and Bridget. Thomas was only one month old when the 1881 census was taken and at that time was the only child listed. The family are shown as living at 21 Pembroke Street Skipton, Yorkshire and his father gave his occupation as an engine man. By the time of the 1891 census the family still live at the same address and the occupation given by his father is a stationary engine driver which suggests he worked on the railways. In 1901 Thomas was still living at home with his parents in Skipton and his occupation was millwright. He was working for William Fawcett, an engineering and Millwright company but had been released due to a lack of work. The company had given Thomas a glowing reference stating he had worked with them for five years and they found him steady, willing and attentive: having no hesitation in recommending him. The memo is addressed to the 'Superintendent of Constabulary', presumably of the Birmingham force.

We also have a second reference for Thomas who had apparently moved to an engineering company called Rushworth Brothers. In a memo dated 8 November 1901 we once again see he was a valued employee only released once more due to scarcity of work. The company state he was quiet, industrious, civil and attentive to all his duties. Finally there is a testimonial from a Justice of the Peace in West Riding. Although not known personally to Thomas, after making enquires with those that did know him, he stated he was informed that Thomas was a perfectly steady and reliable young man suitable for the police force.

On 1 February 1902 Thomas joined Birmingham City Police and was given the warrant number 7419. It wasn't long before Thomas received his first award when in February 1903 he was complimented for assisting in the capture of a thief who had escaped from a colleague (PC A124 Watson). This was followed by the only blemish on his record when he was reported for being under the influence of alcohol in the early hours of 2 October 1904. For this Thomas had his leave stopped but his record does not show the duration of this sanction. On 26 September 1906 he was again complimented for vigilance leading to the arrest of two warehousemen detected a month earlier in the early hours of 24 August. On 20 January 1910 he was further complimented for the arrest of thieves at night. In October of this year he transferred to the C Division however no reason is given for this and it is possible that this was simply a redeployment. Another explanation is that he moved division following his marriage to Nellie Lavinia Russell in 1910. Before this marriage he was living in single men's quarters at Moseley Street Police Station but in the 1911 census he is shown as living with Nellie at 33 Abbey Street, Birmingham. As previously mentioned Nellie's younger sister Edith married another policeman Jack Allen three years later in 1914. Of Thomas's two other policemen brothers-in-law, William Woodyatt left the police in 1914 and William Robinson didn't join the police until after the strike. The late PC Harry Paragreen had also been a part of the family but sadly died in 1918 during the Spanish flu epidemic.

On 5 February 1912 Thomas was awarded a gratuity of one guinea and complimented for the arrest at night of a thief loitering with intent. This was followed in July 1916 when he was again awarded a gratuity of one guinea and complimented for courageous conduct in stopping a runaway horse.

Throughout his service Thomas had shown that he was a very capable officer being conscientious, vigilant and courageous and he was also able to demonstrate his skill when rendering first aid in May 1917 to a person with a compound fracture of the leg. For this he was complimented once again and awarded his 1st stripe of merit.

The final entry on Thomas's service record is dated 4 August 1919 when he was reported by Superintendent Arthur Penrice for being absent from duty on Saturday 2 August 1919 and participating in a police strike. Thomas's brother-in-law PC Jack Allen also went on strike on 2 August and the pair were dismissed.

From Thomas's family we know that at the time he was dismissed the couple had four children: George John Joseph was born in 1911 (George sadly died aged only 22 in 1934), Winifred Mary who was born 27 June 1913, Lilian Margaret born 11 August 1914 and Olive M E born 7 October 1917 - just 22 months old at the time of the strike. The couple were to have a 5th child (Veronica H R) in 1922. Thomas was one of several dismissed officers who went to work at Cadbury's in Bournville and he became a chocolate maker. He is still shown in this trade in the 1939 register but went on to become the night watchman at the company. His grandchildren still remember him bringing home misshaped chocolates in a blue sugar bag and how excited they were.

Thomas and Nellie lived most of their married life at 11 Belgrave Terrace, Soho Road, Handsworth where Thomas died in 1957 aged 76.

Thomas's grandson Anthony Dutton worked for Staffordshire Police from 1957 to 1969. We are very grateful to Thomas's family (particularly Stan Russell, great-grandson of Nellie's parents and his second cousin Miriam Watkins) for providing information and pictures.

PC E121 Arthur John Moore

Arthur John Moore was born on 22 June 1892 in Worcestershire to parents Charles and Ellen. In the 1901 census the family lived in Village Street, Great Hampton. Arthur is shown as one of six children at the address and his father gave his occupation as a foreman platelayer. By the time of the 1911 census the family are still living in Great Hampton however Arthur, now 19 years old, is shown as working on the railway as a platelayer, the same as his father, perhaps they were working together? Soon after this census, Arthur joined Birmingham City Police on 11 March 1912 and was given the warrant number 8695. His service in the police started well when on 17 June 1914 he was awarded a gratuity of one guinea and complimented for courageous conduct in stopping a runaway horse.

With no blemish on his record he resigned to join HM Forces on 15 November 1915, becoming Gunner 66745 in the 78 Siege Battery of the Royal Garrison Artillery. Upon enlistment he gave his home address as 14 Highgate Place, Moseley Road. Birmingham. We also get a brief description of him as his enlistment papers state that he was 5' 11" tall, weighed 168lbs and had very good physical development. Whilst in military service he married Annie Pragnell on 18 January 1916 at Holy Trinity Church, Bordesley but was only to have a few months with her before he embarked from Folkestone on 15 April 1916 and landed in Boulogne, France. On 25 July 1918 he was informed that he had been awarded the Croix de Guerre for acts of bravery before the enemy. On 21 September 1918 the couple had a daughter and called her Dorothy Ellen. For his service with the Army he was to receive the British War Medal, Victory Medal and the aforementioned Croix de Guerre.

On 14 January 1919 Arthur went on to the Army reserve list and re-joined Birmingham City Police a few days later. The final entry on his police service record is dated 4 August 1919 when he was reported by Superintendent Daniel Long for being absent from duty on Saturday 2 August and for participating in a police strike for which he was dismissed.

Having been dismissed from the police service it is apparent that Arthur was keen to get back into employment as there is a letter in his military service papers collection dated 23 September 1919 from the London and North Western Railway requesting a reference as Arthur had applied to be a porter with the company. It makes note of the years spent with the Army but does not make mention of his police service. For many years Arthur worked for the famous Birmingham architect Alfred Cheatle at his home Chalford House, Sutton Coldfield, as a gentleman's gardener, also acting as his gunbearer/beater on hunting days at an estate in Tamworth.

In the 1939 register the family are shown as living in 317 Erdington Road, Aldridge. At this time Arthur stated his occupation was a gardener. Arthur joined the Home Guard during the war but unfortunately the exercises weakened his heart. Arthur died on 10 December 1956 making him 66 years of age.

With thanks to Arthur's granddaughter Carol for information and the picture.

PC C131 John Thomas Morgan

Thomas Morgan was born on 29 March 1882 in Uwchygarreg, Montgomeryshire to parents John and Margaret. The 1891 census shows that Thomas is the younger of two children at the address and Margaret's mother also resides with them. John Morgan gives his occupation as a farmer. By the time of the 1901 census the family are still residing at the same address however Thomas is now shown as the eldest of two children. His occupation is shown as farmer's son so perhaps he is now working with his father.

Within two years of this census Thomas joined Birmingham City Police on 21 August 1903 and was given the warrant number 7276. For almost three years his service progressed well but on 15 April 1906 he was suspended. There is an explanation when we learn that he had been drunk on night duty and for this he had his leave suspended until further orders. This comment is later endorsed that his leave was reinstated on 29 October, six months later. On 14 December Thomas was quarrelling with PC Edwards in Bloomsbury Street Station. Clearly the chief constable took a dim view of his actions, whatever they were, and deemed them serious enough to transfer Thomas to the C Division and cautioned him that any future quarrelling would render him liable to dismissal.

Thomas married Cassandra Caroline Christina Clarke in 1910 and in 1911 the couple are shown as living at 60 Crabtree Road, Birmingham and would go on to have two children. On 27 November 1912 he was complimented for vigilance for the arrest of men loitering at night on two occasions. On 2 May 1917 he was awarded a gratuity of one guinea and complimented for the arrest (in company with PC C145 Campbell) of warehousebreakers. This was followed on 2 January 1918 when he was again awarded a gratuity of one guinea and complimented, this time in a case of poisoning. Unfortunately this good record was not to last when Thomas again came to the attention of the Chief Constable. He was reported for neglect of duty for failing to render assistance on 9 June to Special Constable George Hall who had a prisoner in custody who afterwards escaped. For this he was cautioned.

The final entry on his record is dated 2 August 1919 when he was reported by Superintendent Arthur Penrice for being absent from duty on Saturday 2 August 1919 and for participating in a police strike.

We are fortunate to have found Thomas in the 1939 register where he is found still to be living in Crabtree Road. He gives his occupation as a carpenter.

There is a record of a Thomas John Morgan dying in Birmingham in 1962. If this is our officer then he would have been 80 years old.

PC C175 Samuel Morland

Samuel Morland was born on 20 November 1883 in Lancashire to parents Samuel and Jane. In the 1891 census Samuel Jnr is listed as one of four children and the family lived in the parish of Bulk in Lancashire. His father gave his occupation as a mercantile clerk. By the time of the 1901 census, Samuel is the second eldest of five children and the family are now living at 11 The Broadway, Lancashire. By this time Samuel is 17 years old and gives his occupation as an apprentice.

At the age of 25 years, on 24 May 1909 Samuel joined Birmingham City Police and was given the warrant number 7744. There was a string of discipline matters that followed and you could be forgiven for thinking that Samuel was not cut out for the life of a policeman. On 7 January 1910 he was reported by Superintendent Monk for damaging his staff (truncheon) and was to pay for its replacement and cautioned as to the care of his accoutrements. This was followed when he was reported on 5 January 1911 having been found lying down on the seat in the cab shelter in Edward Street on Christmas Eve for which he was stopped one days leave. The third incident was reported on 29 April 1911 when he reported drunk for night duty on 13 April for which he was again stopped one days leave. He apparently settled down thereafter.

In the 1911 census Samuel is shown as living in single men's quarters at Kenyon Street Police Station aged 27. On 28 April 1912 he married Annie Marie in the parish of St Mark's, Birmingham. The first and only award shown for Samuel came on 18 June 1919 when he was awarded a gratuity of two guineas and complimented for good duty in two cases at petty sessions and for rendering first aid. The final entry on his service record is dated 2 August 1919 when he was reported by Superintendent Arthur Penrice for being absent from duty on Saturday 2 August and participating in a police strike, for which he was dismissed.

In the 1939 register Samuel is living with Annie and two daughters in Birmingham. His employment is now shown as a coach motor trimmer. There is a record of a Samuel Morland who died in Birmingham in 1967 at the grand age of 83 years.

PC A115 John Morledge

John Morledge was born in January 1880 in Birmingham to parents John and Eliza Morledge. In the 1891 census John is shown as one of six children living in George Street, Birmingham, his father giving his occupation as a brass dipper. In the 1901 census widowed Eliza is shown as the head of the family with four of her children. John had joined the Army in the Royal Warwickshire Regiment and was fighting in the Boer War so is not captured in the census.

John joined Birmingham City Police on 11 November 1902, aged 22, and was given the warrant number 7218. On 28 August 1904 he married Alice Hyam from Balsall Heath. The first six years of his police service were uneventful but in 1909 he was awarded a gratuity of one guinea and complimented for courageous conduct when stopping two runaway chain horses.

In the 1911 census John is living with his wife Alice and her brother at No. 3 back of 179 Irving Street, Birmingham. The next and last significant entry on his service recorded is dated 2 August 1919 when he was reported by Superintendent George Monk for being absent from duty on Saturday 2nd August 1919 and for participating in a police strike for which he was dismissed.

John and Alice had three daughters in total but only one, Florence Lillian, survived infancy. Florence and her husband emigrated to South Africa to run a tea plantation.

Tragically they disappeared and were presumed killed in uprisings. It is believed that John worked as a taxi driver following the police strike. In the 1939 register both John and Alice are shown as living in gas Street, Birmingham. John gives his occupation as a church caretaker. John died aged 70 in 1950.

With thanks to Ken Rainbow, John's great nephew, for the picture and information.

PC E76 Claude Morrison

Claude Morrison was born in Linthorpe, Yorkshire on 29 December 1884 to parents Douglas and Eleanor. In the 1891 census he is shown as the youngest of five children and the family are still living in Linthorpe. Interestingly his father gave his occupation as a police constable. By the time of the 1901 census the family have moved and are living at 26 Newstead Road in Middleborough. Claude is now 17 years old and gave his occupation as a bricklayer. His father (by this time 54 years old) gave his occupation as a retired police officer.

In 1903 Claude married Louisa Ward from Durham and on 12 December that same year he joined Birmingham City Police and was given the warrant number 7317. He did not have to wait long before receiving his first recognition for good work when on 8 June 1904 he was awarded a gratuity of one guinea for the arrest of thieves in a prepayment gas meter case. On 20 November 1905 he was however cautioned for being absent from his beat for 15 minutes and then being found sitting down in a wash house in Lodge Road. It was five years before the next significant entry on his service record when on 28 September 1910 he was awarded a gratuity of one guinea for good police duty leading to the conviction of men stealing brass.

In the 1911 census Claude is shown living with his wife Louisa and three young children at 74 Mott Street, Birmingham. On 14 December 1911 Claude found himself disciplined for the first of three incidents in just four months. The first: for parading on duty 15 minutes late he was stopped one days leave. The second: on 6 January 1912 for parading 18 minutes late for duty he was again stopped one days leave. Finally on 29 April for being off his point duty beat and gossiping to a civilian, telling his sergeant a deliberate lie and being insolent to him, Claude was reprimanded and stopped one days leave. He finished 1912 on a good note when on 4 December he was awarded a guinea and complimented for the arrest of a man loitering with intent.

On 29 September 1913 Claude was reported by Sergeant Lees for being in a coffee house in Summer Lane at 4:16am on the morning of 26 July, also for neglect of duty when he failed to find a dwelling house door insecure the following day and for being insolent to his sergeant at the same time and place. For this matter he was reduced in class and pay by one shilling. On 9 October that year Claude was transferred to the E Division however there is no explanation for this or what division he was on beforehand. From 1915 his conduct improved: on 15 July 1915 he was awarded a gratuity of one guinea and complimented for courageous conduct in stopping a runaway horse. This was followed on 2 February 1916 by another compliment and award of a guinea when stopping another runaway horse, followed on 3 July when he was awarded a gratuity of one guinea for rendering first aid to someone with a severed tendon.

Perhaps Claude's worst discipline offence took place on 4 June 1917 when he was found to be asleep whilst on protection duty and under arms at 4:50am on 14 May 1917. For this matter he was cautioned by the Judicial Sub-Committee. The final entry on his service record dates form 2 August 1919 when he was reported by Superintendent Daniel Long for being absent from duty on Saturday 2 August and participating in a police strike.

In the 1939 register both Claude and Louisa are living at 24 Venetia Road, Birmingham with two of their daughters. At this time Claude has given his occupation as being a bricklayer and furnace setter.

The final information we find for Claude is an entry concerning his death which is recorded on 23 May 1948 in Birmingham. He was 64 years of age. It is apparent that he had done reasonably well for himself as he left £1369 to his widow Louise.

PC A47 George Reginald New

George Reginald New was born on 13 August 1888 to parents George and Julia. In 1891 George is the eldest of two children and the family are living in Areley Kings, Worcestershire. George senior is a carpet weaver. The 1901 census shows the family living in Black Road, Worcestershire. George is now the second eldest of six children – perhaps his older sister was living with relatives in 1891?

In October 1913 George married Winifred Bessie Evans and the couple's first child Winifred Annie was born in June 1914.

George joined Birmingham City Police on 1 March 1915 and was given the warrant number 8954. On 9 December 1915 George was attested into the Coldstream Guards and gave his home address as 4 Trenville Avenue, Fulham Road, Sparkhill. From his attestation papers we learn that he declared previous military service, having served with the 7th Worcestershire Territorial Force and being discharged on 13 April 1910. We are also fortunate to have his description: he was 5' 11" tall, weighing 162 pounds with brown hair, blue eyes and in good health.

George was immediately placed in the Army reserve and returned to police duties. On 4 May 1916 he was reported for being absent from his special duty for a period of 45 minutes, the report does not detail the circumstances but he was cautioned for the matter. On 6 December he is reported by Richard Brown for 'disturbing his peace' at 4 Trenville Avenue by sawing wood and hammering and in addition, for making 'improper overtures' towards his wife on 28 October 1916. It should be remembered that this was George's home address so presumably this was a dispute with a neighbour. Whatever the explanation he gave for these two incidents, it was clearly accepted as his record is simply marked 'Explained.'

In 1917 their second child (George Thomas) was born on 22 April which must have been hard for the family as on 23 April 1918 George was mobilised and became private 27554 New, being posted to the 13th Company Coldstream Guards. On 11 October 1918 he was promoted to lance corporal and embarked to France on 28 November with the 3rd Battalion Coldstream Guards. He returned and re-joined Birmingham City Police on 31 March 1919 and was given a new warrant number of 8925 and again placed on the Army reserve list.

The last entry on his police record states that he was reported by Superintendent George Monk and dismissed for participating in a police strike on 2 August 1919.

In 1939 George is still living at the Trenville Avenue address together with his wife and their son George. George senior's occupation is electrical fitter. George died on 28 February 1951. It is apparent that he had done well for himself: the family are shown as living at 51 Wilton Road, Birmingham and the sum of £1,773 2s 1d was left in his Will to his wife. This was no small amount in 1951 and is worth over £50,000 in 2019.

PC E146 George Newman

George Newman was born on 3 November 1884 in Warwickshire to parents George and Harriot. In the 1901 census George is showing as being the second eldest of four children living at 95 Bevington Waste, Warwickshire. His father's occupation is shown as agricultural labourer.

George joined Birmingham City Police on 17 October 1904 and was given the warrant number 7419. He was recognised early in his career - on 8 August 1907 George was awarded certificate of the Royal Humane Society for 'restoring animation' (drowning).

In the 1911 census George is showing as living with his wife Mabel Martha (who he married in 1908) and their one year old daughter Gertrude Emma at 30 Theresa Road, Sparkbrook, Birmingham.

On 11 June 1912 George was complimented in police orders for vigilance in the arrest of a shop lifter. He was complimented again on 13 June 1913 for the arrest of a thief loitering and trying doors at night.

Clearly a bit of a thief taker – on 13 October 1913 George was awarded a gratuity of a guinea and complimented for vigilance at night in the arrest of two thieves loitering. On 17 June 1914 he was awarded a gratuity of a guinea for courageous conduct in stopping a runaway horse.

The final entry on his police record informs us that he was reported by Superintendent Daniel Long for being absent from duty on Saturday 2nd August and participating in the police strike.

In the 1920 electoral register George and Mabel are showing as living at 218 Heather Road Birmingham however by 1925 Mabel is shown as living at the address on her own. We next have an address for George when the 1939 register is conducted. Whilst Mabel still resides alone in Heather Road giving her occupation as a paid domestic, George is shown as residing at 10 Berkley Road East Birmingham working as a tube bench labourer. George died in 1961 aged 76.

PC B148 Albert Oakes

Albert Oakes was born in Westhoughton Lancashire on 27 March 1886 to John and Ellen Oakes. His father was a collier by trade. In the 1901 Census John is not shown and Ellen is recorded as the head of the household in Wood Street, Westhoughton. Albert was the youngest of three children. Albert, now 15 years old, is shown as a coal hewer drawer, his two sisters were working as cotton weavers. Perhaps with Ellen on her own, this is the reason that they also had a boarder by the name of William Whittaker. It may be the case that he worked with Albert as he is also shown as a hewer.

On 15 July 1907 Albert Joined Birmingham City Police with the warrant number 7608.

24 February 1908 saw the first of several comments of good work when he was awarded a gratuity of one guinea for rendering first aid at the scene of a poisoning. It wasn't all plain sailing for Albert

though, as on 25 January 1909, Mr Harry Lewis made a complaint against him for using improper language at 12.25am on 10 January. It is clear Albert was required to provide an account on this complaint and his reply was deemed appropriate and the only comment on his record is the word 'Explained' with no action being taken. Later that year saw his second award: on 27 October he is awarded one guinea for courageous work in stopping a runaway horse.

In the 1911 census Albert is shown as living with his wife Dora in Wheeleys Road Edgbaston. They also have a young daughter by the name of May Edna who is only 7 months old. A third award follows on 15 July 1915 when Albert was granted a gratuity of a guinea and complimented for his skill in rendering first aid at a poisoning.

A second blemish on his record followed on 1 July 1918 when he was reported for failing to work a portion of his night beat during the night of Saturday 1 and also for being insolent to his inspector when being spoken too. He was cautioned for this. This was followed on 24 July 1919 when he was reported for being under the influence of drink and refusing to work his beat at 9.25pm on Saturday 19 July 1917. These incidents may have contributed to his thought process of joining the strike, as just over a fortnight later the final entry on his record on 4 August he is reported by Superintendent Edwin Bennett for being absent from duty on Saturday 2 August and participating in the police strike. He was immediately dismissed. Albert was the only officer from the B Division that went on strike – perhaps most of the officers got on better with their senior officers there?

In the 1939 register record both Albert and Dora are shown as residing in Oakington Manor Drive in Wembley. Their daughter (May Edna) is not showing as living with them however three other people are. Albert is shown as being a member of the ARP.

PC A122 William Padbury

William Jesse Padbury was born on 21 February 1891 to parents William and Mary Padbury. In the 1911 census William is showing living with his parents at Fenny Compton. Interestingly both father and son are shown as working for the Great Western Railway Company as platelayers.

William joined Birmingham City Police on 19 May 1913 with the warrant number 8305. On 11 December 1915 joined the Army, immediately being placed onto the reserve list and returned to policing.

On 22 March 1917 he was reported as being absent from quarters at Digbeth Police Station from 9pm on 1 March until 1.45am 2 March whilst being on the sick list. He was fined one day's pay.

Shortly after this on 2 May 1917 William was awarded a gratuity of a guinea and complimented for having displayed skill in rendering first aid (artificial respiration).

On 15 May 1917 William was mobilized and joined the Royal Garrison Artillery as Gunner 159444. He married Ellen Edwards on 17 October 1917 and had a home address in Wellington Road, Edgbaston. On 1 January 1918 he joined the British Expeditionary Force (BEF) in France as part of the 186 Siege Battery. He was demobilized on 29 January 1919 and returned to the police force although stayed on the Army reserve list. He was awarded both the British War Medal and Victory Medal for his war service.

The next and final entry on his police service record states he was reported by Superintendent George Monk for being absent from duty on Saturday 2 August 1919 and participating in a police strike and was therefore dismissed from the service.

On 16 December 1919 William and Ellen had a son called William G Padbury who is showing as living with them in the 1939 register. William is again working for the railway, Ellen is an unpaid domestic and their son is working as a house decorator. There is also a person by the name of Walter Sewell recorded at the address. He worked for the railway too and is presumably a boarder.

William died on 30 August 1964, leaving £281 to Ellen. At the time of his death he is showing as living in Deerpark Drive, Warwickshire.

PC E248 James Parker

It has not been possible to establish any information about the early life of James Parker. The only information we have comes from his service record.

He joined Birmingham City Police on 11 March 1914 with warrant number 8441 at the rate of 27/- per week. He stated that he was single and 21 ½ years old making him born around September 1892

On 2 February 1916 James was awarded a gratuity of a guinea and complimented for courageous conduct in stopping a runaway horse. A few months later on 3 July he repeated this courageous act and received a further guinea and compliment in police orders.

On 5 March 1917 James resigned to join His Majesties Forces and re-joined Birmingham City Police on 14 March 1919 with the new warrant number 8909.

The final entry on the ledger reports that he was reported by Superintendent Daniel Long for being absent from duty on Saturday 2 August and participating in the police strike.

PC E38 John Frederick Parker

John Parker was born in 1887 to parents Frederick and Emily Parker in Caythorpe, Lincolnshire. In the 1891 census the family were still living in Caythorpe. Frederick gave his employment as a game keeper and John is one of five children shown at the address. By the time of the 1901 census another child had been born making John one of six children at the address.

On 25 September 1907 John joined Birmingham City Police and was given the warrant number 7627. It wasn't all plain sailing for John in his service, as on 8 December 1910 it is recorded that he was found lying drunk on the footway in Pershore Road whilst off duty. He had been suspended on 3 December but returned to duty on the 8th having been fined one week's pay and cautioned. By the time of the 1911 census John is confirmed as living in single men's quarters at Edward Road Police Station.

On 18 September 1912 John was awarded a gratuity of one guinea and complimented for rendering first aid to a person with a severed jugular vein. This was followed by more good first aid work when on 16 April 1913 he was again awarded one gratuity and complimented; this time for skill tending to a person with internal haemorrhaging. On 29 September that year a complaint was made by a Mr Bertie (ex-Birmingham Police) following his arrest by John for being drunk & disorderly in Hobmoor Road, Small Heath on 16 August the previous month. Also arrested was his son for the offence of attempting to rescue his father. Whatever the nature of the complaint, John's record is endorsed 'Explained' and no further action is taken. On 16 October 1913 it was reported that he had been absent from a portion of his beat for 30 minutes and found asleep in an entry in Anderton Road during the night of 12 October. For this offence he was stopped one day's leave.

As 1914 progressed there were mixed fortunes for John. On 17 June he was awarded a 1st stripe of merit and complimented for courageous conduct in stopping a runaway horse however this was followed with a complaint on 15 October when it was reported that a Mr Noble complained that whilst he was the licensee of the Hay Mills Tavern, in January 1914, John had borrowed 30/- from him and had not paid it back. For this matter John was severely cautioned for borrowing money off the publican and ordered to pay it back forthwith. But the year ended on a high when on 16 December he was awarded a guinea and complimented for rendering first aid to a person with an internal haemorrhage. John had demonstrated his first aid skill throughout his service and was again to do so as it is reported that on 16 June he was awarded yet another guinea and complimented when dealing with a person with a fractured leg.

The final entry on his service record is dated 4 August 1919 when he was reported by Superintendent Daniel long for being absent from duty on Saturday 2 August and for participating in a police strike.

PC E246 Ernest Parsons

Ernest Parsons was born in Northampton and became the second eldest of five children of Annie Maria and Lewis Parsons. His father's occupation was dock constable, based at Cardiff Docks in Wales.

In February 1915 Ernest joined Birmingham City Police with warrant number 8589. In December 1915 Ernest was attested to the Army, signing up for the Coldstream Guards – his three brothers also served in HM Forces during the First World War.

He was called up for service in March 1917, serving under regimental number 21910 in a reserve battalion. In May 1917 Ernest was complimented in police orders and awarded a guinea for skill in rendering first aid for a case of varicose veins, presumably this incident happened prior to his leaving for the Forces.

During the war Ernest was out of action for almost a

month in November 1918 after receiving as a gunshot wound to his knee whilst in the field. Ernest returned to the police in February 1919 and was issued a new warrant number of 8823.

On 2 August Ernest was reported by Superintendent Daniel Long for being absent from duty and participating in a police strike, for which he was dismissed. His brother Richard was an officer in the Metropolitan Police but he does not appear to have gone on strike in 1919.

In the 1939 register Ernest is living with Mary and their only child, Leslie. His occupation is shown as a foreman gardener and he worked at Calthorpe Park – he is pictured here in the garden. He continued to work there until one day in June 1949 when he collapsed whilst at work. He was taken to the General Hospital but died shortly afterwards, aged just 55.

With thanks to Ernest's granddaughter Sharon Harding for information and pictures. Sharon also served as a police officer from 1/4/1978 to 31/3/2008 with West Midlands Police.

PC C120 George Fredrick Potter

It has not been possible to confirm details about George's early life. We know that he joined Birmingham City Police in November 1913, aged 20, and was given warrant number 8404.

In June 1915 he was suspended after being reported by Superintendent George Monk for being drunk when coming off duty at Kenyon Street Police Station. He was later reinstated and cautioned by the Judicial Sub-Committee.

In November 1918 he resigned to join HM Forces, returning to Birmingham City Police in February 1919 and given a new warrant number of 8819. The final entry on his record is from 4 August 1919 when he was reported by Superintendent Arthur Penrice for being absent from police duty on 2 August 1919 and participating in a police strike, for which he was dismissed.

PC A106 Charles Frederick Pretty

Charles was born in April 1885 in Yorkshire to parents Henry and Sarah. In the 1901 census Charles is the middle child of five and his father's occupation is shown as railway signalman. The family are living in Saddleworth.

In March 1907 Charles joined Birmingham City Police and was given warrant number 7575. He was in trouble quite early on in November 1907, being reported for failing to parade for duty, then reporting himself sick and failing to see the divisional police surgeon before returning to duty. You might think he did not know the procedures, being so young in service, but his record highlights that this is the second occasion for which he has not followed correct procedures when reporting sick. His leave was stopped until further notice.

The 1911 census shows Charles living in single men's quarters at Moseley Street. In February 1912 Charles is back in the good books after being complimented and awarded a guinea for vigilance at night in the arrest of two men loitering with intent. In 1915 Charles marries Charlotte Carter. In June 1919 he received his second compliment and guinea reward for the arrest of a shop breaker. The final entry on his record is from 2 August when Superintendent George Monk reported him for being absent from police duty and participating in a police strike that same day, for which he was dismissed.

In the 1939 register Charles and Frederick were living together in Birmingham and Charles was working at Cadburys as a chocolate checker. He died in 1956 aged 71.

PC C77 John Henry Price

John was born in April 1885 in Heath, Staffordshire, to parents Thomas and Nina. In the 1901 census John is the fourth eldest of eight children. Thomas's occupation is shown as general labourer and the family are living in Heath Town.

In July 1906 John joined the Birmingham City Police and was given warrant number 7516. In September 1909 John was reported for being drunk whilst coming off duty at 2pm, for which his leave was stopped for one day. In November 1910 he married Margaret Kate Colley and the couple went on to have three children. In the 1911 census Henry and Margaret are living at George Street West, Birmingham.

In February 1916 John was complimented and awarded a guinea for courageous conduct in stopping a runaway horse. He was again complimented and awarded a guinea for skill in rendering first aid to a patient suffering from burns in May 1918. John's third and final compliment comes in June 1919 when he was again awarded a guinea for courageous conduct in stopping a runaway horse.

The final entry on his record comes on 2 August when he was reported by Superintendent Arthur Penrice for being absent from duty and participating in a police strike on the same day, for which he was dismissed.

In the 1939 register John is shown as an electric welder, living in Birmingham with Margaret and sons John and Eric. There are others living at the address but these were redacted in the 2015 release of the 1939 register. He died in 1947 aged 62.

PC E217 Joseph Thomas Priest

Joseph was born in 1888 in Darby End, Worcestershire to parents David and Ann. The 1891 census shows the family living with David's father in his pub. This was handy as David was a brewer! There is also a servant living in the pub, and David's father's step-son. By the 1901 census David had died and Joseph is living with his sister and their grand-parents (now showing as retired licensee) in a premises marked as 'priests building' in Darby Street, Rowley Regis. Joseph's mother Anne is not present at the address.

In 1908 Joseph joined the Armed Forces in the Royal Horse Artillery with regimental number 53200.

In 1911 Joseph is living with his mother and her new husband along with a boarder in Smethwick. His occupation is shown as carpenter/joiner. He married Sarah Mildred Farmed in October 1911.

In September 1913 Joseph joined Birmingham City Police and was given the warrant number 8358. In February 1917 he resigned to join HM Forces and a month later his first daughter was born. Joseph and Sarah had four children in total. He returned to the police in March 1919. The final entry on his record is when he was reported by Superintendent Daniel Long for being absent from police duty and participating in a police strike on 2 August, for which he was dismissed.

Joseph died in 1929 in Birmingham, aged 41.

PC A60 William Joseph Pugh

William was born in January 1888 in Stoke Prior, Worcestershire to parents Richard and Dinah. In the 1901 census William is the second youngest of five children, Richard is working as a salt drawer at the salt works and the family are living in Stoke Prior.

In April 1908 William joined Birmingham City Police and was given warrant number 7683. In October 1917 he was reported by his inspector for being absent from court when his cases were called, leading to eight youths being discharged for vagrancy offences. He may have had a good reason for leaving court however he was severely cautioned for failing to inform the dock officer that he was leaving and where he would be found. In 1911 he is recorded on the census as living in Moor Street Police Station along with several other constables.

In January 1918 William was complimented and awarded a guinea for skill in rendering first aid in a case of severed arties. The final entry on his record comes on 2 August when he was reported by Superintendent George Monk for being absent from duty and participating in a police strike on 2 August, for which he was dismissed.

In 1923 William married Agnes Greaves and he was living with her in 1939 and working as a warehouseman at Cadburys – another beneficiary of the Cadbury family's offer of support to the strikers. He died in 1979 aged 91.

PC E103 Frederick Valentine Sabin

Frederick was born on 14 February 1877 in Warwick to parents Frederick and Mary. In the 1891 census Frederick senior is an agricultural labourer and Frederick Valentine is working as an agricultural ploughboy, presumably with his father.

Frederick joined Birmingham City Police on 12 January 1900 and was given the warrant number 6954. His career did not get off to a good start as he has a discipline entry dated 11 October 1900 when he is reported after refusing to convey an important message from Small Heath Police Station to a detective when requested, for which he had his leave stopped.

In the 1901 census he is showing as living with other officers on the Coventry Road in Birmingham – this is likely to be within the Small Heath Police Station on the Coventry Road.

Small Heath Police Station, Coventry Road

By the 1911 Census Frederick is showing as living in Burlington Road Birmingham with his wife of five years (Ellen Naomi) together with their three children. Sadly Ellen died in 1915 leaving Frederick to bring up their three young children. Frederick had a cousin by the name of Florence May who moved in with Frederick after the death of Ellen to look after the children.

For 19 years he had a fairly unremarkable career and we have to wait until 16 June 1919 until he receives his only gratuity of one guinea, and was complimented for rendering first aid to a person with a fractured leg.

The final entry for Frederick is dated 2 August when he is reported by Superintendent Daniel Long for being absent from duty on Saturday 2 August and participating in the strike, for which he was dismissed.

On the 1920 electoral register the couple are shown as having moved to Emily Road, Birmingham and they are still at that address for the 1939 register, which also shows that Frederick and Florence are by that time married. Frederick's occupation is shown as an undertaker's assistant. He is also a member of the ARP as a decontamination officer.

He died aged 74 years in 1952.

PC C66 Lewis Shaw

Lewis Shaw was born in Honley, near Huddersfield on 10 October 1882 to parents John and Mary. His father was a woollen weaver by trade and the family lived in a mill workers terraced house surrounding the mill. Lewis was the second eldest of five children and in the 1901 census his occupation is shown as a woollen cloth dyer.

Lewis Joined Birmingham City Police on 29 September 1904 and was given the warrant number 7395. Upon joining as an unmarried man he would have been required to move into single quarters. It is likely that he went straight into Kenyon Street Police Station single men's quarters as he has a discipline entry on his record dated 17 July 1905 when he was cautioned for being absent from Kenyon Street quarters whilst on sick leave without permission.

Lewis was involved in the first crime where fingerprint evidence was used to secure a conviction in Birmingham. On the night of 6 October 1905. Two men by the name of George Eccles and Dennis Kennedy attempted to break into the Britannia Inn in Tower Street. In addition to the two jemmies left, they broke one of the windows, Kennedy leaving behind a finger print on the inside of the glass. For the first time in the history of the investigation of crime in Birmingham the court had to consider finger print evidence. Kennedy was arrested the day after the incident and impressions of his fingers taken on specially prepared paper by Superintendent Monk. This was sent to Scotland Yard where they were photographed and enlarged showing eleven *"striking similarities"* on the third finger and eight *"distinct similarities"* on the second finger. PC Lewis Shaw gave evidence that he had seen four men, including Eccles and Kennedy, in Hampton Street. He concealed himself in an entry to watch and saw Eccles and Kennedy getting over the gate of the Britannia Inn. Eccles was arrested on the night by a PC Ollis but Kennedy had escaped only to be arrested the following day by Detective Sparks and identified by PC Shaw. The fate of Kennedy was thus sealed with both the eyewitness evidence from Lewis and fingerprint evidence submitted by Detective Sergeant Munro of New Scotland yard. As you would imaging this 'new' type of evidence was challenged in court but was subsequently accepted and both men found guilty.

Mr Parfitt, prosecuting, said in his address to the jury regarding PC Shaw, *"In twenty years' experience I have never heard a man give his evidence so fairly and carefully"*.

As a direct result of this on 22 November Lewis was awarded the 1st stripe of merit for vigilance leading to the arrest of burglars and for his straightforward evidence given in court.

There are two further discipline offences reported in his record during 1906. The first on 26 May was for fighting with PC Bromley in the single men's quarters on 18 May for which he had his leave stopped. The second incident dated 10 December, when in the company of a prisoner (Alfred Harborne) who had been arrested for street betting, he went into a public house. For this he was reprimanded.

On 21 December 1910 he was awarded a gratuity of one guinea and complimented for the arrest of two warehousebreakers.

In the 1911 census Lewis is shown as residing in single quarters at Bridge Street West. In the summer of 1912 Lewis married May Lily Nicholls. They had a son Joseph who was born a year later but sadly died in infancy.

On 17 June 1914 Lewis was again awarded a gratuity of one guinea and complimented for the arrest of two slot meter thieves. There was a further award on 16 December 1914 when he was awarded a gratuity of one guinea and complimented for rendering first aid to a women who had had her throat cut by her husband.

Lewis and May's first daughter Edna was born in 1915. On 8 February 1916 he was again awarded a gratuity of one guinea and complimented for his first aid skills again whilst dealing with a fractured leg. The final award to Lewis is dated 2 May 1917 when he was awarded the 2nd stripe of merit and complimented for the arrest of shop breakers. His second daughter (Hilda) was born in 1918.

The final entry on his service record informs us that he was reported by Superintendent Arthur Penrice for being absent from duty on Saturday 2 August 1919 and participating in the police strike.

On the 1939 register Lewis is shown as living with his wife and daughters in Coralie Street Birmingham and Lewis is employed as a press stamp operator making military buttons.

He died in 1943 Birmingham aged 60. *With thanks to Alan Sharkey for sharing his research on PC Lewis Shaw.*

PC A71 William Sinclair

There is limited information on William Sinclair as the name is not uncommon however we do know that he was born in about 1882 in Scotland. He was to join Birmingham City Police on 17 July 1908 and was given the warrant number 7700.

In the 1911 census William Sinclair is shown as living as a boarder in Wrentham Street, Birmingham which was the home address of Edward Taylor and his wife Annie. Edward's six children are also shown as living at the address along with a further boarder.

On 18 January 1916 a complaint is recorded against William by Mrs Vaughan who alleged that whilst her son was in custody he was assaulted and rooms were illegally searched without a warrant. This was not taken any further as the lady failed to show up and follow up the complaint.

On 30 January 1912 he is complimented for the arrest of thieves. This was followed on 11 June 1912 when he was again complimented for the arrest of a man stealing brass. On 2 January 1918 he was awarded a gratuity of one guinea and complimented for rendering first aid to someone with a fractured arm.

William Sinclair gave evidence to the Desborough Committee which is included earlier in this book. He was clearly well thought of by his fellow officers and senior officers to have been put forward for this role.

The final entry on his record is made on 2 August 1919 when he is reported by Superintendent George Monk for being absent from duty on Saturday 2 August 1919 and for taking part in the police strike.

In the 1939 register there are two William Sinclairs of the right age living in Birmingham – however one of them is working as a chocolate concher, likely at Cadburys, and it is known that Cadburys offered jobs to the strikers so our money is on this man being the former officer.

PC A44 Frederick Smith

With a name such as Frederick Smith it is difficult to get much background information but we do have a service summary sheet for him.

Born around 1889 in Devonshire, Frederick joined Birmingham City Police on 29 July 1909 and was given the warrant number 7750. As an unmarried officer he would have been placed into single quarters. It is probably that he went straight in accommodation at Duke Street Police Station as the 1911 census shows him as a 22-year-old constable living with 11 other officers at that station.

Frederick has two awards on his summary. The first was on 16 December 1914: he was awarded a gratuity of one guinea and complimented for his first aid skills when performing artificial respiration. The second award is recorded on 2 January 1918: he was again awarded a gratuity of one guinea and complimented for the arrest of a shop breaker.

The final entry for Frederick is on 2 August when he is reported by Superintendent George Monk for being absent from duty on Saturday 2 August 1919 and for participating in the police strike.

PC A58 William Henry George Smith

There are far too many people of this name to confirm any details of his early life but we do have a one page summary of his police service.

William joined Birmingham City Police on 22 January 1915 at the age of 18 which makes him born around 1897.

On 10 February 1917 William was disciplined. It is reported that he was absent from his special protection post (armed) for 26 minutes on 22 January 1917. For this he was cautioned. Various sites required special protection during World War One including railway stations and other locations thought vulnerable to air attack.

William resigned to join the Armed Forces on 5 March knowing of course that he would be allowed to re-join the police when his military service finished. Nothing is known of his military service but we do know that he re-joined the police service on 11 January 1919.

On 16 June 1919 William was awarded a gratuity of one guinea and complimented for the arrest of thieves for loitering with intent at night.

The final entry on his police summary is dated 2 August when he is reported by Superintendent George Monk for being absent from duty on Saturday 2 August 1919 and participating in the police strike for which he was dismissed.

PC E116 Arthur Henry Stone

Arthur Henry Stone was born on 8 August 1884 in Branstone, Staffordshire to parents George and Jane. In the 1901 census Arthur is shown as a 16-year-old brewer's labourer and resided in Village Street, Branstone but he was also a very keen sportsperson taking up football, cricket, boxing and walking. He played for several football clubs over the following years and went on to be captain of one of them.

In 1908 Arthur married Nellie Williams at Burton on Trent. He joined Birmingham City Police on 4 August 1909 and was given the warrant number 7755. He is described as being English and 5' 9 ¾". This was not the end to his sporting career as he joined the E Division football team. The following year on 27 October he was awarded a gratuity of one guinea and complimented for courageous conduct in stopping a runaway horse.

In the 1911 census the couple are shown as living in Vincent Crescent, Balsall Heath together with their two sons Arthur and Sydney. Also at the address is his brother-in-law Herbert Williams. In 1912 there was another addition to the family when Violet was born. He was complimented on 11 December 1913 for the arrest of meter thieves and on 2 May 1917 he was again awarded a gratuity of a guinea and complimented for courageous conduct in stopping another runaway horse.

It wasn't all awards for Arthur as on 28 May 1918 he was reported by Superintendent Daniel Long for using obscene language towards PC Comley whilst on duty in Coventry Road and was disciplined. As a matter of interest PC Comley also struck in 1919 and was dismissed. His fourth and final award was made on 2 October 1918 for rendering first aid to a person with a double fracture to both legs and severed artery.

The final entry on his ledger is dated 2 August 1919 when he is reported by Superintendent Daniel Long for being absent from duty and for participating in the police strike. He was dismissed from the force. During this year a fourth child was added to the family when William was born and in 1922 Margaret was born.

Arthur's family informed us that sometime after leaving the police he joined the Bass Worthington Security Dept.

In the 1939 register Arthur is shown as living in Tutbury, Staffordshire together with Nellie. His occupation is shown as a brewery watchman. He died in Lichfield in 1968 aged 83.

With thanks to Arthur's grandson Arthur and his wife Shirley for information and the picture of Arthur.

PC E81 John Teahan

John Teahan was born on 19 September 1874 in Killarney, Kerry, Ireland. We know that he joined Birmingham City Police on 28 April 1900 with the warrant number 6984. He presumably moved into single men's quarters at that time as he is shown as living at Mosely Street Police Station in the 1901 census. It is apparent that he did not adapt well to the regulations that governed police officers at that time as he found himself disciplined several times in the early years. On 27 December 1900 he was fined two days' pay for absenting himself from quarters without leave to do so. Just three weeks later he was again disciplined when he absented himself from his beat for 25 minutes and was found by Sergeant Robbins sitting down in Kyatts Road Tram Office warming himself by a fire. His punishment was having his leave stopped until further orders.

On 19 February 1903 things appeared to be looking up for John when he was complimented for zeal and vigilance in the arrest leading to the conviction of a shoplifter. Unfortunately this good work was not to last and on 4 February 1905 he was found drunk. Although off duty he was in uniform and was suspended immediately. He resumed duty however his leave was stopped again and not restored until 27 July. This did not deter him from producing good police work however, perhaps he was keen to make up for this, shall we say - error of judgement? Thus on 17 May his record is endorsed to say that the Chief Constable was pleased at his prompt action: when discovering a broken window he entered a canal boat and arrested four men leading to their conviction. In 1906 John married Catherine Mary Moran and would have undoubtedly moved out of single quarters. From here on until the police strike John had a promising career and completed much good work. He was awarded a gratuity of one guinea for tact and ability when arresting a thief, followed on 30 December 1908 when he was awarded another guinea and complimented for skill when rendering first aid in a drowning case. This was followed two weeks later when he was awarded a Royal Humane Society certificate for a case of drowning - presumably for the same incident.

His service following this was fairly unremarkable but he kept himself out of any trouble with senior officers. In the 1911 census he is shown as living at 93 Bradford Street together with his wife and two young daughters Catherine and Mary Ann. The couple were to have two further children: Julia and John. His final award was several years later on 2 October 1918 when he was awarded the 1st stripe of merit for rendering first aid at an incident where he dealt with a severed artery.

The final entry for John was when he was reported by Superintendent Daniel Long for being absent from duty on Saturday 2 August 1919 and for participating in the police strike, for which he was dismissed.

In the 1939 register John is shown as living at 178 Alcester Street, Birmingham. He has given his trade as a muffel fireman. He died in Birmingham at the age of 86.

PC E24 Charles Henry Thomas

Charles Henry Thomas was born 14 February 1878 to parents Charles and Sarah. In the 1881 census Charles (senior) gave his occupation as a police sergeant and the family are living in a court in Sherlock Street. Charles (junior) has a younger brother of nine months. By the 1891 census the family are shown as living in Great Brook Street, Duddeston. Charles senior has now been promoted to inspector and there have been additions to the family as Charles is now shown as the oldest of four children.

The 1901 census informs us that the family are living at Duke Street Police Station in Aston. Charles senior is shown as superintendent of the station and therefore had the privilege of having larger quarters with his family also living with him. There are 25 police constables listed in single quarters at the station. Charles junior, now 23-years-old, is shown as an insurance agent. On 6 February 1902 Charles followed in his father's footsteps by joining Birmingham City Police, he was given the warrant number 7158.

Charles Thomas senior had quite a distinguished career and joined Birmingham Borough Police on 21 August 1873. After a slow start he was promoted to sergeant on 22 March 1881 and to inspector on 25 October 1887. He went on to be promoted to superintendent in June 1896 and was one of two officers recognised by the Watch Committee for their valuable services in the conviction of persons who caused the death of PC Philip Gunter. He was specially promoted to superintendent 3rd class on £230 per year. He resigned on pension on 22 February 1909.

In 1903 Charles junior was to marry Edith Elizabeth Pett in Aston. His service was not all plain sailing: on 13 February 1904 it was reported that he was under the influence of drink and was using threatening and abusive language toward PS Boon and striking him with his hand in Kenyon Street Police Station. He was disciplined and had his leave stopped, being instructed to apologise to Sergeant Boon. There is an additional comment against his discipline entry informing us that his leave was re-instated on the 21 June 1904. On 17 June 1905 a second discipline is shown when he was cautioned for gossiping on his beat on 5 June.

On 26 April 1906 he was complimented for rescuing three persons at a fire before the fire brigade arrived. Five months later on 26 September he was awarded a gratuity of one guinea for stopping a runaway horse. This wasn't the only runaway horse he stopped, as he was complimented a second time for this on 20 April 1907. On 20 January 1910 he was again complimented for his vigilance in the arrest of two warehouse breakers. On 28 September 1910 he was awarded a gratuity of one guinea and complimented for the arrest of a man leading to a conviction for stealing a tool bag and for good work.

By the time of the 1911 census Charles is shown as living with Edith in South Avenue, Handsworth. The couple now have three children. On 22 October 1913 he was cautioned for being drunk off duty and was initially suspended. He was cautioned and his next class deferred for 12 months. On 16 December 1914 he was awarded a gratuity of one guinea for rendering first aid to a person with severed arteries. Clearly first aid was a strength for Charles as he was again awarded a guinea and complimented for dealing with a person with varicose veins. On 5 June 1916 he was reported by Superintendent Daniel Long for being drunk on duty at Mosely Street Police Station.

The final entry on his service record is dated 2 August 1919 when he was reported by Superintendent Daniel Long for being absent from duty on Saturday 2 August 1919 and for participating in a police strike for which he was dismissed.

In 1920 the electoral role show that the family moved to Eversley Road, Small Heath where they remained for several years. By 1930 they are shown as living in Clements Road, Yardley.

In the 1939 register Charles is shown as living Wellclare Road, Sheldon and still living with his wife, he gives his occupation as a die cast foreman. He is still shown at the address in 1955.

PC E210 George Mordue Thompson

George Mordue Tompson was born on 19 May 1891, Chirton, Tynemouth in Northumberland. The surname spelt both Thompson & Tompson appears throughout his records. Born to parents Lancelot and Elizabeth, the 1901 census shows he was the eldest of two children. His father gave his occupation as coal miner hewer. By 1911 George is also working as a coal miner.

George married Margaret Sarah Spowart on 26 December 1912 in Ashington Northumberland. He joined Birmingham City Police on 18 April 1915 and was given the warrant number 8715. Later that year on 10 December he was attested to the Coldstream Guards and immediately posted to the reserve to await future mobilization. He continued his service with Birmingham City Police but there is nothing of note over the following years until 2 January 1918 when he was awarded one guinea and complimented for the arrest of a thief for stealing a magneto from a canal boat. Just a few months later on 23 April 1918 he was called to the colours and resigned to join HM Forces to enter service as Private 26338 Thompson with the Coldstream Guards. From his medical records we have a description of him at the time: he was 5' 9 ¾ tall, weighed 154lbs, with brown hair, blue eyes and a fresh complexion and of good physical development. He is also shown as living at 2 Midland Grove, Edward Road in Balsall Heath. He embarked from Southampton for France on 23 November 1918, disembarking in Le Havre France the following day after being posted to the 3rd Battalion.

George was not to spend long overseas and returned to England on 2 January 1919. Less than three weeks later on 20 January he re-joined Birmingham City Police. The final entry on his police service record is dated 2 August 1919 when he was reported by Superintendent Daniel Long for being absent from duty on Saturday 2 August 1919 and for participating in a police strike.

In the 1939 register George is shown as still living with Margaret at 148 Tenby Road, Birmingham and gives his occupation as a grocery warehouseman. There are no children shown at the address. There is a record of a George M Thompson of the correct age dying in Birmingham in 1958 age 67.

PC E262 Thomas Mansergh Thorne

Thomas was born on 21 April 1888 to parents Robert and Henrietta in Ireland. In the 1901 census Thomas is shown as one of three children living at 2 Thornhill Birdhill, Tipperary. Also shown as living at the address are Robert's mother and a male servant. In the 1911 census the family have moved next door and both Robert's mother and the servant are no longer living with the family.

Thomas joined Birmingham City Police on 14 March 1914. The first two years of his service were fairly uneventful, but on 2 February 1916 he was awarded a gratuity of one guinea and complimented for skill in rendering first aid to a person with a fractured forearm. On 14 August 1915 he resigned to join His Majesties Armed Forces. He was given the regimental number 37055 and joined the Royal Welch Fusiliers. He was to win a Military Medal as a corporal. This is a medal won for bravery in the field. He also went on to become an acting regimental sergeant major (RSM) and an acting warrant officer.

Thomas re-joined Birmingham City Police on 31 March 1919, which is also the year when he was to marry Brenda May Oldham. The final entry on his police service record is dated 2 August 1919 when he was reported by Superintendent Daniel Long for being absent from duty on 2 August and participating in a police strike.

The electoral register 1925 – 1935 shows that Thomas was residing at King Edward's Grammar School 293 Bristol Road, Birmingham. The reason for living at that address is most likely explained in the 1939 register where he again gives this address and gives his occupation as a school caretaker.

It is difficult to say with certainty when Thomas died but it is likely that he is the Thomas Thorne who died in 1963 at Thornhill, Tipperary, Ireland.

PC C116 Charles William Thorpe

Charles Thorpe was born in 1873 in Suffolk to parents John and Jane. In the 1881 census he is one of three children, including his stepbrother Thomas. His father gives his occupation as an agricultural labourer and the family live Chalk Terrace, Ixworth, Suffolk. In the 1891 census Charles has the same occupation.

By December 1897 Charles has married his wife Elizabeth and joins Birmingham City Police, being given the warrant number 6810. By the time of the 1901 census Charles is shown as living with his wife in Birmingham and the couple have a nine month old daughter. On 27 July 1903 Charles was cautioned by the Judicial Sub-Committee for not rescuing a man by the name of Thomas Boyce who had fallen into the canal near Spring Hill and was drowning.

Charles was again disciplined on 28 December 1908 for being drunk on duty. For this matter he was initially suspended but was re-instated three days later and had his leave stopped for just one day. Two years later on 26 January 1910 he was awarded a guinea and complimented for stopping a runaway horse. Just a few months later he was awarded his first stripe of merit for rendering first aid to a man with a severed artery.

By the time of the 1911 census the family are living at 57 Southfield Road, Birmingham. Charles now has three daughters although the eldest was not shown on the 1901 census (potentially she was living with family members). Of note is that there are three visitors shown as being at the address. One of these is a man by the name of Henry Joseph Preece who is shown as a prison warder. This is an interesting connection and it is likely that he worked at Winson Green Prison, so we can't help but wonder what (if any) role he may have had in the future strike? Charles's career settled down over the next few years, perhaps being a family man agreed with him but it was not to last. His summary shows he was reported on 14 June 1914 for being drunk and was suspended. There is another entry on 18 June where it is documented that he was drunk in Lyttleton Road one morning whilst on plain clothes duty. He was again stopped one day's leave. After almost 22 years' service there is a final entry on his summary dated 2 August 1919. He was reported by Superintendent Arthur Penrice for being absent from duty on Saturday 2 August and for participating in a police strike, for which he was dismissed.

We have been unable to confirm additional information for Charles as there are several people of the same name. There is a record of a Charles Thorpe dying in Birmingham in 1933, if this is the same Charles Thorpe he would have been 60 years old.

PC C99 Joseph Walker

Joseph was born in Hucclecote, Gloucestershire in January 1893 to parents Frederick and Eliza. In the 1901 census Joseph is living with his father (shown as William F Walker) in the parish of Hucclecote and is one of eight children. Sadly William is shown as being widowed and with his youngest child only two years old, he gives his employment as a milk salesman.

Joseph joined Birmingham City Police on 27 November 1912 and was given the warrant number 8634. When he joined he stated he was single and 19 years old. Two years later Joseph married Mary Nancy Harford on 9 November 1914 in the Kings Norton district. His service was uneventful but he was attested into the Coldstream Guards as Guardsman 23593 on 10 December 1915 before being placed immediately onto the Army reserve to continue with his police duties. On 23 April 1918 he resigned from the police to join His Majesties Armed Forces.

Upon joining Joseph gave his home address as 10 Orford Road, Park Road, Hockley, Birmingham. He is described as being 6' 2" tall, weighing 161lbs with dark brown hair, dark complexion and brown eyes. He remained in the UK (London) for the duration of the war, re-joining the police in January 1919.

On 16 June 1919 Joseph was awarded a gratuity of a guinea and complimented for courageous conduct when stopping a runaway horse. The final entry on his summary sheet is dated 2 August 1919 when he was reported by Superintendent Arthur Penrice for being absent from duty on Saturday 2 August and for participating in a police strike.

Soon after the strike Joseph was seeking alternative employment. There is a letter dated 19 September 1919 from the London Northwestern Railway (LNWR) to his Army headquarters at Buckingham Gate, London requesting a reference for Joseph. He had applied to the LNWR for employment. Three days later his colonel replied stating his character was good. It is not known if Joseph was successful with this application.

Further information on Joseph is difficult to confirm as there are several people of the same name from that period. There is a recorded death of a Joseph Walker of the right age in Birmingham dated 1921. If this was ex-PC Walker then he would have been just 28 years old.

PC C113 Edmund Wallace

Edmund was born in January 1892 in Marylebone, London to parents Walter and Mary. In 1901 the family lived in Buckingham with his father giving his occupation as a railway engine driver. Edmund is shown as the eldest of three children. In the 1911 census, aged 19, he is recorded as working in a butchers shop.

Edmund joined Birmingham City Police on 18 May 1914 and was given the warrant number 8479. His summary sheet informs us that he had transferred from the Buckinghamshire Police where he had already served almost two years. Edmund was living in single quarters in Kenyon Street Police Station in 1915, and was attested into the military on 10 December but immediately placed on the reserve list and returned to policing duties. He had a fairly uneventful career until he resigned on 23 April 1918 to join the HM Forces the same day. He was posted two days later as Guardsman 25790 in the 13th Company Coldstream Guards and described as being 5' 11" tall, with light brown hair and a fresh complexion with blue eyes. On 20 April 1918 Edmund married Mary Agnes Murtagh at St Francis Church Handsworth, with the couple now living at 100 Wood Lane, Handsworth Wood. He is shown as being demobilized on 6 February 1919 and re-joined Birmingham City Police three days earlier on the 3rd. The final entry on his summary sheet is dated 4 August 1919 when he was reported by Superintendent Arthur Penrice for being absent from duty on Saturday 2 August 1919 and for participating in a police strike.

In 1924 Edmund and Mary had decided to make a new life for themselves as there is a record of the two of them obtaining ticket numbers 1308 & 1309 on the SS Barrabool with one way tickets to Melbourne, Australia. Their previous address is recorded as 25 Oscott Road, Perry Barr and his occupation was declared as a rubber worker. On 19 May 1953 both Edmund and Mary are showing as boarding the ship Orion, part of the Orient Line and returning to England. Travelling with them is Joan Wallace so presumably they have had a daughter born in Australia. Edmund now lists his trade as a tramway employee. He died in 1968 in Victoria, Australia and is buried in Box Hill Cemetery.

PC C269 Ernest Walters

Ernest Walters was born in Wolverhampton on 11 December 1884. In the 1901 census he is shown as living with his older brother Arthur and sister-in-law Gertrude. Both Ernest and Arthur were spectacle frame makers.

Ernest joined the regular army on 3 February 1904. He enlisted as Gunner 33467 Walters and was posted to 119 Battery Royal Artillery Regiment. It is apparent that he already had some military experience as his service papers show that he served in the 3rd Battalion South Staffordshire Regiment which was a unit of part time militia.

On 28 February 1906 he married Ellen Howe in a registry office in Bristol and together the couple were to have seven children between 1908 and 1920.

After completing three years' service on 3 February 1907 Ernest left the military and was placed on the army reserve list. At the time of leaving he gave his address as being 88 Burleigh Road Wolverhampton, and gave his trade as a brass dresser. It is evident that he was intent on joining the police service as a document signed at the time of leaving states that he intends to serve in a constabulary although which one is not stated. It also states that his character is very good, and that he is sober and trustworthy.

Ernest joined Birmingham City Police on 8 July 1907 and was given the warrant number 4596. Within six months he was disciplined for the first of several times when on 30 January 1908 he was cautioned for failing to examine a premises that had been broken into.

In the 1911 census he is shown as residing with his wife and six-week-old son Leonard together with a Mr and Mrs Rainey at 74 Wellington Road, Edgbaston, Birmingham. The relationship here is not certain but it is evident that the house belongs to the Rainey household. Ernest is shown as a constable of course but Ellen is shown as a servant. It is also unclear if this is at that address or another.

On 5 June 1912 he was reported by Superintendent George Monk for being under the influence of drink when in company with PC Dexter, using obscene language and assaulting an unknown man on Monument Road. At the same time he was also dealt with for a complaint from a Mrs Parker in Osler Street, for using obscene language towards her. For this matter he was reduced from 3rd to 4th Class constable. He had to wait until May the following year to be reinstated to 3rd Class and promoted to 2nd Class. Unfortunately he was not to keep this increase in pay for long as by 29 September 1913 he was reported by Sergeant Lees for being in a coffee house in Summer Lane whilst on duty. For this matter he was again reduced to 3rd Class. Things did not improve for Ernest as on 8 January 1914 it is recorded that he was drunk in New Summer Street on New Year's Day and for striking Acting Sergeant Day several times on the face with his fist. Although not stated it is apparent he was suspended as the record states that he was re-instated and severely cautioned and this case would be referred to should there be any further incident.

There may have been a sense of relief when on the outbreak of war he was called to re-join the military on 7 August. Ernest was in France before the month was out. He served with several different artillery batteries whilst overseas but on 2 June 1915 he was sentenced to 28 days No. 1 field punishment for being found guilty of drunkenness. No. 1 field punishment consisted of the convicted man been shackled in irons and secured to a fixed item, often a gun wheel or similar. He could only be thus fixed for two hours in 24, and not for more than three in four days or for more than 21 days in his sentence. This punishment was often known as the crucifix and due to its humiliating nature was viewed by soldiers as unfair. In 1916 conscription was introduced and Ernest had his service extended. For this he received a £20 bonus, a substantial amount of money at that time. During the German offensive in March 1918 Ernest was wounded. He is shown as receiving a gunshot wound however he received injuries to his face, hand, right leg and knee which would be more consistent with being hit by counter battery shellfire from German guns supporting infantry attacks. He left the military in February 1919 and was again placed on the reserve list. For his service in the Great War he was later to receive the British War Medal, Victory Medal and the 1914 Star.

He re-joined Birmingham City Police on 10 February 1919 and was given a new warrant number, this being 8820. The final entry on his record states he was reported by Superintendent Arthur Penrice for being absent from duty on Saturday 2 August 1919 and participating in the police strike.

In the 1930s Ernest was working as a gatekeeper and may have done some form of metal work according to his family. The 1939 register shows that Ernest and Ellen are still married living in Greenwood Avenue, Birmingham. Ernest lists his occupation as a charge hand for metal pressings.

Ernest died at the age of 86 in Solihull in 1971.

With thanks to Ernest's great-grandson Matthew Walters for providing the picture and information on Ernest's life.

PC C285 John James Latimer Warriner

John James Latimer Warriner was born in 1893 in Westmoreland to parents George and Margaret. The family address in the 1901 census is Church Street, Westmoreland. He is shown as the youngest of three children and his father gives his occupation as a railway engine driver.

We do not know why John moved away from his parents address but the 1911 census shows him living as a boarder with the Brennan family who were an elderly couple living in Lonsdale. John gives his employment as a railway porter.

John joined Birmingham City Police on 31 March 1914 and was given the warrant number 8636. From what little information survives for John, his police career appears fairly uneventful. There is one award listed for him when on 2 July 1914 he was awarded a guinea and a humane certificate from the Society for the Protection of Life from Fire for his rescue of a man from a burning house. This extra money would no doubt came in handy as John was to marry Nancy Bond less than three weeks later on 20 July.

On 10 December 1915 John was attested into the Armed Forces but was immediately placed onto the reserve list and continued his service with Birmingham City Police. His service papers show that he was now living in Spring Hill Avenue, Birmingham. He resigned on 2 April 1918 and was mobilised on 23 April. Two days later he was posted as Private 25872 to the Coldstream Guards at Caterham in the 13th Company which was a reserve battalion. His service records give us a good description and inform us that John was is 5'9 ½" tall, weighed 154lb, had dark hair with a fresh complexion, brown eyes and 'good physical development'. He continued to serve until he was placed on the Army reserve in January 1919 and re-joined Birmingham City Police on 6 January.

The final entry on John's summary is dated 2 August 1919 he was reported by Superintendent Arthur Penrice for being absent from duty on Saturday 2 August 1919 and for participating in a police strike.

There is a John J L Warriner that is shown as dying in Lancashire in 1937 at just 43 years of age. There is also a record of a Nancy Bond dying in 1938 in Westmoreland where the couple you may recall originate from. Additional information for Nancy informs us that at the time of her death she was a widow so it is highly likely that we have the correct John Warriner and tragically both died young.

PC C264 Francis Thomas Warwood

Francis Warward was born in Astwood Bank, Feckenham, Worcestershire in April 1874 to parents Thomas and Rebecca. In the 1881 census the family are shown as living in Forgate Street, Feckenham and Francis is shown as the 3rd eldest of seven children. His father gives his occupation as a rural postal messenger. By the time of the 1891 census the family are living in Feckenham Road and Francis is one of 10 children although the eldest is no longer living at the address. His father has now changed his trade and is shown as a milk seller. Francis is 16 and has a job as a needle brusher.

On 4 March 1901 Francis joined Birmingham City Police and was given the warrant number 7044. The following year he married Edith Harriet Gould. His police career started promisingly when on 1 July 1903 he was awarded a gratuity of a guinea for vigilance and tact in the arrest of a notorious burglar. We do not know when Francis and Edith set up home themselves but by the time of the 1911 census they were living at 18 Arley Road in Bournbrook, Birmingham and have two young

daughters. This address is a small terraced house that still stands today but they made room for a boarder, perhaps the early signs were there that officers were struggling financially. He continued to work his way up through the pay scales and on 18 September 1912 he was awarded a gratuity of a guinea and complimented for courageous conduct in stopping a runaway horse. Six months later on 16 April he repeated the act when he stopped a second runaway horse. On 3 July 1916 he was awarded another guinea and complimented for the arrest of youths shop breaking and on 2 January 1918 he was awarded the 1st stripe of merit and complimented for administering first aid and yet again stopping a runaway horse. His final award was on 16 June 1919 when he was awarded the 2nd stripe of merit and complimented for good police duty for assisting another officer in a case of robbery, stopping a runaway horse and arresting a juvenile thief.

On 2 August 1919 Francis was reported by Superintendent Arthur Penrice for being absent from duty that day and for participating in a police strike

Francis died in 1938 aged just 63 years old.

PC A18 William Charles Waters

There are many records relating to different William Waters' but the most promising based on age and being a fairly local man is William Charles Waters born in Worcestershire in 1888 to parents George and Mary. In the 1891 census he was one of six children and his father gave his occupation as a farm labourer. One of the children listed is an elder brother to William by the name of Frank. By the time of the 1901 census three more children appear making a total of nine children. When the 1911 census was conducted there is a William Waters living with his brother 'Frank' in Anderton Street, Ladywood. His occupation is given as a railway worker.

What is certain is that William Waters joined Birmingham City Police on 15 April 1912 and was given the warrant number 8817. His career was fairly uneventful, his one and only award in his service was on 16 December 1914 when he was awarded a gratuity of a guinea and complimented for the arrest of a warehousebreaker. The following few years were without incident for William but in 1917 he received a series of complaints. Starting with 5 February when he was complained of by Mrs Connelly of the Central Hotel, Moor Street for failing to deal with a woman who had taken an overdose. He was reduced in class and cautioned for this matter. On 22 March 1917 he was fined one day's pay for being absent from quarters at Digbeth Police Station whilst being on the sick list. The third matter reported was an allegation by Captain Coventry of the Royal Military Police that William was rude to him however the record states that there was no case to answer.

The final entry of note is dated 2 August when he was reported by Superintendent George Monk for being absent from duty on 2 August 1919 and participating in a police strike.

The 1939 register reveals a William Waters living in Birmingham and one living in Worcestershire, it hasn't been possible to confirm if our William is one of these.

PC E147 John Whapples

John Whapples was born in 1883 in Barton-Under-Needwood, Staffordshire to parents John and Martha. In the 1891 census John was one of five children, with his father giving his occupation as a general labourer. The family address is in Aylestone Road, Leicestershire. In the 1901 census, John (now 18-years-old) is shown as a labourer at a gas works. Interestingly his father is shown in the same line of business, perhaps at the same company. His mother Martha died in 1898 aged only 46. In 1902 John (junior) married Blanch Flora Beeby in Leicester.

On 8 August 1905 he joined Birmingham City Police and was given the warrant number 7472. On 12 December 1907 John was disciplined for being absent from his beat for two hours and 20 minutes. His leave was stopped but later reinstated. On 23 March 1908 he was disciplined for drinking a glass of ale twice whilst on duty the previous December. For this he was reduced from 4th to 5th class. On 3 March 1910 he was disciplined for perhaps his worst act when he was suspended for being insubordinate and refusing to work his beat. For this matter he was severely cautioned, although he was reinstated. On 30 March 1911 he was disciplined for not reporting himself when visited in Coventry Road and being insolent when spoken to about it by his sergeant. His leave was stopped for two days.

By the time of the 1911 census we find John living with Blanch at 16 Grosmont Avenue, Grosmont Villa, Oldfield Road, Birmingham, together with their four children. He received his only award on 15 June 1913 when he was complimented for his actions when rescuing persons from a burning dwelling house, but this was followed on 1 July 1918 when he was reported for highly improper conduct by following another occupation whilst off duty.

The final entry on his record dated 4 August 1919 states he was reported by Superintendent Daniel Long for being absent from duty in Saturday 2 August and for participating in a police strike.

John and Blanch remained in Birmingham, living in Sparkbrook in the 1920s. Tragically Blanch died in 1929 and John followed 19 years later in 1948, aged 65.

PC E106 John Williams

It hasn't been possible to confirm any details about John Williams' early life. He joined Birmingham City Police on 11 March 1914 and was given the warrant number 8903. Upon joining it is recorded that he was single and 22 years old making his year of birth around 1892. The first award won by John was on 2 February 1916 when he was awarded one guinea and complimented for his first aid skills when rendering first aid to a person with two fractured legs. The following year on 14 May 1917 John resigned to join His Majesty's Forces. His record shows that he re-joined Birmingham City Police on 10 March 1919. The last entry on his summary states that he was reported by Superintendent Daniel long for being absent from duty on Saturday 2 August 1919 and for participating in a police strike, for which he was dismissed.

PC C118 Edward Wilson

Edward was born in November 1884 in Driffield, Yorkshire to parents William and Mary. In the 1891 census William's occupation is shown as assistant ironmonger. Also living at the family address is Edward's older brother Arthur and their four-year-old cousin Richard. By 1901 William is a joiner carpenter and Edward is presumably working alongside him, as his occupation shows as joiner carpenter apprentice. William's nephew is still residing with the family.

Edward joined Birmingham City Police on 22 August 1904 and was given the warrant number 7387. Shortly after joining on 15 March 1905, he was disciplined for failing to assist another officer moving prisoners from cells to the prison van three days earlier. For this, Edward's leave was stopped until 20 May 1905 and his appointment deferred for six months. Later that year on 9 December he was complimented for his actions at a fire in Crabtree Road.

In 1908 Edward married Gertrude Elizabeth Hyde in his birthplace of Driffield. His name is recorded as William Edward for the marriage registration. In the 1911 census he is shown as living with his wife Gertrude and older brother Arthur at the aptly named Gertrude Place, Brookfields, Birmingham. This year also saw Edward awarded a guinea and complimented for the rescue of persons in a fire. On 2 May 1917 he was again awarded a guinea and complimented for praiseworthy action at another fire. On 4 August 1919 there is a final entry for Edward when he is reported by Superintendent Arthur Penrice for being absent from duty on 2 August 1919 and participating in a police strike.

There is a Gertrude Wilson on the 1939 register living with a William Wilson in Leeds, you may recall Edward was recorded as William Edward Wilson on his marriage registration, so it is likely this is the former officer and his wife.

PC A81 Albert Woods

Albert was one of nine children born to Thomas and Sarah Woods. He was born in Wigston, Leicestershire on 30 January 1884. The family lived in Moat Street, Leicestershire. His father's occupation was a railway signalman in the 1891 census. In the 1901 census Albert is working as a boot sprigger.

On 26 July 1902 Albert joined the Coldstream Guards with the regimental number 4764 and enlisted for 12 years' service. In a subsequent medical he is shown as being 5' 10 ½" tall with blue eyes, having brown hair, weighing 149 pounds and in perfect health. On 24 March 1903 Albert is shown as being promoted to lance corporal. It is apparent that he cut his military service short as on 26 July 1905 after three years Albert left the Army although he remained on the reserve list.

Albert is shown as joining Birmingham City Police on 7 December 1908 and was given the warrant number 7722. On 4 January 1911 Albert married Eliza Ann Collings at the Methodist Church, South Wigston, Leicester. We are informed by the 1911 census that the two of them resided in Langley Road, Small Heath, Birmingham, and soon afterwards in 1912 their first child Colin was born. When Britain declared war on Germany on 4 August 1914 Albert was not recalled to HM forces unlike many other officers, as he had ceased to be a reservist on 25 July, only the previous month! It is apparent that he made the decision not to volunteer for war service although it is shown on his service record that he was 'lent' to the War Office as an Army drill instructor on 8 September 1914, no doubt due to his previous military service. It is evident these duties were on an ad hoc basis as he was back on police duty when awarded one guinea and complimented for an arrest of warehouse breakers on 16 December 1914. In 1915 the couple had their second child when Horace was born. An entry on his police service record on 7 May states he 'resumed' police duty, so presumably he had spent a further period with the military.

He was again awarded a guinea and complimented on 2 October 1918 for his vigilance and arrest of warehouse breakers. During this year his only daughter Hilda was born. This leads us to the final entry we have for Albert on his police record. After nine years of exemplary service he was reported by Superintendent George Monk for being absent from duty on Saturday 2 August 1919 and participating in the police strike and dismissed.

On the 1939 register Albert he is shown as a foreman (gas services) living in Warwick Road, Birmingham. He died in 1956 aged 71.

PC C297 George Arthur Wright

George Arthur Wright was born in January 1893 in Burton-on-Trent to Arthur and Sarah Jane Wright. Arthur's occupation is recorded as brewer's labourer and George is the middle of three children, living in Village Street, Branstone, Burton on Trent. The 1911 census shows George working in Derbyshire as a farm servant living with the Morris family at their farm in Kilburn.

George joined Birmingham City Police on 14 December 1914 and was given the warrant number 8578. Less than 12 months later on 15 November 1915 he resigned to join His Majesties Forces. He joined the Royal Garrison Artillery on 15 November (the same day as he resigned) with a regimental number of 66762. During his service he was with the 78th Siege Battery as a gunner. This battery served in France and Belgium. He was later to be awarded both the British War Medal and the Victory Medal. George is shown as being discharged on 13 March 1919 and re-joining Birmingham City Police two days later on 17 March 1919, being given a new warrant number of 8913. The final entry on George's record is from 4 August when he was reported by Superintendent Arthur Penrice for being absent from duty on 2 August and participating in a police strike.

Sunday 3 August 1919

PC E255 Bernard Herbert Evans

Bernard was born in December 1893 in Oakthorpe, Leicestershire, to Henry and Selina Evans. In the 1901 census Henry is the oldest of three siblings living with his parents and his father is working in a colliery. In the 1911 census Henry now has three younger siblings, the family are living in Ashby Woulds, Leicestershire, and Henry is working alongside his father as a coal miner. The census tells of hidden tragedy in the family, with the number of children born living to Henry and Selina as 10, but only five of them still living.

In September 1913 Bernard joined the Birmingham City Police and first came to the notice of his superiors for being absent from single men's quarters in March 1916 when he returned home at 2:20am. His punishment was to have one day's leave stopped. After signing up with the Armed Forces in December 1915 Bernard was called up in March 1917 as private 21901 with the Coldstream Guards.

He married Elsie Betteridge in June 1917 and a son, Bernard William Henry, followed in October 1917. The couple went on to have two more children. Bernard returned to the police in January 1919. The final entry on his record was when he was reported for being absent from duty and participating in a police strike on 3 August 1919. He was reported by Superintendent Daniel Long and dismissed.

Bernard remained in Birmingham and in 1939 his occupation is showing as an aeroplane assembler. He is living with wife Elsie and their three children.

He died in 1966, aged 72.

PC C76 Thomas George Fuller

Thomas was born in August 1893 in Kingston-Upon-Thames to Thomas and Emma Jane Fuller. In the 1901 census Thomas is living with two older siblings and an older cousin, along with his parents. His father's occupation is shown as 'carman (parcels)'. By the 1911 census Thomas is working as a baker.

In March 1913 Thomas joined the Birmingham City Police with warrant number 8274. In August 1916 he married Florence Jane Munslow in Handsworth and they had their first son Thomas Harry in 1917. In May 1918 Thomas was complimented and awarded a guinea for skill in rendering first aid in a burns case and again in October 1918 for an individual with varicose veins.

The final entry on his record is when Superintendent Arthur Penrice reported him for being absent from duty on Sunday 3 August and participating in a police strike, for which he was dismissed. Thomas's brother-in-law (his wife's sister's husband) was also an officer in the force – Robert (known as Bill) Turley was a sergeant at the time of the strike and retired in 1946 to Wales. Bill didn't go out on strike – another example of the strike dividing families.

Thomas's wife felt that he lost his calling after he was dismissed from the police. Eventually he started up a coal business with his son called T.G. Fuller and son. Thomas and his wife were very kind people - in the late 1930s they fostered a 14-year-old Jewish Polish girl Sabina, whose mother managed to smuggle her out of Danzig before ending up in Auschwitz herself. The girl's father had already died and she later found out her mother had died during the War. In the 1939 register Thomas is living with Florence, Thomas, their younger son Don and Sabina in Birmingham. Thomas and his eldest son are working as coal merchants. Thomas and Florence also adopted an 11-month-old girl in 1944.

Thomas Fuller with his son Don around 1935

Thomas died in 1964 aged 71. Tom junior died the following year from a heart attack.

With thanks to his granddaughters Joanna Silvester and Rosalyn Fuller for the pictures and additional information.

PC E70 George Edwin Harvey

It has not been possible to establish any details about George's early life, but we know he joined Birmingham City Police on 18 September 1914 with warrant number 8536. His service record is uneventful with no compliments or misconduct reports, simply entries stating increases in pay and promotions up the pay scale through length of service and efficient work.

The only entry of relevance is from 4 August when Superintendent Daniel Long reported him for being absent from duty on 3 August and participating in a police strike, for which he was dismissed.

PC E272 John Thomas Woodhouse

There are several people of the same name and similar age making it very difficult to establish any details about the early life of John Woodhouse. What we do know from his police summary sheet is that he joined Birmingham City Police on 7 December 1914 and was given the warrant number 8567. He also stated he was married and his age was 20 years old. His police service was uneventful but he appears in a picture of the Birmingham City Police Gymnastics Class dated January 1915. Unfortunately it seems he was moving slightly when the picture was taken, making him blurry in an otherwise perfect group picture.

The final entry dated 4 August 1919 informs us that John was reported by Superintendent Daniel Long for being absent from duty on 3 August 1919 and participating in a police strike.

PC C261 Herman Cole

Herman was born in January 1892 in Merthyr Tydfil, South Wales, to George and Emily. The census in 1901 shows George working as a coal hewer, Emily is not at the family address (possibly visiting somewhere else as George is shown as married and not widowed?) and Herman has an older brother and sister and a younger brother living with him in Merthyr Tydfil.

The 1911 census shows Herman working as a colliery tipper (working above ground). His father is a colliery worker underground and one younger brother is a miner (the other being at school). In December 1911 Herman married Ada Gertrude White and the couple had four children.

Herman joined Birmingham City Police in December 1913 with warrant number 8635. He was reported by Superintendent George Monk for failing to arrest four men who had stolen a diamond ring from a woman at a house in Handsworth and cautioned in January 1916. The following month he was complimented and awarded a guinea for good police work in the arrest of warehouse breakers.

In December 1915 Herman signed up with the military and joined the Army reserve. He was called to the colours in April 1918 as Private (Guardsman) 4850 in the Welch Guards and returned to the police in January 1919. Herman was one of the last officers to join the strike and absented himself from duty on Monday 4 August 1919, being reported by Superintendent Arthur Penrice – which is particularly unfortunate as surely word had spread to many officers that the strike had failed by this point and his dismissal could have been avoided if he had gone on duty.

Ada died in 1938 and the 1939 register shows a widowed Herman living in Birmingham and working as a cinema manager.

Herman died in June 1964 in Nottinghamshire, aged 72.

PC E237 Alfred Homer Creswell

Alfred was born in Prestwich, Manchester in 1887 to Homer and Mary. In 1891 Alfred was living with his mother and father, widowed grandmother, two older sisters and a younger sister in Harpurhey, Manchester. Homer's occupation is shown as plumber and painter. By 1901 the family were living in Cheshire. At 13, Alfred was working as a part time cotton spinner.

Enlisting for the Army in May 1909, in the 1911 census Alfred was living in Army barracks in Hampshire. Alfred served with 2nd Battalion of the Grenadier Guards and also the Guards Machine Gun Regiment.

Alfred joined the Birmingham City Police in June 1912 with warrant number 8239. A year later he was in trouble when he was reported by his sergeant for highly improper conduct towards two fellow constables, insolence towards the sergeant and further reported for refusing to obey an order once back at Moseley Street Police Station. With barely 12 months service he was lucky to keep his job – instead being cautioned and reduced a class as punishment.

On 4 August 1914 Alfred left the police to join HM Forces, serving as a lance corporal with regimental number 1541. He is on the absent voters list showing as a police officer living at Moseley Street Police Station. He re-joined the police on 7 March 1919, being paid 50/- a week. The final entry on the record indicates Alfred joined the strike in its final stages on 4 August 1919, when he was reported by Superintendent Daniel Long and dismissed.

In 1922 Alfred married Martha Bennett. In the 1939 register Alfred is living with Martha and their children Henry, Mary and Margaret in Cheshire. Alfred's occupation is shown as 'foreman navvy – heavy work'. In June 1960 Alfred died, whilst still living in Cheshire.

PC C139 Frank Jones

Frank Jones was born around 1888 in Wichenford, Worcestershire to parents John and Charlotte. In the 1891 census Frank is the youngest of five children and John is recorded as a farm labourer. By 1901 Frank is shown as living at 57 Castle Hill, Ockeridge in the parish of Whitley, Worcestershire, together with only his father who at this time was a game keeper.

On 4 July 1910 Frank joined Birmingham City Police and was given the warrant number 7811, stating

that he was single and 21 years old. In 1911 he was living in single men's quarters in Kenyon Street. We know that Frank was in the tug of war team in 1911 as his picture is taken from the group picture when they were declared amateur champions of England. Their trainer and coach was Inspector Arthur Penrice.

The first years of his police service were fairly uneventful until 12 November 1914 when he was reported by Inspector Boon for drinking In the Leopard Inn whilst on duty the previous 4 November. For this matter his was fined one day's pay. He was further disciplined on 3 January 1916 when he was reported by Superintendent Monk for neglect of duty for not arresting four men who had stolen a diamond ring to the value of £10, from the finger of Walter Heathcote. For this matter he was cautioned and reduced in pay by the Judicial Sub-Committee.

On 24 April 1918 he resigned to join HM Forces, becoming Private 172958 Frank Jones of the Machine Gun Corps, returning to Birmingham City Police on 24 February 1919 and given the new warrant number 8875. The final entry on his police service record informs us that on 4 August 1919 he was reported by Superintendent Arthur Penrice for being absent from duty on Monday 4 August 1919 and for participating in a police strike.

PC E180 Frederick Redley

Frederick Redley was born on 25 September 1888 in Northampton to parents James and Ellen. In the 1901 census James's occupation is shown as a shepherd and Frederick was the younger of two children at the address. The 1911 census shows the family had moved to Little Brington in Northampton but Frederick is now the only child resident with his parents. Both father and son are shown as labourers.

Aged 24 Frederick joined Birmingham City Police on 14 July 1913 and was given the warrant number 8347. The following year on 23 December 1914 he married Ethel Gertrude Eales at the Parish Church, Long Buckley, Northampton.

On 5 July 1915 Frederick was awarded a gratuity of a guinea and complimented for his first aid skills when rendering aid to a person with a fractured leg. This was to be the only award earned by Frederick in his policing service. There was an addition to the family on 9 November when the couple had a son who they called Albert John.

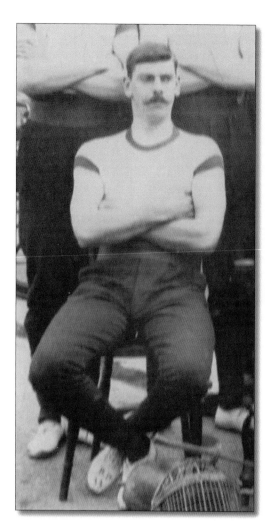

On 10 December 1915 Frederick was attested into the Coldstream Guards but was immediately placed onto the Army reserve the following day and returned to police duties.

On 23 April 1918 Frederick resigned to join the Armed Forces as Private 25779 in the Coldstream Guards giving his home address as Kenhelm Road, Small Heath. He subsequently embarked from Southampton on 23 November 1918, landing the following day at Le Harve (France) and served with the 3rd Battalion Coldstream guards. On 24 February 1919 he returned to Birmingham City Police but remained part of the Armed Forces Reserve.

The final entry on his police records show that he was reported by Superintendent Daniel Long for being absent from duty on Monday 4 August and participating in the police strike. He was dismissed from the force.

The 1939 register shows us that Frederick and Ethel are living together residing at The Farm on Sampson Road, Birmingham, and his occupation given is a Park Keeper. He died at the grand old age of 89 in 1977.

Who were the senior officers?

99% of the officers were reported by three senior officers – the superintendents in charge of the A, C and E Divisions. But who were those men and what are their stories?

Daniel Long

Daniel Long joined Birmingham City Police in February 1884 with his previous occupation recorded as baker. He proceeded through the ranks becoming sergeant in November 1894, inspector in October 1901, chief inspector in October 1911 and superintendent in February 1916. He spent much of his career on the D Division, moving to E Division upon promotion to chief inspector.

Daniel was complimented once for detecting crime in 1889 and once for courage in 1896, receiving a stripe of merit on each occasion.

The 1889 incident was on the recommendation of the court recorder, concerning the arrest of warehousebreakers, for which Daniel was awarded a £3 gratuity. The 1896 compliment which earned him his 2nd stripe of merit, relates to his courageous conduct in stopping a runaway horse on New Street in November 1895.

At various times he was the coach on the cricket team and also a shooting team, as the picture below shows.

Superintendent Long retired on superannuation on New Year's Eve 1926 after completing 42 years' service with the Birmingham City Police.

Superintendent Daniel Long seated centre, proudly displaying a shield won by the rifle team

George Monk

George joined Birmingham Borough Police in September 1881, eight years before it became a city. He had previously been working at Birmingham prison as a warder. He was promoted to sergeant in December 1886 and inspector in December 1889. In July 1897 after three months' probation he was promoted to superintendent – taking over the leadership of the A Division.

During his career he received three compliments for detecting crime. He received one misconduct entry for being drunk on duty very early in his career in December 1881.

In June 1896 George received a £5 gratuity from the North Western Railway Company for vigilance in catching thieves – this was significant compared to the one guinea reward most officers were awarded!

In 1906 George's second daughter married Detective Frank Ainge of the Detectives Department with the Birmingham police. Many of the C Division were present at the wedding. George also took the lead on the role of coach on various teams such as the first aid team and the billiards team. He is seen below – seated second from the right.

On 23 September 1923 George died whilst still serving, having spent over 40 years with the Birmingham police. He was accorded a funeral with full police honours and thousands of people lined the streets to watch the procession. The Chief Constable Charles Haughton Rafter was present, along

with Assistant Chief Constable Cecil Moriarty, Chief Superintendents Boulton and Burnett, Superintendents Long, Penrice, Cook, May and Bennett, the Chief Constable of Wolverhampton as well as senior officers from West Bromwich and 36 men of the fire brigade. There were also many police pensioners present. George was clearly very highly thought of.

Arthur David Penrice

Arthur Penrice had a long and distinguished career. After serving seven years in the Grenadier Guards (receiving the Queen's South Africa Medal), he joined Birmingham City Police in April 1903 as a 5th class constable. He rose through the ranks quickly – becoming a sergeant in December 1908 and an inspector in October 1911 shortly before Birmingham expanded and the Birmingham Police inherited officers from Handsworth and other locations. Arthur was stationed at Handsworth and he remained on the C Division throughout subsequent promotions – a sign he was doing well and was respected by the men. We also know he was coach and trainer of the Birmingham Police Tug of War Team in 1911 – a team which became amateur champions of England.

In September 1914 Arthur was lent to the War Office as an army drill instructor, returning in February 1915. Before he became an inspector he was assaulted and injured on duty on four separate occasions. Throughout his career he received five compliments for detecting crime, two for first aid and three for courage. This included helping to solve an attempted murder, prompt action dealing with a severe scalp wound and effectively dealing with a fire in a picture house and controlling the subsequent crowd.

In July 1916 Arthur became chief inspector and July 1918 he was promoted to superintendent of the C Division. In 1923 the Hockley Brook overflowed and Arthur was quick to render services and courageously rescued individuals at risk of drowning. He also helped to assist those rendered homeless by the disaster and was commended by the Watch Committee and awarded a Royal Humane Society certificate for his courageous conduct.

In 1926 Arthur received the King's Police Medal for services to policing. He received over 60 letters from local businesses, other police forces, the Grenadier Guards and local dignitaries congratulating him on the achievements. Arthur retired on superannuation on 31 May 1928.

Arthur Penrice is seated centre and striker Frank Jones is standing second from the left.

What happened after the strike?

Recruitment of replacement officers occurred almost immediately – with 63 recruits being examined on 13 August, 48 of these being accepted and allocated to the divisions affected by the strike[cxxxii].

The Birmingham branch of NUPPO had experienced a brief life and a painful death.[cxxxiii]

The police union initially tried to support striking officers and their families but this became too much of a financial burden to bear. Bear in mind any officers living in force provided accommodation would have effectively become homeless unless they had family they could move in with. The little monetary support given by trade unions was not stretching far and by the end of August the executive urged the former officers to take employment elsewhere wherever possible, retaining only a small number of individuals on the union payroll in order to continue to fight their cause.[cxxxiv]

The Birmingham Post and Gazette were heavily critical of the striking officers and supported the Home Office and Birmingham Watch Committee's stance on not reinstating any of the men. The Post on 5 August stated harshly:

'The unfortunate dupes are left to shift for themselves, as after all, they ought to be. They entered onto a great gamble and have lost. They have only themselves and their leaders to blame for the consequent suffering – and suffering there must be, because they cannot possibly be readmitted into the force they so wantonly deserted'

The paper continued to pour cold water on the strike action – claiming on 7 August that the most serious consequence in Birmingham of the strike action was that the prosecution of a publican for serving outside licensed hours had to be postponed because the police witness was on strike[cxxxv].

Birmingham officers who had remained on duty urged Rafter to hold an enquiry to identify the 'real' offenders and exculpate and rehabilitate those who were deserving. He declined. A delegation from A Division also failed to convince him to reinstate the strikers. Further evidence of Rafter's views on the situation (if needed!) was provided when he banned a voluntary collection on behalf of strikers in 1920[cxxxvi].

On 12 August the Birmingham Watch Committee decided to adopt the new scale of pay for all constables and sergeants and pay the balance of arrears on the following Friday; with striking officers having missed out on significantly improved scale of pay by just days. On 15 August the Watch Committee announced that any officers currently on a reduced scale of pay (due to misconduct or minor indiscretions) would have that reduction cancelled and their new scale of pay calculated as if the reduction had not been in place. It was stated that the Committee 'remembered that these men were not involved in a recent regrettable transaction.'[cxxxvii]

On 29 August the creation of a new national police organisation was discussed in police orders – what we now know as the Police Federation. It was described as an organisation for every officer under the rank of superintendent, divided into branch boards which enabled each rank to discuss issues regarding welfare and efficiency of the police. The order also reinforced the provision in the Police Act 1919 prohibiting any officer from being a member of a trade union and the responsibility of officers to remain loyal to the force and not to cause disaffection.[cxxxviii]

On 30 August it was stated in police orders that a copy of the Police Act 1919 had been placed in every station for the perusal of any member of the force who desires. In October it was stated that men returning from the Armed Forces should be given a copy and also information in relation to the branch boards, in order to familiarise themselves with the new provisions. It was also highlighted in October (as elections began for the representatives for the new branch board) that members of the First Police Reserve are also included as members of the force, and should all be given copies of the Police Act[cxxxix].

It was evident that the prospect of further strike action was not far from the mind of the chief constable. Indeed the railway strike late September 1919 had caused all leave to be stopped for members of the force, who were all recalled for duty. Even band practice and evening classes were stopped temporarily, as the need for resource was so great.

In the Judicial Sub-Committee minutes of 29 September 1919 Rafter received a letter from the National Federation of Discharged and Demobilised Sailors and Soldiers asking if police officers would be allowed to join the federation. After some consideration of the aims and purpose of the federation, Rafter decided that members of the police force could not be permitted to join. This was closely followed in the minutes by the Chief Constable submitting letters both from the Branch Union of the Railwaymen and a letter from the District Trade Union Industrial Council. Although the contents of the letters are not known it is apparent that the union were asking for leniency for the officers who had been dismissed for going on strike. In reply:-

'Resolved: That the Unions be informed that the Committee cannot alter their previous decision.'

It was at this time that the Rafter apparently received the first applications for reinstatement from officers who had been dismissed for striking, these being from ex PCs Parker, Cartwright, Baggott, Morgan and Barker.

'Resolved: The applications be not granted[cxl].

In October the secretary of the Birmingham branch (and one of the striking officers) Arthur James Green, wrote a letter to the Trade Union Council asking them to place the matter before their members to offer support for the former officers and prison warders. Of particular concern was the prison warders due to be evicted from their houses, owned by the prison service. Arthur also points out that a public meeting was being held on 21 October and the union would welcome the presence of members to ensure a great gathering to discuss the matter of reinstatement of the officers and warders and the proposed evictions[cxli].

When members of the NUPPO executive visited Edward Shortt to ask about reinstating the strikers, particularly as the Metropolitan Police were advertising for new officers to fill their places, he stated that these men had shown themselves to be unreliable and therefore they could not be trusted again.[cxlii]

At the Judicial Sub-Committee on 27 October 1919 a report was received bearing twenty six signatures urging that a full and impartial enquiry into the causes of the police strike should be held.

The sub-committee decided that the Watch Committee be recommended to refuse the application on the grounds that it is not within their province to hold such an inquiry, particularly as an enquiry had been made in each case and ample warning of the result of striking was given to each member of the police force in police order dated 30 May 1919. The sub-committee were of the opinion that no further investigations was necessary[cxliii].

In the same Watch Committee minutes the Chief Constable was congratulated as to how he made arrangements for extra police assistance in the recent railway strike.

Nationally, there was a clear distinction between officers recruited before and after the Police Act 1919 – with older officers with more service resenting newer colleagues who gained increased opportunities, significantly better pay and improved working conditions without having been through any of the earlier struggles to attain them[cxliv]. There was also a difference in success rates for promotion – with the officers who joined pre-1919 struggling to pass the exams that were solely paper based. There were arguments in the Desborough Committee's reports that promotions not be based solely on examinations because of the importance of 'initiative, tact, judgment, and other personal qualifications which cannot be gauged by means of an examination paper.' However this did not happen and the recommendation for experience to be taken into account was also ignored[cxlv]. In Birmingham initial exams were deliberately simple and easy so as not to 'place men at a disadvantage who had not been prepared for the examination laid down by the new law'.[cxlvi] This did not have the desired effect and many officers who had joined before the Great War found themselves failing the new exams.

The Chief Constable was trying to gather information on the strikers from the divisional superintendents in January 1920[cxlvii]:

From the Chief Constable to Superintendents

Police Strikers

Will Superintendents please send in to Chief Office as early as possible a list of the men who went out on strike, giving their record in the Police Service; and if they have served in the Army, any Distinctions they had won or what Superior Rank they had attained.

Also, any particulars regarding each man which has come to the Superintendent's knowledge.

The records might conveniently be sent in on form 498, specimen attached, and the remarks column on that form used for the particulars of Army Service; or any other information to hand.

In the Judicial Sub-Committee meeting of 1 March 1920 the Chief Constable reported that he had just received part 2 of the Desborough Report, which had recently been issued, but he had not yet had the opportunity of considering it. He wished, however, to draw the attention of the sub-committee to the paragraph recommending an increase in leave to members of the force, and as the annual leave season for members of the Birmingham force commenced on the 1st of the month he asked for an early decision in the matter[cxlviii].

Under the new proposals it was suggested that constables and sergeants should receive 14 days of annual leave, which with 50 days weekly leave would make 64 days of leave a year for these ranks. Until now constables and sergeants had been allocated nine days annual leave. This was agreed and the officers subsequently had their annual leave increased by over 50% and the Chief Constable was authorised to recruit the necessary increase in men to cover the increased leave provision.

In May 1920 there was a debate at the Birmingham Council meeting regarding some remuneration for the police strikers, particularly with regards to their contributions to the superannuation fund which had subsequently been lost on account of their being dismissed. Alderman Beard argued that the contributions were actually part of the men's salaries and there was a certain amount reasonably due back to them. The Watch Committee was asked to consider paying an amount to the men on account of the money they had paid into the fund – this was defeated. Former Sergeant Edward Taylor (as a locally elected councillor) was on the council and claimed 'some of the men who are on duty in your police force now have deceived us and they will deceive you.' Mrs Cadbury pleaded that the punishment meted out was already enough.[cxlix] It is clear the Cadbury family had sympathy for the strikers and several were still working for Cadbury in the 1939 register.

In March 1920 the force was offering voluntary classes in police duties to support officers wanting to take newly created promotion exams to progress through the scales of pay and receive increments[cl]:

Voluntary classes in police duties on divisions

Examinations will be held by the direction of the Home Office in accordance with Part 1. of the Desborough Report, which requires examinations to be held for Constables who have attained five years' service or over, with a view to their obtaining further advancement. A Constable of five years' service who is of good conduct and efficient and who passes a qualifying examination may receive a special advance of one increment in the scale of pay, and the following year a second special advance of one increment, so that a Constable may attain the maximum ordinary scale of pay after 8 years' service.

In London, many serving officers made donations towards the former officers and their families on payday, particularly at Christmas, for which Jack Hayes was keen to express his thanks. It is unclear whether the same actions occurred in Birmingham.

When the Police Federation was officially established, Jack Hayes made representation to the Central Committee asking for support in getting the former officers reinstated. This came after the committee had openly recognised the action of the 1918 strikers, for which the service as a whole were indebted. Unfortunately however, the Federation representatives were not keen on the idea of making representation to the Home Office on the matter.

In May 1920 His Majesty's Inspector of Constabulary Sir Leonard Dunning's report into the police strike of 1919 was published. It acknowledged that recognition of the union was the major cause of the strike, however it also highlighted that the Police Bill gave the police all the privileges of a trade union without the right to withhold their services:

"The value of a policeman's service depended on the faithful observance of promises to serve the King in the office of constable, and to give truthful evidence. The first promise was the one any honest man could make without the sacrifice of independence, and he could at any time release himself by resignation but if, whilst still bound by it, he deliberately refused to perform it, he forfeited the respect of his fellow man. Special weight had in the past been given to the evidence of police, but men who broke their promise of faithful service showed the promise meant little to them. To allow such men to retain their office was to put the life, liberty and reputation of others in peril. Though but a minority took part in the proceedings, the whole body had suffered the loss of public confidence, and it would take every effort of the rest for them to regain for themselves the high position in public esteem which had been lost.[cli]"

The Birmingham Trades Council recognised that reinstatement was the best that could be hoped for and that the union would not be recognised. They continued to pass resolutions into 1920 and there were sustained attempts to raise money on behalf of the strikers and their families. The Birmingham Labour movement eventually pulled together a token financial contribution of £20 per man in 1925[clii].

In May 1924 a committee was appointed to enquire into 'the claims of the Men Dismissed from the Police and Prison Services in account of the strike of 1919'.

The focus of the committee was the plea from the men that they be allowed to return to the various police forces from which they were dismissed, or at the very least be entitled to the return of their pension contributions.

The committee heard evidence from Chief Constables and Watch Committees of all those forces involved in the strike. The strikers themselves were represented by Jack Hayes, a Met striker who later became an MP and was known as 'the bobbies MP'.

Evidence was heard to the effect that the strike was based not on disloyalty to their police forces, but misguided loyalty to their comrades and that there was no further possibility of another strike and the suffering of the men and their families had already seen them severely punished for their actions.

The various authorities all agreed that reinstatement was not an option - not least for practical difficulties in the smaller forces, but mainly for the message it would send out to other officers and the disadvantage it would place on them in terms of promotion prospects etc. It was felt that the strikers had demonstrated a disregard for their oath of office and therefore they could not be allowed to return. The men presented evidence that serving officers unanimously supported the reinstatement but this was not enough.

Birmingham's situation was discussed as part of the evidence of individual forces and it was established that the force's Representative Committee, in its early stages of operation during 1918/19, had sent a deputation to the Watch Committee and asked for the union to be recognised and no members to be victimised. The committee had stated they were unable to recognise the union.

The events of the strike in Birmingham was discussed and the chairman of the Watch Committee informed the strike committee that out of the 119 officers (presumably not including Edwin Foster, the first police reserve officer):

- Three had died
- One was in a mental institution
- 82 were in the employment of others
- 11 were working for themselves
- One had gone abroad
- 12 had left the city
- Two had returned to their own homes
- Three are known to be unemployed
- Four cannot be traced

The committee reported in Dec 1924 and in concluding, highlighted that they were unable to arrive at a unanimous decision regarding reinstatement. The majority were against but sympathised with the men's economic struggles and the inherent unfairness of the refusal to return pension contributions. The committee authorised police authorities to use their discretion to return the deductions to the men who had not already had them. At this point Birmingham was still maintaining a tough line and refusing to give any strikers their contributions back.

The total number of striking officers in relation to forces was given: 2,400
- 1,056 Met out of 18,200 (5.8%)
- 58 City of London out of 970 (6%)
- 120 Birmingham out of 1,320 (9.1%)
- 954 Liverpool out of 1,874 (50.9%)
- 114 Birkenhead out of 180 (63.3%)
- 63 Bootle out of 77 (81.8%)
- 1 Wallasey out of 120 (0.8%)

The Police Pensions Act 1926 gave various provisions for ex-officers to apply for the return of their pension contributions. In April 1925 the Watch Committee stood firm on previous decisions regarding the strikers and said it saw no reason to depart from those decisions. They did not favour legislation being introduced that would change this. However they soon had a change of heart, reporting in May 1925 that the previous comments be rescinded and that if legislation was considered necessary, the committee supported this provided that Local Authorities were empowered to give retrospective effect in the case of all men dismissed on the understanding that the Watch Committee had the discretion to return the whole or part of the deductions in cases of hardship to wives and children[cliii]. In 1925 the force unofficially assisted strikers and helped them to find employment.[cliv]

By 1927 when the legislation was in, many former officers were applying for their contributions back – not just the strikers. In July 1927 a report was submitted by the Chief Constable from men requesting their contributions to be returned, including 14 strikers who gave their current wages (six of whom worked at Cadburys, three of these having the highest wages of all the men on the report) and a further two strikers who provided no details as to their wages. All the names were accepted bar the requests of three former strikers (Bailey, Bullock and Jackson). The committee stated the first two names would be considered further if the men would provide details as to their current financial situations and clearly many of the strikers' requests were approved. One additional striker appears to have been initially included in the 'approved' list however, and that decision was rescinded in October 1927 with no reason given[clv].

The remnants of NUPPO eventually formed the Police Strikers' Association – in an article in the Daily Mirror on 8 November 1948 – it was reported that 200 former Metropolitan police officers dismissed during the strike, had gone to a meeting and been told that their 29 year struggle had failed and they had been continuously let down by successive Prime Ministers. One of the former officers was M.P. Harry Goodrich. It would seem several of the men got involved in politics after being dismissed. Just before they marched out of the hall they had agreed to change their name to the London Police Strikers Association. After 29 years presumably they no longer wished to be reinstated but instead were campaigning for an apology and recognition.

Why did they strike?

It is highly likely they were disillusioned by the propaganda coming out of the NUPPO executive in London and the discontent about lack of recognition, this was stirring up feelings of unrest in Birmingham. Some of these men will have seen how long it took for changes to be implemented, even after going through Parliamentary committees – so perhaps they did not realise how close the other changes in the 1919 Act were, and at the same time distrusted the idea of the Police Federation, feeling it was forced upon them and their own union pushed aside.

All of them will have known how successful the 1918 strike was – with the officers being promised a significant pay rise and their jobs back. It is likely that most (if not all) of the Birmingham strikers felt if enough men went on strike they could not possibly all be sacked.

Reynolds and Judge make a very important point in *'The Night the Police Went on Strike'* – they highlight that a great deal of officers were returning from the military at a time where police forces were trying to enforce discipline in the strongest ways and stamp down on any misconduct, particularly during Macready's early years of trying to establish control of his force. Rafter was also well-known for being a strict disciplinarian with a penchant for military regulation and order. Many of the ex-military officers had already had their fill of extreme discipline and order in the Armed Forces and could not tolerate it for much longer back at home.

There are also a number of important points to make about why more officers didn't answer the call to strike – aside from the obvious ones of the already promised increase in pay and the risk of losing their job and pension. It would appear many of the grievances of the Birmingham Police were economically driven – therefore when these were resolved a lot of the vigour and enthusiasm within the NUPPO Birmingham branch dissolved. As previously mentioned the officers didn't only risk losing their jobs, but also the substantial pay increase and their pensions. For some of them this was quite significant – Sergeant Taylor for example lost a pension of £140 per annum and Sergeant Doughty missed out on a pay rise from £161 to £292[clvi].

It has also been highlighted that relations between the public and the police in Birmingham pre-WWI were generally pretty good. And whilst many were perhaps unhappy with the tight regulations imposed by Rafter, he had instigated many good practises within the force – including a training school to be proud of, a representative committee for officers to discuss and air their grievances and ever improving working conditions. It is likely he had the grudging respect of many of his men. He was also consistent – whereas some other forces experienced change and uncertainty with new Chief Constables, Rafter had already been in post 20 years by 1919, and went on to serve another 16 before he died (still in post) in 1935. He had also been commended for outward facing changes he had implemented to the police service (such as advocating crime prevention advice and segregation of juveniles at court) and early implementation of the Defence of the Realm provisions during WWI which had saved the citizens of Birmingham from Zeppelin raids. In addition, Rafter was responsible for introducing policewomen to Birmingham in 1917 and was a much respected character in police circles nationally.

The vast majority of the strikers were commended for courageous conduct during their service, putting themselves in danger to stop runaway horses and rescuing individuals from fires and canals. There are compliments and awards on most of their records for effectively rendering first aid to individuals suffering from broken bones, burns or varicose veins and delivering artificial respiration. A great many of the men had families to feed and were working long hours in hard working conditions for low pay. The Desborough Committee's research showed that the income of an officer with two or more children barely covered all the expenses being occurred in the family home. It has been mentioned earlier that some men in some police forces were requesting permanent night duty so that they could fall into the one family bed as soon as their wife and children were out of it, and others felt obliged to take on other occupations in order to make ends meet. No one can doubt how hard it was to be a police officer during the early 1900s, often being assaulted on duty and reverting back to working a seven day week during part of World War One.

Only one officer in Birmingham had less than a year's service – Albert James Pout had just over three months in the job when the strike was called. 39 officers had between 4 and 6 years' service and 26 had 7-10. 22 had 11-14 years' service and 30 had 15-19 years' service. Most notably two officers had over 20 years' service – Charles William Thorpe had almost 22 years and Sergeant Edward Charles Taylor had almost 23.

The Cadbury family were very supportive of the men, offering jobs to many of the former officers, several of whom were still working there by 1939. Mrs Cadbury also fought for them to get their pension contributions back in 1920, claiming they had suffered enough.

The strike split families apart with some officers striking where other family members did not. Thomas Fuller's brother-in-law remained in the force until the 1940s. Fellow strikers and brothers-in-law Jack Allen and Thomas Mooney joined the strike but their brother-in-law William Henry Robinson, joined the Birmingham force on 20 August 1919, less than a month after the strike. He served 30 years as a police officer and then returned to the force as a First Police Reserve in 1950. Family members have told us this did not cause any problems within the family, and subsequently two members of later generations joined the police – the niece of Harry Paragreen (another brother-in-law who died during the Spanish flu epidemic) and William Robinson's grandson. A true policing family!

Criticism has quite rightly been given to the role of organised labour in the strike. After initially offering considerable support and visibly supporting the union, thus encouraging the strike action and plans of inexperienced trade union activists, there was little support given to the officers after they had actually taken the step of going on strike. A. V. Sellwood stated that *'little support except for lip service, had been forthcoming for the 'police brothers' when the crisis had exploded, leaving them among it victims'*[clvii]. James Henry Thomas (general secretary of the National Union of Railway Workers) had publicly committed to NUPPO but privately issued concerns that immediate striking would lead to revolution. When the only physical support from organised labour materialised in support of the striking policemen – in the form of 750 railway and London underground workers – Thomas urged them to return to work and they did. Another potentially promising (but ultimately disappointing) voice of support came from the Birmingham and District Joint Committee of Engineering Trade Unions, who passed a resolution expressing admiration for the strikers and pledged to pressure the government to withdraw the Police Bill. [clviii] When the men left their posts, they really were on their own.

Conclusion:

So why did 120 men, several of whom were months away from getting their pensions, who had just been promised a significant pay rise (and had already received a large amount of back pay), risk their jobs and their pensions by going out on strike? We have come to several conclusions:

1) The summer of 1918 was fresh in everyone's minds. They did not believe they would be sacked if enough officers went on strike.

2) The rhetoric coming from NUPPO exec and organised labour locally were overly encouraging and pushing for strike action, overpromising on numbers and support. The executive indicated they had all gone out on strike themselves, when really they had not.

3) NUPPO numbers in Birmingham were higher than Charles Rafter wanted to believe. Many union men were part of the first and second representative committee created by Rafter for the men to make representation to the Chief Constable and Watch Committee. It is likely more officers went on strike but quickly went back to duty, with the number of union members most of these officer probably felt they could not all be sacked. But unluckily for those that did, the small number meant they could indeed be sacked and replaced.

4) Many distrusted the idea of the federation and wanted to fight for the union which they thought had achieved a lot including significant pay increase. They were not consulted on the Police Act 1919 and felt it was being thrust upon them.

5) Many of the men had just left military conditions and were willing to fight to ensure working for the police was different. Some may have also been suffering from Post-Traumatic Stress Disorder.

One might also question why, out of six divisions, did the men primarily come from three of those divisions (with one lone striker coming from a fourth)? A number of officers claimed that there were other strikers who simply went back on duty when it was clear the numbers were not as anticipated. Were the senior officers on the other divisions more tolerant and allow the men to go back on duty, shielding them from the superintendent? Or was there more discontent on the A, C and E divisions – perhaps from overbearing supervision? We also need to take into account that the C Division had the NUPPO branch leader, Sergeant Edward Taylor, and therefore C Division would have been hearing lots of pro-union information coming from a trusted colleague, making them more likely to take action. They also had branch secretary Sergeant William Doughty amongst their ranks. A Division had PC Arthur Green, who later became the branch secretary and E Division had assistant branch secretary PC Charles Henry Thomas. This is likely to have made a big impact on the men of those three divisions.

Men like Edward Taylor believed in the greater good - he could have simply tolerated any of his grievances for another two years but instead he fought for what he believed in, the union and the good he thought it could do for men around the country, putting his job and his pension on the line. Even though he personally didn't want to strike, he believed in democracy and went with what he was told the majority had voted for. The men were lied to by the union executive and organised labour. The government and Chief Officers could possibly have been more open and consultative about the Police Act 1919. The resulting effect was that the police service lost a lot of good men that day, men who had put themselves at risk for members of the public whilst policing and who had fought for their country.

Hindsight is a wonderful thing and it is easy to consider 'what if's. What we do know is that things are very different today - across most police forces and open culture exists where officers are able to ask questions of chief officers and are consulted on key changes. The Federation is consulted and representatives across the force are able to take up grievances and issues on behalf of its members, whilst also supporting them through injuries and misconduct cases. Social media and TV documentaries give a far greater insight into policing than was ever possible previously. There are still many problems within policing - some the same today as 100 years ago - but there are ways and means for these to be addressed, with far more support available for officers than in the early 1900s.

The creation of the Police Federation

On 8 October 1919 the Birmingham City Police started to elect their branch boards[clix]:

'Election of Branch Boards

The Representative Committee held a meeting on Tuesday 7th October 1919 for the purpose of making arrangements for the election of Branch Boards in this Force for the Police Federation, as provided in Section 1. of the Police Act 1919, when it was decided to hold the elections on Monday 20th October.

All members below the rank of Superintendent will be eligible to vote. Each member will have one vote which must be given to a Candidate, in his own particular rank, and attached to the Division on which the voter serves.

Chief Inspectors will be eligible to vote, and stand as Candidates for the Board of Inspectors.

On each Division the Constables will elect one Constable, the Sergeants one Sergeant, and the Inspectors one Inspector. The Boards will thus consist of six Inspectors, six Sergeants and six Constables.

Each Board will be separate, and each will elect its own Chairman and Secretary. The three Boards, or any two may by agreement sit together for all purposes of common interest'.

On 17 October the candidates for the Branch Boards of the Police Federation were published in police orders[clx] and on 21 October it was reported that the following officers had been successful in being elected to the first ever Birmingham City Police Branch Boards[clxi]:

Division	Inspectors	Sergeants	Constables
A Division	J. Cartwright	4 G. Barrett	21 F. Bond
B Division	H. Cook	11 S. Shereston	52 J. Doughty
C Division	W. Mountford	12 E. Randall	249 W. Archer
D Division	A. Ainge	2 T. Lawrence	133 C. Twamley
E Division	F. Wasley	2 E. Cowley	115 G. Ware
R Division	G. Barnes	2 S. Allen	97 H. Collins

The election had been overseen by former honourable secretary of the representative board Sergeant William Clowes. The first board meetings were held on 6 November 1919 and later that month deputations representing each board attended the Judicial Sub-Committee with initial requests, giving a very useful insight into what was bothering officers at the time of the strike. The following month the Judicial Sub-Committee reported the following queries were raised and subsequent responses given[clxii]:

From the joint inspectors, sergeants and constables branch board:

- Creation of a social club to address inadequate refreshment provisions for officers engaged on special duty and for recreation & pastime of members of the force: the Chief Constable reported the only difficulty he could see was identifying suitable premises and he asked for any suggestions to be forwarded to him. The Watch Committee were supportive of the request and awaited further information. Separate to this, the Chief Constable was making arrangements to establish a canteen in the Victoria Law Courts for officers engaged in the centre of the city.

Issues raised by the joint sergeants and constables branch board:

- Requirement for annual leave to be taken between 1 April and 31 October: it was established that the previous Representative Board had already raised this issue and arrangements were made for leave to be taken between March and November, with those taking leave in the colder months to be able to take leave in the summer months the following year.
- A request for all lady clerks to be dispensed with, now there was no shortage of male labour, as it was felt that women were not conducive to discipline in departments! The Watch Committee stated this was outside of the purview of the boards as it did not concern the welfare and efficiency of the force.
- A request for men attached to the R Division from other divisions to be transferred to that department after six months or returned to their own division. It was confirmed that this was standard practise in normal times.
- The board requested they be able to make a 2d contribution per member per week to the police orphanage, which the Watch Committee were pleased with.

Issues raised through the constables branch board:

- Requests were made for officers failing to progress through the classes through a lack of 'efficiency' to be provided with a confidential report outlining why this was the case. The Watch Committee determined this to be outside the scope of the board but also highlighted that men were provided with reasons regarding any failure to progress.
- A request was made concerning officers on evening duty attending classes at the police training school and this depriving other officers of their evening off (in order to cover the absence). The Watch Committee highlighted the abnormal position the force was in, with an unusually high level of recruits in school (329) and that it was impossible to address this situation at present without causing detriment to the force. This high number was likely down to replacing the dismissed officers from the strike and also officers who had not returned from the Armed Forces or had returned unfit for duty.
- To amend the overalls for point duty men, reduce the amount of time on point duty from four hours to two and to subsequently ensure both men allocated to the point duty received the allowance. This matter was referred to the Chief Constable.
- That special duty pay be paid promptly and at the end of each month. The Chief Constable assured the officers that no time would be lost in his office processing the payments, but that the force was reliant on whoever was making the payment for the duty.
- Lighter headgear for summer weather was requested but the Watch Committee was of the opinion that this was unnecessary.
- When weekly leave is stopped due to an emergency, men should be allowed to take this leave at a time suitable for them and likewise, when weekend leave is stopped that men be allowed to take two consecutive days together at a time convenient for them and their families. The Watch Committee deemed that whenever practical this request would be met, however the operational needs of the force must come first.

The Birmingham branches of the Federation had gotten off to a rocky start – in 1925 when the Federation sent out a questionnaire regarding temporary pay cuts, the branches sent it out to their members with detailed instructions on how to vote and what they should vote for – circumventing any true reflection of the opinion of the men[clxiii].

By the 1930s the Police Review was publishing articles written by men complaining about the lack of action and success of the Federation, which was at risk of becoming an organisation that simply complained about things, without delivering any change.

The big success of the Birmingham branches came in 1938 when they won a ten year battle to remove the Birmingham split shift system, which had been operating since 1882. It had been implemented on the argument that split shifts caused less strain on a policeman's health. The men however did not appreciate the system – which required that eight hour shifts be split over 12 hours, with a four hour break in the middle. Including travel time it was often not worth going home which meant the men would have to hang around Birmingham in the intervening period. In 1903 officers requested a return to the eight hour shift system but the Watch Committee had deemed it 'inconvenient and unworkable'.[clxiv] The Federation took up the argument in 1928 and stated that the existing system did not give officers to change to enjoy the Sports Ground – the Watch Committee did not agree and stated long continuous shifts would make the men less likely to want to do physical activity, and would also place 'heavy strain upon a man's physique and a continuing lowering of the vitality, with a resultant increase in liability to sickness'.[clxv]

Over subsequent decades the Birmingham City Police Federation continued to earn the respect of its officers, making representations to senior officers and the Watch Committee and supporting members through difficult times in their service. In 1974 when West Midlands Police was formed it migrated into the West Midlands Police Federation, now also supporting officers from Coventry, Wolverhampton, Walsall, Dudley, Solihull and Sandwell.

The West Midlands Police Federation state: 'The Federation today represents the interests of over 136,000 police officers, bringing together their views on welfare and efficiency to the notice of the government and all opinion formers. The Federation negotiates on all aspects of pay, allowances, hours of duty, annual leave and pensions. It is consulted when police regulations are made, dealing with training, promotion and discipline.

It takes an active interest in a wide range of subjects, which affect the police service, and puts forward its views on the members' behalf. Thus, it not only acts as a staff association, but also as a professional body, able to influence not only living standards, through pay and other benefits, but also the development of professional standards.'[clxvi]

The Police Family

Several stories have surfaced during the research for this book of descendants or families of striking officers who have continued with policing careers either shortly after the strike or generations later.

The Russell sisters and their descendants:

In an incredible family story, between them the four Russell sisters (Nellie, Edith, Beatrice and Elsie) married five police officers - strikers Jack Allen and Thomas Mooney, former officer William (Billy) Woodyatt (who retired in 1914), Harry Paragreen (who sadly died during the Spanish flu epidemic in 1918) and William Robinson who joined the force in August 1919.

E Division – Moseley Street c1912. William Woodyatt is far left on the front row

Below - wedding of Thomas Mooney and Nellie Russell on 3 October 1910. All 4 sisters, 2 brothers, parents, and PC Harry Paragreen are on the photo, 2nd man from the left is PC Joe Harris, the policeman in uniform is unfortunately unknown but the man to his left is Bert Harding another policeman. Joe Phillips, one of the first recipients of the King's Police Medal for extreme gallantry in 1911, is standing next to Thomas and is presumably his best man.

Birmingham City Police swim team between 1912 and 1918 – Harry Paragreen is second from left on the front row

PC William Robinson who served from 1919 to 1949 before returning as a First Police Reserve

Paul John Robinson

The grandson of William Robinson, Paul Robinson, is a serving officer with Avon and Somerset Constabulary.

Paul is the son of William's son John Robinson. He joined the special constabulary in Warwickshire between 1993 and 1995. He then moved to the Metropolitan Police in 1995, from there he transferred in 2004 to Somerset and Avon Police, where he is still based in 2019.

Tony Dutton

Tony is the grandson of striker Thomas Mooney. In 1956 Tony became a cadet in Staffordshire County Police and that year he was in the boxing team for the Smethwick Division of Staffordshire County Police. He won his bout and they won the force annual boxing tournament. In February 1957 he went to the Police Training School at Mill Meece, Staffs. During the late

1950's he did a training course for divisional noddy bikes (the Velocette LE). Tony is second from the right on the middle row.

Tony was at Piddocks Road, Smethwick, as a cadet. As a policeman his number was 373 and he spent time at West Bromwich Police Station, Greets Green, All Saints, Hamstead, near Great Barr and Cannock, where he was a motor patrol driver. Tony left the Force in February 1969.

Sharon Harding (nee Parsons) – granddaughter of Ernest Parsons

Sharon's grandfather was Birmingham striker Ernest Parsons. Sharon joined West Midlands Police in April 1978 and served until the end of March 2008. Ernest's son Leslie (Sharon's father) was not in the police family and was actually a scientist. Sharon is one of three children and served mostly on the B Division in Birmingham.

Sharon (left) and Ernest (above)

Mike Hodgkiss – grandson of John Hodgkiss

Mike Hodgkiss joined West Midlands Police in 1975 and retired in 2006. His brother David also served with West Midlands Police.

Mike could have left in 2005 after completing 30 years' service, but it was quite a difficult time for community cohesion in the West Midlands and in his role as deputy Head of Diversity and Inclusion, Chief Constable Chris Simms asked him to stay an extra 12 months. He worked on every division in the then Central and Eastern Divisions and has some very fond memories of his very first unit at Stechford and the last team he worked with. During his career he was awarded a Royal Humane Society Award for Saving Life and he shook Bill Clinton's hand!

Geoff Reader – grandson of Thomas Frederick Jones

Geoff is the grandson of Thomas Frederick Jones, he joined Birmingham City Police in 1962 as a cadet straight after leaving school. During his time as a cadet Geoff spent time in an international youth camp in Austria which was an incredibly challenging and moving experience. Geoff was enrolled into the regulars in October 1964, initially being posted to Cotteridge and then Longbridge until he resigned in 1973.

After a quick taste of life outside the force Geoff re-joined in October 1973. He became part of West Midlands Police in the 1974 amalgamation and spent his career working as the 'station officer', on the motorway and in roads policing, in accident enquiries and also in the force control room.

Geoff retired in January 1995 on an ill-health pension, less than 60 days before completing 30 years' service.

Ada Bowers – great grandson of Walter Giblett (Metropolitan Police striker)

Former West Midlands Police Detective Superintendent Ada Bowers also has a strike family connection. Ada recently discovered his great grandad was an officer in the Metropolitan Police who was dismissed for going on strike in 1919. It is likely he also took part in the 1918 strike with the majority of the force being involved in that action.

His name was Walter Giblett, he was born in Eaton Socon, Bedfordshire around 1881, married his wife Ada in Brentford in 1896 and in 1911 was living at 8 Fenelon Street.

In March 1906 he joined the Metropolitan Police with the warrant number 92947 and the collar number 76. His division on joining was F (Paddington), which would have included Kensington, and he remained in that division with that divisional number throughout his career. He was dismissed on 1 August 1919 for participation in the police strike that year.

His son William Arthur (born in 1907), died suddenly in 1922 aged just 15. Walter's daughter Phyllis was born in 1909, married aged 23 in 1932, with her father's occupation recorded as taxi driver. His other daughter Kathleen Doris, born in 1910, is Ada Bowers grandmother.

The above photograph is Walter and Ada around 1920 – shortly after the strike.

Ada joined West Midlands Police in December 1976 and retired as a detective superintendent in October 2008. Here he is pictured as a constable early in his service and an inspector in 1989.

Birmingham City Police.

REVISED SCALE OF PAY.

SUPERINTENDENTS.

							Deductions for Superannuation Fund. 2½ per cent.	
After 8 years in rank	...	...	...	...	£280 per annum	...	£7 0 0 per annum.	
,, 7 ,,	...	...	...	...	270 ,,	...	6 15 0 ,,	
,, 6 ,,	...	...	...	...	260 ,,	...	6 10 0 ,,	
,, 5 ,,	...	...	...	...	250 ,,	...	6 5 0 ,,	
,, 4 ,,	...	...	...	...	240 ,,	...	6 0 0 ,,	
,, 3 ,,	...	...	...	...	230 ,,	...	5 15 0 ,,	
,, 2 ,,	...	...	...	...	220 ,,	...	5 10 0 ,,	
,, 1 ,,	...	...	...	...	210 ,,	...	5 5 0 ,,	
On appointment	...	...	...	...	200 ,,	...	5 0 0 ,,	

CHIEF INSPECTORS.

On appointment, £160 per annum, increasing at intervals of not less than two years to £180. The amount of increase and intervals to be at the discretion of the Watch Committee.

INSPECTORS.

Special Class	...	...	...	...	57/8 per week	...	1/5½ per week.
1st Class—after 6 years in rank	...	...	...	54/- ,,	...	1/4 ,,
2nd Class— ,, 3 ,, ,,	...	...	...	50/- ,,	...	1/3 ,,
3rd Class—on appointment	...	...	...	47/6 ,,	...	1/2½ ,,

SERGEANTS.

Long Service Class—after 9 years in rank	...	43/- per week	...	1/1 per week.
1st Class—after 7 years in rank	...	...	42/- ,,	...	1/0½ ,,
2nd Class— ,, 5 ,,	...	...	...	41/- ,,	...	1/- ,,
3rd Class— ,, 3 ,,	...	...	...	40/- ,,	...	1/- ,,
4th Class—on appointment	...	...	...	38/- ,,	...	11½d. ,,

CONSTABLES.

*Star Class—after 20 years' service	...	...	36/- per week	...	10½d. per week.
4th Long Service Class—after 15 years' service	35/- ,,	...	10½d. ,,
3rd ,, ,, ,, 13 ,,	...	34/- ,,	...	10d. ,,
2nd ,, ,, ,, 11 ,,	...	33/- ,,	...	10d. ,,
1st ,, ,, ,, 9 ,,	...	32/- ,,	...	9½d. ,,
1st Class— ,, 7 ,,	...	31/- ,,	...	9d. ,,
2nd ,, — ,, 5 ,,	...	30/- ,,	...	9d. ,,
3rd ,, — ,, 3 ,,	...	29/- ,,	...	8½d. ,,
4th ,, — ,, 1 ,,	...	28/- ,,	...	8d. ,,
5th ,, —(on appointment)	...	...	27/- ,,	...	8d. ,,

*Subject to special conditions with regard to good conduct and efficiency.

Allowances.

Rent—

Superintendents resident in Stations are allowed house, coal, gas and water free.

Inspectors resident in Sub-stations are allowed house, coal, gas and water free.

Inspectors non-resident in Stations, both Uniform and Detective, are allowed 6s. a week for house rent.

Sergeants (married) necessarily paying 6s. 6d. a week and not exceeding 8s. per week of rent are allowed 1s. per week.

Constables (married) necessarily paying 6s. a week and not exceeding 8s. a week of rent are allowed 1s. per week.

Boots—

An allowance for boots is made as follows :—

Superintendents	...	...	...	£2	10	6	a year
Inspectors	...	...	...	...	2	0	0	,,
Sergeants	...	...	...	...	2	0	0	,,
Constables	...	...	...	...	1	10	0	,,

Point Duty—

Constables engaged on point duty regulating traffic receive an allowance of 1s. a week while so engaged.

Office Duty—

Reserve Office Sergeants at Divisional Stations receive an allowance of 5s. per week whilst they perform that duty.

Office and Departmental—

An allowance at the undermentioned rate is made to Inspectors, Sergeants, and Constables bona-fide employed as clerks in the Chief Constable's offices, Detective Office, and other offices of the Chief Constable's Department, including the Street Trading, Explosives, and Coroner's Departments :—

Inspectors	...	...	...	...	3s. a week
Sergeants	...	...	...	...	3s. ,,
Constables	...	...	...	...	2s. ,,

Detective Allowances—

		Plain Clothes (including Boots).		Incidental Expenses
Superintendent	...	£12 a year	...	4s. a week
Inspectors	...	...	£12 ,,	...	4s. ,,
Sergeants	...	...	£10 ,,	...	3s. ,,
Constables	...	...	£10 ,,	...	3s. ,,

An allowance for plain clothes on the above scale is made to members in various Departments.

An allowance is made to officers performing duty in plain clothes at Divisional Stations of £5 a year for clothing.

Merit.

Sergeants and Constables may obtain Merit Stripes. Sergeant's first stripe carries 1s. a week, and second stripe the same : total 2s. a week, called "full merit." Constable's first stripe carries 6d. a week, the second stripe 6d., and the third 1s. : total 2s. a week, called "full merit." A Constable holding the first or second stripe on promotion to the rank of Sergeant holds the Sergeant's first stripe of merit, carrying 1s. If he holds a Constable's third stripe (full merit) he obtains a Sergeant's full merit.

Deductions.

SICK—When not hurt on duty, ~~2s. for the first day~~ and 1s. for each ~~subsequent~~ day.

LODGING—Single sergeants or constables accommodated in Police Station, 1s. per week. Married sergeants or constables accommodated in police or station quarters, 2s. 6d. per week.

Leave.

	Annual.	Monthly.			Annual.	~~Monthly.~~ *one days*
Superintendents ...	14 days.	None specified.		Sergeants ..	10 days.	~~2 days.~~
Inspectors...	...	10 ,,	,,		Constables ...	9 ,,	2 ,, *rest in seven*

Pensions.

The maximum scale under the Police Act, 1890, without age limit.

[C14147]

CONDITIONS OF SERVICE

OF THE

BIRMINGHAM CITY POLICE.

————

1. Each Constable will be enrolled for one year on probation, and if then recommended by the Chief Constable as fit, will be appointed by the Watch Committee. A Constable on probation may be dismissed by the Chief Constable for unfitness, negligence, or misconduct.

2. Each member of the Force shall devote his whole time to the Police service of the City. He must not, directly or indirectly, carry on any trade or calling; nor can he be permitted, without the consent of the Chief Constable, to live at any place where any member of his family carries on business.

3. He shall serve where appointed, and reside in the City and in his Division, and within a reasonable distance of the Station to which he is attached, unless otherwise permitted by the Chief Constable.

4. He shall not, directly or indirectly, be interested in any publichouse or beerhouse. He is prohibited from borrowing money from publicans, beerhouse keepers, or other tradesmen, or being in any way indebted to them. He may not reside in a house licensed for the sale of intoxicating liquors.

5. He shall conform to all rules, orders, regulations, fines, and deductions now in force, or as the Watch Committee may frame for preventing neglect or abuse, and making the City Police efficient in the discharge of their duties, and shall promptly obey all the orders of the Chief Constable, and others placed in authority over him.

6. He shall appear in his complete Police uniform at all times when on duty, unless otherwise directed; but he may wear plain clothes when off duty.

7. He shall at all times provide himself with a respectable suit of plain clothes to the satisfaction of his Superintendent.

8. In consideration of receiving a boot allowance he shall provide himself with such boots as are directed by the Regulations.

9. Single men on joining will not be permitted to marry until they have been in the Force one year, and received permission of the Chief Constable.

10. Such debts owing by him as the Watch Committee or Chief Constable directs to be paid shall be paid by him forthwith.

11. He shall not belong to or subscribe money to the funds of any political or party society.

12. He shall have no claim to any stolen or unclaimed money or property, or other money or property found by him, or that may have come into his possession in the execution of his duty; and he shall deliver up all such money and property to his Superintendent; to be accounted for in accordance with the regulations relating to lost or stolen property.

13. He shall not retain any money or other thing given to him by way of fee, reward or presentation, without permission of the Watch Committee on the recommendation of the Chief Constable.

14. His pension will be calculated upon the amount of his pay, from which a deduction of $2\frac{1}{2}$ per cent. is made for superannuation, and not on the amount of any extra pay or allowance he may receive.

15. He will not be entitled to pay if absent from duty without leave.

16. He will make written applications for promotion from one Class to another, when such promotion falls due; otherwise his promotion may be delayed; and the Watch Committee reserve the right to defer promotion or to reduce his pay for misconduct or inefficiency.

17. He will be required to pass an educational test before receiving his first promotion, and may be called on for similar tests as to efficiency before further promotion.

18. He will be required to obtain first, second, and third class St. John Ambulance Certificates within three years of his joining the Force, and to attend revision class each year subsequently, to keep up his efficiency in rendering "First Aid" to the injured.

19. He shall not resign or withdraw himself from his duties or from the Force unless allowed to do so in writing by the Chief Constable; or unless he shall have given the Chief Constable one month's previous notice in writing, at the same time assigning a reason for so doing. If he resign or withdraw without such leave or notice, he is liable to forfeit all pay due and to be charged before a Magistrate.

20. He is liable to immediate dismissal for unfitness, negligence, or misconduct, independently of any other punishment to which by law he may be subject. The Watch Committee may remove him from the service by dismissal or otherwise.

21. A Constable dismissed from the Police Force, or who resigns or ceases to hold office, shall forthwith deliver up all articles of clothing, accoutrements, appointments, and other necessaries that have been supplied to him for the execution of his duties. They do not become his property; and he shall also deliver them up whenever called upon to do so, complete and in good order. If such clothing or appointments have in the opinion of the Chief Constable been unduly worn or improperly used or damaged, a deduction from the pay then due to the Constable shall be made, sufficient to make good the damage or supply a new article.

22. A certificate of good character in the Police service will not be given if the Constable has been dismissed the service; has frequently been guilty of misconduct; has been guilty of serious misconduct; has not served one year; has left the Force without giving one month's notice; or if he does not apply for the certificate within six months after leaving the Force.

𝔅irmingham 𝔔ity 𝔓olice.

REVISED SCALE OF PAY.
(To date from 2nd SEPTEMBER, 1918.)

SUPERINTENDENTS (Merit).

Deductions for Superannuation Fund, 2½ per cent.

At the discretion of the Watch Committee, not to exceed	£450 per annum ...	£11 5 0 per annum.

SUPERINTENDENTS.

After 6 years in rank	£410 per annum ...	£10 5 0 per annum.
,, 5 ,, ...	400 ,, ...	10 0 0 ,,
,, 4 ,, ...	390 ,, ...	9 15 0 ,,
,, 3 ,, ...	380 ,, ...	9 10 0 ,,
,, 2 ,, ...	370 ,, ...	9 5 0 ,,
,, I ,, ...	360 ,, ...	9 0 0 ,,
On appointment	350 ,, ...	8 15 0 ,,

CHIEF INSPECTORS (Merit).

At the discretion of the Watch Committee, but not to exceed	£312 per annum ...	£7 16 0 per annum.

CHIEF INSPECTORS.

After 4 years in rank	£296 8 0 per annum ...	£7 8 0 ,,
,, 3 ,, ...	286 0 0 ,, ...	7 3 0 ,,
,, 2 ,, ...	275 12 0 ,, ...	6 18 0 ,,
,, I ,, ...	265 4 0 ,, ...	6 13 0 ,,
On appointment	254 16 0 ,, ...	6 7 0 ,,

INSPECTORS (Merit).

the discretion of the Watch Committee, but not to exceed	£4 14s. 0d. a week ...	s. d. 2 4 per week.

INSPECTORS.

After 4 years in rank	87/- per week ...	2 2 per week.
,, 3 ,, ,, ...	85/- ,, ...	2 1 ,,
,, 2 ,, ,, ...	83/- ,, ...	2 1 ,,
,, I ,, ,, ...	81/- ,, ...	2 0 ,,
On appointment	79/- ,, ...	2 0 ,,

SERGEANTS.

After 9 years in rank	65/- per week ...	1 7 per week.
,, 8 ,, ,, ...	64/- ,, ...	1 7 ,,
,, 7 ,, ,, ...	63/- ,, ...	1 7 ,,
,, 6 ,, ,, ...	62/- ,, ...	1 6 ,,
,, 5 ,, ,, ...	61/- ,, ...	1 6 ,,
,, 4 ,, ,, ...	60/- ,, ...	1 6 ,,
,, 3 ,, ,, ...	59/- ,, ...	1 5 ,,
,, 2 ,, ,, ...	58/- ,, ...	1 5 ,,
,, I ,, ,, ...	57/- ,, ...	1 5 ,,
On appointment	56/- ,, ...	1 5 ,,

CONSTABLES.

After 20 years' service	53/- per week ...	1 4 per week.
,, 15 ,, ...	52/- ,, ...	1 3 ,,
,, 8 ,, ...	51/- ,, ...	1 3 ,,
,, 7 ,, ...	50/- ,, ...	1 3 ,,
,, 6 ,, ...	49/- ,, ...	1 2 ,,
,, 5 ,, ...	48/- ,, ...	1 2 ,,
,, 4 ,, ...	47/- ,, ...	1 2 ,,
,, 3 ,, ...	46/- ,, ...	1 2 ,
,, 2 ,, ...	45/- ,, ...	1 1 ,,
,, I ,, ...	44/- ,, ...	1 1 ,,
On appointment	43/- ,, ...	1 1 ,,

Allowances.

Rent—

Superintendents resident in Stations are allowed house, coal, gas and water free.

Superintendents non-resident in Stations are allowed £45 a year for house rent.

Inspectors resident in Sub-stations are allowed house, coal, gas and water free.

Inspectors non-resident in Stations, both Uniform and Detective, are allowed 6s. a week for house rent.

Sergeants (married) necessarily paying 6s. 6d. a week and not exceeding 10s. per week of rent are allowed 2s. per week (21/5/17).

Constables (married) necessarily paying 6s. a week and not exceeding 10s. a week of rent are allowed 2s. per week (21/5/17).

Boots—

An allowance of £2 12s. od. per annum for boots is made to all ranks.

Point Duty—

Constables engaged on point duty regulating traffic receive an allowance of 1s. a week while so engaged.

Motor Drivers—

Motor drivers receive 2s. 6d. a week while so engaged.

Office Duty—

Reserve Office Sergeants at Divisional Stations receive an allowance of 5s. per week whilst they perform that duty.

Office and Departmental—

An allowance at the undermentioned rate is made to Inspectors, Sergeants, and Constables bona-fide employed as clerks in the Chief Constable's Office, Criminal Investigation Department Office, and other offices of the Chief Constable's Department, including the Street Trading, Explosives, and Coroner's Departments:—

Inspectors	...	...	...	...	3s. a week
Sergeants	...	...	...	...	3s. ,,
Constables	...	...	...	...	2s. ,,

Allowances in C.I. Department (Detectives)—

Plain Clothes.		
Superintendent	...	£18 a year.
Inspectors ...	...	£18 ,,
Sergeants	...	£15 ,,
Constables ...	...	£15 ,,

Incidental Expenses.

Eight shillings a week is paid to all ranks in C.I.D. to meet the extra expense caused by irregular hours of duty, small payments for information, and other expenses incidental to Detective duty.

An allowance for plain clothes on the above scale is made to members in various Departments.

Officers performing duty in plain clothes on Divisions receive the plain clothes allowance at the above rate.

Merit (non-pensionable).

Sergeants and Constables may obtain Merit Stripes. Sergeant's first stripe carries 1s. a week, and second stripe the same : total 2s. a week, called "full merit." Constable's first stripe carries 6d. a week, the second 6d., and the third 1s.: total 2s. a week, called "full merit." A Constable holding the first or second stripe on promotion to the rank of Sergeant holds the Sergeant's first stripe of merit, carrying 1s. If he holds a Constable's third stripe (full merit) he obtains a Sergeant's full merit.

Deductions.

SICK—When not hurt on duty, 1s. for each day.

LODGING—Single sergeants or constables accommodated in Police Station, 1s. per week. Married sergeants or constables accommodated in police or station quarters, 2s. 6d. per week.

Leave.

	Annual.	Monthly.		Annual.	
Superintendents ...	14 days.	None specified.	Sergeants ...	10 days.	One day's rest in seven.
Inspectors... ...	10 ,,	One day's rest in seven.	Constables ...	9 ,,	

Pensions.

The maximum scale under the Police Act, 1890, without age limit.

Travelling and Subsistence Allowance: Individual Duty.

Subsistence allowance will be paid to Police Officers when absent from the City on duty, when such absence necessarily extends over four hours, namely:—

			Superintendents.	Inspectors.	Sergeants. Constables.
Breakfast	...	If leaving home before 8 a.m.	3/6	3/-	2/6
Dinner	...	If absent between 1 and 2 p.m.	6/-	4/-	3/-
Supper	...	If not returning home until after 6 p.m.	3/6	3/-	2/-
Bed...	...	If necessary	7/-	6/-	5/-
Total	...	Per day, not exceeding	20/-	16/-	12/6

CONDITIONS OF SERVICE

OF THE

BIRMINGHAM CITY POLICE.

1. Each Constable will be enrolled for one year on probation, and if then recommended by the Chief Constable as fit, will be appointed by the Watch Committee. A Constable on probation may be dismissed by the Chief Constable for unfitness, negligence, or misconduct.

2. Each member of the Force shall devote his whole time to the Police service of the City. He must not, directly or indirectly, carry on any trade or calling; nor can he be permitted, without the consent of the Chief Constable, to live at any place where any member of his family carries on business.

3. He shall serve where appointed, and reside in the City and in his Division, and within a reasonable distance of the Station to which he is attached, unless otherwise permitted by the Chief Constable.

4. He shall not, directly or indirectly, be interested in any publichouse or beerhouse. He is prohibited from borrowing money from publicans, beerhouse keepers, or other tradesmen, or being in any way indebted to them. He may not reside in a house licensed for the sale of intoxicating liquors.

5. He shall conform to all rules, orders, regulations, fines, and deductions now in force, or as the Watch Committee may frame for preventing neglect or abuse, and making the City Police efficient in the discharge of their duties, and shall promptly obey all the orders of the Chief Constable, and others placed in authority over him.

6. He shall appear in his complete Police uniform at all times when on duty, unless otherwise directed; but he may wear plain clothes when off duty.

7. He shall at all times provide himself with a respectable suit of plain clothes to the satisfaction of his Superintendent.

8. In consideration of receiving a boot allowance he shall provide himself with such boots as are directed by the Regulations.

9. Single men on joining will not be permitted to marry until they have been in the Force one year, and received permission of the Chief Constable.

10. Such debts owing by him as the Watch Committee or Chief Constable directs to be paid shall be paid by him forthwith.

11. He shall not belong to or subscribe money to the funds of any political or party society.

12. He shall have no claim to any stolen or unclaimed money or property, or other money or property found by him, or that may have come into his possession in the execution of his duty; and he shall deliver up all such money and property to his Superintendent; to be accounted for in accordance with the regulations relating to lost or stolen property.

13. He shall not retain any money or other thing given to him by way of fee, reward or presentation, without permission of the Watch Committee on the recommendation of the Chief Constable.

14. His pension will be calculated upon the amount of his pay, from which a deduction of $2\frac{1}{2}$ per cent. is made for superannuation, and not on the amount of any extra pay or allowance he may receive.

15. He will not be entitled to pay if absent from duty without leave.

16. He will make written applications for promotion from one Class to another, when such promotion falls due; otherwise his promotion may be delayed; and the Watch Committee reserve the right to defer promotion or to reduce his pay for misconduct or inefficiency.

17. He will be required to pass an educational test before receiving his first promotion, and may be called on for similar tests as to efficiency before further promotion.

18. He will be required to obtain first, second, and third class St. John Ambulance Certificates within three years of his joining the Force, and to attend revision class each year subsequently, to keep up his efficiency in rendering "First Aid" to the injured.

19. He shall not resign or withdraw himself from his duties or from the Force unless allowed to do so in writing by the Chief Constable; or unless he shall have given the Chief Constable one month's previous notice in writing, at the same time assigning a reason for so doing. If he resign or withdraw without such leave or notice, he is liable to forfeit all pay due and to be charged before a Magistrate.

20. He is liable to immediate dismissal for unfitness, negligence, or misconduct, independently of any other punishment to which by law he may be subject. The Watch Committee may remove him from the service by dismissal or otherwise.

21. A Constable dismissed from the Police Force, or who resigns or ceases to hold office, shall forthwith deliver up all articles of clothing, accoutrements, appointments, and other necessaries that have been supplied to him for the execution of his duties. They do not become his property; and he shall also deliver them up whenever called upon to do so, complete and in good order. If such clothing or appointments have in the opinion of the Chief Constable been unduly worn or improperly used or damaged, a deduction from the pay then due to the Constable shall be made, sufficient to make good the damage or supply a new article.

22. A certificate of good character in the Police service will not be given if the Constable has been dismissed the service; has frequently been guilty of misconduct; has been guilty of serious misconduct; has not served one year; has left the Force without giving one month's notice; or if he does not apply for the certificate within six months after leaving the Force.

BIRMINGHAM CITY POLICE.

REVISED SCALE OF PAY.
(To date from 1st April, 1919).

SUPERINTENDENTS.

		Deduction for Superannuation Fund.
After 4 years in rank.	£520 per annum.	£13. 5.0 per annum.
" 3 " " "	£510 "	£12.15.0 "
" 2 " " "	£490 "	£12. 5.0 "
" 1 " " "	£470 "	£11.15.0 "
On appointment.	£450 "	£11. 5.0 "

CHIEF INSPECTORS.

After 4 years in rank.	£415 per annum.	£10. 7.6 per annum.
" 3 " " "	£405 "	£10. 2.6 "
" 2 " " "	£395 "	£ 9.17.6 "
" 1 " " "	£385 "	£ 9.12.6 "
On appointment.	£375 "	£ 9. 7.6 "

INSPECTORS.

After 4 years in rank.	£360 per annum.	£ 9. 0.0 per annum.
" 3 " " "	£350 "	£ 8.15.0 "
" 2 " " "	£340 "	£8.10 .0 "
" 1 " " "	£330 "	£ 8. 5.0 "
On appointment.	£320 "	£ 8. 0.0 "

SERGEANTS.

After 5 years in rank.	112/6 per week.	2/9d. per week.
" 4 " " "	110/- "	2/9d. "
" 3 " " "	107/6 "	2/8d. "
" 2 " " "	105/- "	2/7d. "
" 1 " " "	102/6 "	2/6d. "
On appointment.	100/- "	2/6d. "

CONSTABLES.

"B" After 22 yrs from appt.	95/- per week.	2/4d. per week.
"B" " 17 " " "	92/6 "	2/3d. "
" 10 " " "	90/- "	2/3d. "
" 9 " " "	88/- "	2/2d. "
" 8 " " "	86/- "	2/2d. "
" 7 " " "	84/- "	2/1d. "
" 6 " " "	82/- "	2/0d. "
" 5 " " "	80/- "	2/0d. "
" 4 " " "	78/- "	1/11d. "
" 3 " " "	76/- "	1/11d. "
" 2 " " "	74/- "	1/10d. "
" 1 "(unless probation is extended.)	72/- "	1/9 d. "
On appointment (on probation.)	70/- "	1/9 d. "

"B". Subject to good conduct and efficiency.

CONDITIONS OF SERVICE

OF THE

BIRMINGHAM CITY POLICE.

1. Each Constable will be enrolled for one year on probation, and if then recommended by the Chief Constable as fit, will be appointed by the Watch Committee. A Constable on probation may be dismissed by the Chief Constable for unfitness, negligence, or misconduct.

2. Each member of the Force shall devote his whole time to the Police service of the City. He must not, directly or indirectly, carry on any trade or calling; nor can he be permitted, without the consent of the Chief Constable, to live at any place where any member of his family carries on business.

3. He shall serve where appointed, and reside in the City and in his Division, and within a reasonable distance of the Station to which he is attached, unless otherwise permitted by the Chief Constable.

4. He shall not, directly or indirectly, be interested in any publichouse or beerhouse. He is prohibited from borrowing money from publicans, beerhouse keepers, or other tradesmen, or being in any way indebted to them. He may not reside in a house licensed for the sale of intoxicating liquors.

5. He shall conform to all rules, orders, regulations, fines, and deductions now in force, or as the Watch Committee may frame for preventing neglect or abuse, and making the City Police efficient in the discharge of their duties, and shall promptly obey all the orders of the Chief Constable, and others placed in authority over him.

6. He shall appear in his complete Police uniform at all times when on duty, unless otherwise directed; but he may wear plain clothes when off duty.

7. He shall at all times provide himself with a respectable suit of plain clothes to the satisfaction of his Superintendent.

8. In consideration of receiving a boot allowance he shall provide himself with such boots as are directed by the Regulations.

9. Single men on joining will not be permitted to marry until they have been in the Force one year, and received permission of the Chief Constable.

10. Such debts owing by him as the Watch Committee or Chief Constable directs to be paid shall be paid by him forthwith.

11. He shall not belong to or subscribe money to the funds of any political or party society.

12. He shall have no claim to any stolen or unclaimed money or property, or other money or property found by him, or that may have come into his possession in the execution of his duty; and he shall deliver up all such money and property to his Superintendent; to be accounted for in accordance with the regulations relating to lost or stolen property.

13. He shall not retain any money or other thing given to him by way of fee, reward or presentation, without permission of the Watch Committee on the recommendation of the Chief Constable.

14. His pension will be calculated upon the amount of his pay, from which a deduction of $2\frac{1}{2}$ per cent. is made for superannuation, and not on the amount of any extra pay or allowance he may receive.

15. He will not be entitled to pay if absent from duty without leave.

16. He will make written applications for promotion from one Class to another, when such promotion falls due; otherwise his promotion may be delayed; and the Watch Committee reserve the right to defer promotion or to reduce his pay for misconduct or inefficiency.

17. He will be required to pass an educational test before receiving his first promotion, and may be called on for similar tests as to efficiency before further promotion.

18. He will be required to obtain first, second, and third class St. John Ambulance Certificates within three years of his joining the Force, and to attend revision class each year subsequently, to keep up his efficiency in rendering "First Aid" to the injured.

19. He shall not resign or withdraw himself from his duties or from the Force unless allowed to do so in writing by the Chief Constable; or unless he shall have given the Chief Constable one month's previous notice in writing, at the same time assigning a reason for so doing. If he resign or withdraw without such leave or notice, he is liable to forfeit all pay due and to be charged before a Magistrate.

20. He is liable to immediate dismissal for unfitness, negligence, or misconduct, independently of any other punishment to which by law he may be subject. The Watch Committee may remove him from the service by dismissal or otherwise.

21. A Constable dismissed from the Police Force, or who resigns or ceases to hold office, shall forthwith deliver up all articles of clothing, accoutrements, appointments, and other necessaries that have been supplied to him for the execution of his duties. They do not become his property; and he shall also deliver them up whenever called upon to do so, complete and in good order. If such clothing or appointments have in the opinion of the Chief Constable been unduly worn or improperly used or damaged, a deduction from the pay then due to the Constable shall be made, sufficient to make good the damage or supply a new article.

22. A certificate of good character in the Police service will not be given if the Constable has been dismissed the service; has frequently been guilty of misconduct; has been guilty of serious misconduct; has not served one year; has left the Force without giving one month's notice; or if he does not apply for the certificate within six months after leaving the Force.

References

[i] The Graphic, 31st January 1874

[ii] A History of Police in England and Wales – TA Critchley, p166

[iii] A History of Police in England and Wales – TA Critchley, p166

[iv] An account of 150 years of policing Birmingham – John Reilly

[v] https://www.british-history.ac.uk/vch/warks/vol7/pp1-3 accessed 4/3/2019

[vi] An account of 150 years of policing Birmingham – John Reilly

[vii] https://api.parliament.uk/historic-hansard/lords/1910/jun/16/police-weekly-rest-day-bill accessed 13/3/2019

[viii] A History of Police in England and Wales – TA Critchley, p172-173

[ix] A History of Police in England and Wales – TA Critchley, p173

[x] A History of Police in England and Wales – TA Critchley, p174

[xi] A History of Police in England and Wales – TA Critchley, p174

[xii] West Midlands Police Roll of Honour: https://www.wmpeelers.com/rollofhonour accessed 27/2/2019

[xiii] Invisible Men: The secret lives of Police Constables in Liverpool, Manchester and Birmingham, 1900-1939 p8

[xiv] 150 years of Policing Birmingham, John Reilly

[xv] Invisible Men: The secret lives of Police Constables in Liverpool, Manchester and Birmingham, 1900-1939 p17

[xvi] Invisible Men: The secret lives of Police Constables in Liverpool, Manchester and Birmingham, 1900-1939 p44

[xvii] Birmingham Police Orders 23rd November 1901 p574, referenced in Invisible Men: The secret lives of Police Constables in Liverpool, Manchester and Birmingham, 1900-1939 p139

[xviii] Invisible Men: The secret lives of Police Constables in Liverpool, Manchester and Birmingham, 1900-1939 p140

[xix] The English Police, Clive Emsley, pp133 referenced in Invisible Men: The secret lives of Police Constables in Liverpool, Manchester and Birmingham, 1900-1939 p142

[xx] Birmingham Police Orders, 30th October 1913 referenced in Invisible Men: The secret lives of Police Constables in Liverpool, Manchester and Birmingham, 1900-1939 p142

[xxi] The Irish Times, 22nd July 1899

[xxii] Jack Hayes MP. HC Deb. 5th Series, Vol. 166, 12th July 1923, Column 1713, referenced in Anthony Wright and Richard Shackleton (eds.) *Worlds of Labour: Essays in Birmingham Labour History* (Birmingham, 1983)

[xxiii] Birmingham City Police Orders, 22/8/1901 page 512

[xxiv] Birmingham City Police Orders, 12/11/1914 p358

[xxv] The Night the Police Went on Strike, Reynolds and Judge, p39

[xxvi] https://collection.nam.ac.uk/detail.php?acc=1976-03-50-66 accessed 2/7/2019

[xxvii] Snow Hill Station No. 2, box of photographs of Snow Hill Station, Library of Birmingham

[xxviii] WK/B11/256, Warwickshire Photographic Survey, Library of Birmingham

[xxix] Invisible Men: The secret lives of Police Constables in Liverpool, Manchester and Birmingham, 1900-1939 p146

[xxx] Invisible Men: The secret lives of Police Constables in Liverpool, Manchester and Birmingham, 1900-1939 p18

[xxxi] A History of Police in England and Wales, TA Critchley, p182

[xxxii] Birmingham City Police Orders 3rd April 1919 639

[xxxiii] Invisible Men: The secret lives of Police Constables in Liverpool, Manchester and Birmingham, 1900-1939 p133

[xxxiv] The Night the Police Went on Strike, Reynolds and Judge, p6

[xxxv] The Night the Police Went on Strike, Reynolds and Judge, p8

[xxxvi] The Night the Police Went on Strike, Reynolds and Judge, p8-16

[xxxvii] The Night the Police Went on Strike, Reynolds and Judge, p19

[xxxviii] https://api.parliament.uk/historic-hansard/written-answers/1919/aug/01/wages-1914-and-1919 accessed 13/3/2019

[xxxix] The Night the Police Went on Strike, Reynolds and Judge, p25-26

[xl] The Night the Police Went on Strike, Reynolds and Judge, p30-31

[xli] The Night the Police Went on Strike, Reynolds and Judge, p31-32

xlii The Night the Police Went on Strike, Reynolds and Judge, p37

xliii The Night the Police Went on Strike, Reynolds and Judge, p41

xliv A History of Police in England and Wales, TA Critchley, p186

xlv http://www.ploddinthesquaremile.co.uk/city-police-people/john-zollner-a-man-of-the-union/ accessed 13/3/2019

xlvi The National Union of Police and Prison Officers, V L Allen, 1958, The Economic History Review vol 11 no 1 pp133-143

xlvii A History of Police in England and Wales, TA Critchley, p186

xlviii The Night the Police Went on Strike, Reynolds and Judge, p4

xlix The Night the Police Went on Strike, Reynolds and Judge, p71

l Picture found on https://www.policeoracle.com/news/1918-strikes-I-rang-Scotland-Yard-and-told-them-there-is-likely-to-be-trouble_96966.html accessed 13/3/2019, original picture located in Police Review and credited to Daily Sketch

li A History of Police in England and Wales, TA Critchley, p189

lii The History of HMIC, the first 150 years, Cowley and Todd 2006, p46

liii The Great British Bobby, Clive Emsley, 2009, p195, referring to the report from the Desborough Committee

liv Desborough Committee evidence p297

lv A History of Police in England and Wales, TA Critchley, p190

lvi A History of Police in England and Wales, TA Critchley, p190-91

lvii Desborough Committee evidence questions 1982 (p110) and 3144 (p166) both referenced in Invisible Men: The secret lives of Police Constables in Liverpool, Manchester and Birmingham, 1900-1939 p153

lviii A History of Police in England and Wales, TA Critchley, p191

lix Invisible Men: The secret lives of Police Constables in Liverpool, Manchester and Birmingham, 1900-1939 p9

lx Invisible Men: The secret lives of Police Constables in Liverpool, Manchester and Birmingham, 1900-1939 p25

lxi The History of HMIC, the first 150 years, Cowley and Todd 2006, p47

lxii Invisible Men: The secret lives of Police Constables in Liverpool, Manchester and Birmingham, 1900-1939 p7-8

lxiii Report of the Committee on the Police Service of England, Wales and Scotland Part II, 1920

lxiv Inspectors in Constabulary Report for year ended 29th September 1912, PP 1913 (76) lii, 663, p107

lxv Invisible Men: The secret lives of Police Constables in Liverpool, Manchester and Birmingham, 1900-1939 p36

lxvi Invisible Men: The secret lives of Police Constables in Liverpool, Manchester and Birmingham, 1900-1939 p56

lxvii Invisible Men: The secret lives of Police Constables in Liverpool, Manchester and Birmingham, 1900-1939 p77

lxviii Birmingham Trades Council minutes (BTCM) 5th October 1918, referenced in Anthony Wright and Richard Shackleton (eds.) Worlds of Labour: Essays in Birmingham Labour History (Birmingham, 1983) (pp. 63-87)

lxix BTCM 10th October, referenced in Anthony Wright and Richard Shackleton (eds.) Worlds of Labour: Essays in Birmingham Labour History (Birmingham, 1983) (pp. 63-87)

lxx BTCM 26th October, referenced in Anthony Wright and Richard Shackleton (eds.) Worlds of Labour: Essays in Birmingham Labour History (Birmingham, 1983) (pp. 63-87)

lxxi Anthony Wright and Richard Shackleton (eds.) Worlds of Labour: Essays in Birmingham Labour History (Birmingham, 1983) p67

lxxii Birmingham City Police Orders 7th October 1918, p257 - 259

lxxiii Birmingham City Police Judicial Sub-Committee minutes 3rd March 1919, 8778

lxxiv Birmingham City Police Judicial Sub-Committee minutes 3rd March 1919 8778

lxxv Birmingham City Police Superintendents reports and confidential letters, 2nd November 1918 referenced in Invisible Men: The secret lives of Police Constables in Liverpool, Manchester and Birmingham, 1900-1939 p77

lxxvi Birmingham City Police Judicial Sub-Committee minutes 3rd March 1919

lxxvii Birmingham City Police Orders 8th April 1919 658

lxxviii Birmingham City Police Orders April 1919 676 - 696

lxxix Birmingham City Police Judicial Sub-Committee minutes 5th May 1919 8882

lxxx The Night the Police Went on Strike, Reynolds and Judge, p179

lxxxi The Night the Police Went on Strike, Reynolds and Judge, p181

lxxxii The English Police, A Political and Social History, Clive Emsley, p134

lxxxiii Birmingham City Police Judicial Sub-Committee minutes 5th May 1919 8887 lxxxiv Anthony Wright and Richard Shackleton (eds.) *Worlds of Labour: Essays in Birmingham Labour History* (Birmingham, 1983) p68

lxxxv BTCM 30th May 1919, referenced in Anthony Wright and Richard Shackleton (eds.) *Worlds of Labour: Essays in Birmingham Labour History* (Birmingham, 1983)

lxxxvi Birmingham Police Orders 29th May 1919 792

lxxxvii Birmingham City Police Judicial Sub-Committee minutes 23rd June 1919 8915

lxxxviii Birmingham City Police Judicial Sub-Committee minutes 23rd June 1919 8920, answers received 30th June 8938

lxxxix Birmingham City Police Orders, 1st March 1920 1895

xc The Night the Police Went on Strike, Reynolds and Judge, p133-134

xci The Night the Police Went on Strike, Reynolds and Judge, p135

xcii The Night the Police Went on Strike, Reynolds and Judge, p137

xciii The Night the Police Went on Strike, Reynolds and Judge, p141

xciv The National Union of Police and Prison Officers, V L Allen, 1958, The Economic Review Vol 11 no 1 pp133-143

xcv The Night the Police Went on Strike, Reynolds and Judge, p182

xcvi The Night the Police Went on Strike, Reynolds and Judge, p181

xcvii The Night the Police Went on Strike, Reynolds and Judge, p182

xcviii Birmingham Post, 2nd August 1919

xcix Anthony Wright and Richard Shackleton (eds.) *Worlds of Labour: Essays in Birmingham Labour History* (Birmingham, 1983) p70

c The Night the Police Went on Strike, Reynolds and Judge, p183

ci Birmingham City Police Judicial Sub-Committee minutes, August 2nd 1919

cii The Night the Police Went on Strike, Reynolds and Judge, p183

ciii The Night the Police Went on Strike, Reynolds and Judge, p183

civ Anthony Wright and Richard Shackleton (eds.) *Worlds of Labour: Essays in Birmingham Labour History* (Birmingham, 1983) p71

cv The Night the Police Went on Strike, Reynolds and Judge, p184

cvi Anthony Wright and Richard Shackleton (eds.) *Worlds of Labour: Essays in Birmingham Labour History* (Birmingham, 1983) p75

cvii Birmingham City Police Orders 3rd August 1919, 976-977

cviii Birmingham NUPPO branch strike leaflet from Library of Birmingham, Birmingham Institutions K/4 / 518835

cix Anthony Wright and Richard Shackleton (eds.) *Worlds of Labour: Essays in Birmingham Labour History* (Birmingham, 1983) p72

cx Birmingham City Police Orders, 4th August 1919

cxi The Night the Police Went on Strike, Reynolds and Judge, p184

cxii Discussion with Geoffrey Read regarding his grandfather Thomas Jones

cxiii The Night the Police Went on Strike, Reynolds and Judge, p184

cxiv The Night the Police Went on Strike, Reynolds and Judge, p185

cxv http://liverpoolcitypolice.co.uk/#/sgt-robert-tissyman-pti/4565694960 accessed 6/5/1919

cxvi Police Strike, A V Sellwood, 1978, p68

cxvii Police Strike, A V Sellwood, 1978, p81

cxviii The Night the Police Went on Strike, Reynolds and Judge

cxix Police Strike, A V Sellwood, 1978, p94

cxx http://liverpoolcitypolice.co.uk/#/sgt-robert-tissyman-pti/4565694960 accessed 6/5/2019

cxxi Helmets, Handcuffs and Hoses – The Story of the Wallasey Police and Fire Brigade Part 1, Noel E Smith, 2001

cxxii Police Strike, A V Sellwood, 1978, 159-163

cxxiii 16 and 22 August two reports of PS Mybroie, referenced in Invisible Men: The secret lives of Police Constables in Liverpool, Manchester and Birmingham, 1900-1939 p159

cxxiv Police Strike, A V Sellwood, 1978, p117

cxxv Liverpool Daily Report Books 7 Feb 1928 PC Barrett - referenced in Invisible Men: The secret lives of Police Constables in Liverpool, Manchester and Birmingham, 1900-1939 p159

cxxvi Invisible Men: The secret lives of Police Constables in Liverpool, Manchester and Birmingham, 1900-1939 p159

cxxvii The English Police, A Political and Social History, Clive Emsley, p135

cxxviii The Night the Police Went on Strike, Reynolds and Judge, p186 cxxix From https://www.geograph.org.uk/photo/4706282 accessed 27/6/2019, licensed for reuse under creative commons license

cxxx East Riding Archives POL/4/5/2/4 and POL/4/5/3/3

cxxxi http://mappingbirmingham.blogspot.co.uk/2013/02/georgian-terraces-2-crescent-that-wasnt.html accessed 28/6/2019

cxxxii Birmingham Police Orders 14th August 1919 1015

cxxxiii Anthony Wright and Richard Shackleton (eds.) *Worlds of Labour: Essays in Birmingham Labour History* (Birmingham, 1983) p65

cxxxiv The Night the Police Went on Strike, Reynolds and Judge, p187 & 188

cxxxv Anthony Wright and Richard Shackleton (eds.) *Worlds of Labour: Essays in Birmingham Labour History* (Birmingham, 1983) p76

cxxxvi Birmingham Watch Committee minutes 15th August 1919 pp108-9, 1st September 1920 and Judicial Sub-Committee minutes 5th July 1920 p163, both referenced in Invisible Men: The secret lives of Police Constables in Liverpool, Manchester and Birmingham, 1900-1939 p157

cxxxvii Birmingham City Police Orders 12th-15th August 1919 1003 - 1016

cxxxviii Birmingham City Police Orders 29th August 1919, 1084-1089

cxxxix Birmingham City Police Orders 7th October 1919, 1258 and 8th October 1919 1265

cxl Birmingham City Police Judicial Sub-Committee minutes, 29th September 1919, 9001 and 9002

cxli Letter from NUPPO to Birmingham Trade Union Council, dated October 19th 1919, Birmingham Institutions K/4 / 518835

cxlii The Night the Police Went on Strike, Reynolds and Judge, p188

cxliii Birmingham City Police Judicial Sub-Committee, 27th October 1919, 9039

cxliv Invisible Men: The secret lives of Police Constables in Liverpool, Manchester and Birmingham, 1900-1939 p114

cxlv The Report of the Committee on the Police Service of England, Wales and Scotland, 1920, Cmd 574, vol. XXII, 539 p10

cxlvi Birmingham Police Orders 21st July 1927, 13108

cxlvii Birmingham City Police Orders 6th January 1920 - 1596

cxlviii Birmingham City Police Judicial Sub-Committee, 1st March 1920, 9186

cxlix Birmingham Daily Gazette, 5th May 1920

cl Birmingham City Police Orders 22nd March 1920 1954

cli Derby Daily Telegraph, 25th May 1920,

clii *BTCM Minutes of Executive of Birmingham Trades Council meeting with Delegates of Joint Committee of Engineering Trade Unions – around 20th Aug 1919* referenced in Anthony Wright and Richard Shackleton (eds.) *Worlds of Labour: Essays in Birmingham Labour History* (Birmingham, 1983) p81 and p82

cliii Birmingham Watch Committee minutes 1/4/1925 1349 & 6/5/1925 1380.

cliv Birmingham Watch Committee Minutes 8th May 1925, p9845, referenced in Invisible Men: The secret lives of Police Constables in Liverpool, Manchester and Birmingham, 1900-1939 p160

clv Birmingham Watch Committee minutes 27th July 1927 and 5th October 1927

clvi Anthony Wright and Richard Shackleton (eds.) *Worlds of Labour: Essays in Birmingham Labour History* (Birmingham, 1983) p73

clvii Anthony Wright and Richard Shackleton (eds.) *Worlds of Labour: Essays in Birmingham Labour History* (Birmingham, 1983) p76

clviii Anthony Wright and Richard Shackleton (eds.) *Worlds of Labour: Essays in Birmingham Labour History* (Birmingham, 1983) p79-82

clix Birmingham City Police Orders 8th October 1919, 1267

clx Birmingham City Police Orders, 17th October 1919 1293

clxi Birmingham City Police Orders 21st October 1919 1314

clxii Birmingham City Police Orders 30th Dec 1919 1549-1554

clxiii Birmingham City Police Orders 2nd May 1925, p9845, referenced in Invisible Men: The secret lives of Police Constables in Liverpool, Manchester and Birmingham, 1900-1939 p162

clxiv Birmingham Watch Committee minutes 15th July 1903 p448-452

clxv Birmingham City Police Orders 30th January 1928 p13779

clxvi https://www.polfed.org/westmids/about-us/history/ accessed 6/6/2019